Applications and Innovations in Intelligent Systems XIII

Ann Macintosh, Richard Ellis and
Tony Allen (Eds)

Applications and Innovations in Intelligent Systems XIII

Proceedings of AI-2005, the Twenty-fifth SGAI International Conference on Innovative Techniques and Applications of Artificial Intelligence, Cambridge, UK, December 2005

Professor Ann Macintosh, BSc, CEng
Napier University, Edinburgh, EH10 5DT, UK

Richard Ellis, BSc, MSc
Stratum Management Ltd, UK

Dr Tony Allen, PhD
Nottingham Trent University, UK

British Library Cataloguing in Publication Data
A catalogue record for this book is available from the British Library

ISBN-10: 1-84628-223-3 Printed on acid-free paper
ISBN-13: 978-1-84628-223-2

Printed in the United Kingdom

9 8 7 6 5 4 3 2 1

Springer Science+Business Media
springer.com

APPLICATION PROGRAMME CHAIR'S INTRODUCTION

A. L. MACINTOSH
Napier University, UK

The papers in this volume are the refereed application papers presented at AI-2005, the Twenty-fifth SGAI International Conference on Innovative Techniques and Applications of Artificial Intelligence, held in Cambridge in December 2005. The conference was organised by SGAI, the British Computer Society Specialist Group on Artificial Intelligence.

This volume contains fifteen refereed papers which present the innovative application of a range of AI techniques in a number of subject domains. This year, the papers are divided into sections on *Applied AI in Information Processing*, *Techniques for Applied AI*, *Industrial Applications* and *Medical Applications.*

This year's prize for the best refereed application paper, which is being sponsored by the Department of Trade and Industry, was won by a paper entitled "Case-Based Reasoning Investigation of Therapy Inefficacy". The authors are Rainer Schmidt of the University of Rostock, Germany, and Olga Vorobieva, from the Sechenow Institute in St.Petersburg, Russia.

This is the thirteenth volume in the *Applications and Innovations* series. The Technical Stream papers are published as a companion volume under the title *Research and Development in Intelligent Systems XXII.*

On behalf of the conference organising committee I should like to thank all those who contributed to the organisation of this year's application programme, in particular the programme committee members, the executive programme committee and our administrator Collette Jackson.

Ann Macintosh
Application Programme Chair, AI-2005

ACKNOWLEDGEMENTS

AI-2005 CONFERENCE COMMITTEE

Dr Tony Allen, Nottingham Trent University	(Conference Chair)
Dr Alun Preece, University of Aberdeen	(Deputy Conference Chair, Electronic Services)
Dr Nirmalie Wiratunga, The Robert Gordon University	(Poster Session Organiser)
Professor Adrian Hopgood, Nottingham Trent University	(Workshop Organiser)
Professor Ann Macintosh, Napier University	(Application Programme Chair)
Richard Ellis, Stratum Management Ltd	(Deputy Application Programme Chair)
Professor Max Bramer, University of Portsmouth	(Technical Programme Chair)
Dr Frans Coenen, University of Liverpool	(Deputy Conference Chair, Local Arrangements and Deputy Technical Programme Chair)
Rosemary Gilligan	(Research Student Liaison)

APPLICATION EXECUTIVE PROGRAMME COMMITTEE

Professor Ann Macintosh, Napier University (Chair)
Richard Ellis, Stratum Management Ltd (Vice-Chair)
Rosemary Gilligan, University of Hertfordshire
Professor Adrian Hopgood, Nottingham Trent University
Mr Richard Wheeler, University of Edinburgh

APPLICATION PROGRAMME COMMITTEE

Nick Adams (Napier University)

Victor Alves (Universidade do Minho)

Ines Arana, (The Robert Gordon University)

Li Bai (University of Nottingham)

Euan Davidson (University of Strathclyde)

Sarah Jane Delany (Dublin Institute of Technology)

Argiris Dentsoras (University of Patras)

Richard Ellis (Stratum)

Florentino Fdez-Riverola (ESEI)

Pablo Gervás (Universidad Complutense de Madrid)

Rosemary Gilligan (University of Hertfordshire)

John Gordon (Applied Knowledge Research Institute)

Catholijn M. Jonker (University of Nijmegen, The Netherlands)

Daniel Kerr (BUPA)

John Kingston (University of Edinburgh)

Paul Leng (University of Liverpool)

Shuliang Li (University of Westminster)

Honghai Liu (University of Aberdeen)

Ann Macintosh (Napier University)

Giles Oatley, (University of Sunderland)

M.A. Salido (Universidad de Alicante)

Wamberto Vasconcelos (The University of Aberdeen)

CONTENTS

APPLICATION KEYNOTE ADDRESS

Legal Engineering: A structural approach to Improving Legal Quality[1]

Tom M. van Engers[2]
University of Amsterdam/Leibniz Center for Law
vanEngers@uva.nl
www.LeibnizCenter.org

Abstract

Knowledge engineers have been working in the legal domain since the rise of their discipline in the mid-eighties of the last century. Traditionally their main focus was capturing and distributing knowledge by means of the knowledge-based systems, thus improving legal access. More and more legal knowledge engineering has become an analytical approach that helps to improve legal quality. An example is the POWER-approach developed in a research programme that is now finished. This programme was run by the Dutch Tax and Customs Administration (DTCA in Dutch: Belastingdienst) and some partners (see e.g. Van Engers et al., 1999, 2000, 2001, 2003 and 2004). The POWER-approach helped to improve quality of (new) legislation and codify the knowledge used in the translation processes in which legislation and regulations are transformed into procedures, computer programs and other designs. We experienced that despite these clear benefits implementation proved to be far from easy. In fact the implementation phase still continues. Adapting research results in public administrations is a tedious process that takes lots and lots of energy and requires continuous management attention. Learning at organisational level proved to be much harder than we thought.

1. Introduction

Getting the right knowledge at the right place at the right time has always been a great challenge for governments since this inflicts the ability to effectuate the legislative power to regulate and control. The Dutch Tax and Customs Administration (DTCA) has developed a method and supporting tools supporting the whole chain of processes from legislation drafting to executing the law by government employees and citizens (see e.g. Van Engers et al., 1999, 2000, 2001,

---

[1] Parts of the material described here have been published before (see e.g. Van Engers 2004).

[2] Tom M. van Engers was programme manager of the POWER research programme and coordinator of the IST funded E-Power project.

2003 and 2004). These method and tools resulted from the POWER research program (Program for an Ontology-based Working Environment for Rules and regulations), a research program that was partly sponsored (the E-POWER project) by the European Commission through the IST 5th framework program.

The POWER approach combines two typical knowledge management approaches; the stock or codification approach and the flow or organisational approach. It offers both a method and supporting tools that support a systematic translation of (new) legislation into the administrations' processes.

The motive behind running the POWER program was that drafting and implementing new legislation is a rather time, energy and money consuming process consisting of many inter-connected processes. These processes are very vulnerable to errors. Not only because of the intrinsic complexity of the law, but also because mostly a large number of people is involved in these processes as wells as of the complexity of these processes themselves. Varying interests have to be aligned and communication difficulties due to differences in technical jargon have to be overcome in both drafting and implementing changes to legislation. The same holds when completely new legislation has to be implemented.

The POWER-method helps to improve the quality of (new) legislation. It also supports codification of the legal knowledge into procedures, computer programs and other designs. One of the advantages thereof is the reduction of the time-to-market of the implementation of legislation and its increased transparency which will lead to reduced maintenance costs and improved services to citizens.

The POWER-approach was developed in a research programme that is now finished. In this paper I will share some of my experiences with you without explaining the POWER-approach in too much detail.

2. Design of regulatory processes

The knowledge and experience needed to create new laws or adapt existing ones, specify, design and implement procedures and systems in legislative domains is very scarce. A (piece of) law should reflect the intentions of the political responsible minister and should also meet some quality criteria such as clarity and consistency from the perspective of the law-enforcement organization. This is the responsibility of the legislation drafters that are responsible for drafting the new law.

The people responsible for implementing the law (i.e. the administration) have to adapt the procedures, processes and information systems to the new law. Also risk diagnosis, assessment procedures and audit measurements have to be designed and implemented as well. This all has to be done while taking political and social-environmental requirements into account. An example of such requirements is the need for diminishing the administrative costs for citizens and businesses.

Between drafting new legislation and enforcement thereof a chain of processes has to be managed and aligned. Preventing errors as early as possible in this chain can save a lot of time and money. Not only at the design stage but even more during the law-enforcement stage. Unintended use or even worse abuse is often due to anomalies in the law. Also, the position of the government is much stronger when involved in a dispute if the law is very clear with respect to the object of disagreement.

Many legislation drafting departments at the different ministries already have their own quality insurance techniques. Furthermore in many cases the ministry of Justice has a special role because they are usually responsible for the overall legal quality of a country. Despite all the effort that's been spend on improving legal quality using traditional measurements, such as co-reading (peer reviewing etc.) many anomalies can still be found in recently drafted legislation. The situation is even worse in situations when existing legislation is adapted.

Quality insurance measurements also exist for the other processes in the chain mentioned. Most attempts to achieve quality improvements however focus at just one of the processes involved. In the approach developed in the POWER-research program we consider each of these processes as equally important. We furthermore stress the importance of managing the chain rather then the distinctive processes themselves.

Finding a way to improve legal quality was just one of the three main goals of the POWER research program. The other two goals are reduction of total cost of ownership (TTO) of the (knowledge-based) systems intended for the support of civil servants or citizens and secondly, reduction of time to market (TTM) i.e. the speed with which these (knowledge-based) systems can be created, and consequently the regulatory power can be effectuated.

The POWER-approach supports the finding of anomalies in legal sources. Central in the approach is the central role for formal (and semi formal) knowledge representations. In the POWER-approach different knowledge representation formats are used. How these knowledge representations are used and how they contribute to improving legal quality is extensively described in other papers (see e.g. Van Engers et al., 1999, 2000, 2001, 2003 and 2004). Amongst them are both procedural descriptions called 'scenarios' (which are more or less comparable to UML action diagrams) and POWER-conceptual models (expressed in UML/OCL). Although scenarios (see section 3) lack the benefits of a strict formal model expressed in UML/ OCL (van Engers et al., 2001 [3] and [4]) they are useful to provide both analysts and experts with a good insight in the legal domain represented, especially when the legislation involved is to be used in a categorization or assessment task. Scenarios also proved to be an excellent means of communication with experts and representatives of disciplines involved in the implementation of legislation (see Van Engers et al. 2002 [7]).

The POWER approach combines two typical knowledge management approaches; the stock or codification approach and the flow or organisational approach. It offers both a method and supporting tools that support a systematic translation of (new) legislation into the administrations' processes. POWER offers a systematic approach can help to improve legal quality.

In contrast to other knowledge modelling approaches the POWER-approach is focused on modelling legal sources rather than expert knowledge. Expert knowledge however is needed to find the correct interpretations but also for efficiency reasons. Starting with representing the (legal) experts' knowledge (using scenarios) helps to find the adequate scope (the legal sources to be analysed). Confronting the expert with differences between the model build out of the experts' knowledge and the knowledge that can be distilled out of the other knowledge sources (specifically the law) causes the legal experts to see things in a different light and has often led to changes in the law.

3. Quality improvement

The quality of the law enforcement depends on the quality of the legislation itself and on the quality of the knowledge systems that are actually used in the client handling processes as well. In previous work (see Van Engers and Boekenoogen 2003) we described some results from a project that was aimed a improving the quality of legislation and the investigation of the consequences of implementing a new law. Others also have proposed approaches form quality improvement both in the legal domain as for knowledge in general (see e.g. Voermans 2000, Preece 1994, Vanthienen 1997 and Spreeuwenberg 2001).

The problem with most verification procedures is that these procedures can only be applied after most of the hard work has already been done, i.e. formalising the knowledge. Since this formalisation process, i.e translating the legislation into a formal representation (van Engers et al., 2001 [5]) and applying a verification process to it, usually takes some time even when it is supported by tools such as the POWER-workbench, a less subtle and profound approach is needed to satisfy the practical needs of legislation drafters and policy makers need feedback. Especially if in the drafting process, where these drafters deal with the politicians and other influential stakeholders feedback is needed in a much earlier stage. Furthermore it is not always necessary to design a (rule-based) system at all. Specifically for this purpose we developed a less labour and time intensive method derived from the original Power-method that helps to find anomalies. That method is called the Power-light method. We can choose to just applying the Power-light if we don't need a formal model for the purposes mentioned before.

The POWER-approach is used to detect anomalies in legislation, but as a regular part of the design of the regulatory processes not as a separate step. Under time pressure we can use the Power-light method which works quite similar, except for the fact that formalization only takes place in the modellers' mind.

How the POWER-method can be used to detects in legislation defects has already been describe in previously published papers (e.g. Van Engers 2004) I refer to those papers for more detailed information about the process and examples. Typical anomalies found are circularities, ambiguous references and missing concepts, gaps in the law and inapplicable regulations.

4. Knowledge representation

Central to the POWER-approach is the creation of a formal knowledge representation of the legal domain at hand. This representation is called the POWER-conceptual model. The representation formalism, design and examples are already described in previous publications (e.g. Van Engers et al 2001 [5]) for readers yet unfamiliar with this approach in this section a very short introduction is given. The POWER-conceptual model is represented in a notation called Unified Modelling Language (UML see D'Souza and Wills 1999). This notation has become one of the most accepted standard notations for representing domain model, but there are many ways to use the notation. The usage defined in the POWER-method, starts by dividing the model in UML packages. The structure of packages within the translated conceptual model is identical to the hierarchy in the legislation (i.e. chapters, sections, articles, members etc.), which allows tracing all conceptual models, and products that will derive from them, to the original legislation. The structure of packages within the integrated conceptual model represents the definition of concepts found in the legislation, and the relationships between these definitions.

Within each UML package, the important concepts found in the legislation are modelled as types and attributes. The references found in the legislation are modelled as an extension to the UML, which we called "Package Reference". A package reference is modelled as a classifier, which represents some not-yet-identified other packages. Finally, the norms within the legislation are modelled in a formal language, named Object Constraint Language (OCL), which is a part of the UML. The Object Constraint Language can for instance determine under which conditions a "Natural Person" becomes a "Tax Payer". One can use OCL in a similar way as one would use a reified first order predicate calculus to express a legal norm.

The conceptual models produced this way (the POWER-model) contain the legal knowledge. When this knowledge is combined with the process and task knowledge, we have a specification for a supporting knowledge-based component.

Before making a formal representation of a certain domain it proved to be helpful to first understand a bit about the legal domain. This is best obtained by looking at how some (prototypical) cases are solved that correspond to a certain target group. The reasoning strategies of legal experts used for the solution of these (hypothetical or real) cases can be represented in a kind of procedural representation like a decision tree which can be expressed in e.g. UML action diagrams. Within the POWER research program we use a special form of such action diagrams which we call 'scenarios' because they represent the possible scenarios of solving cases (see also Van Engers et al. 2002 [7]).

We experienced that developing such scenarios at the start of the knowledge modelling process helped both knowledge analysts and legal experts to understand the domain better, especially in case of modelling new or complex legislation.

Entitlement to a government subsidy for day nursery

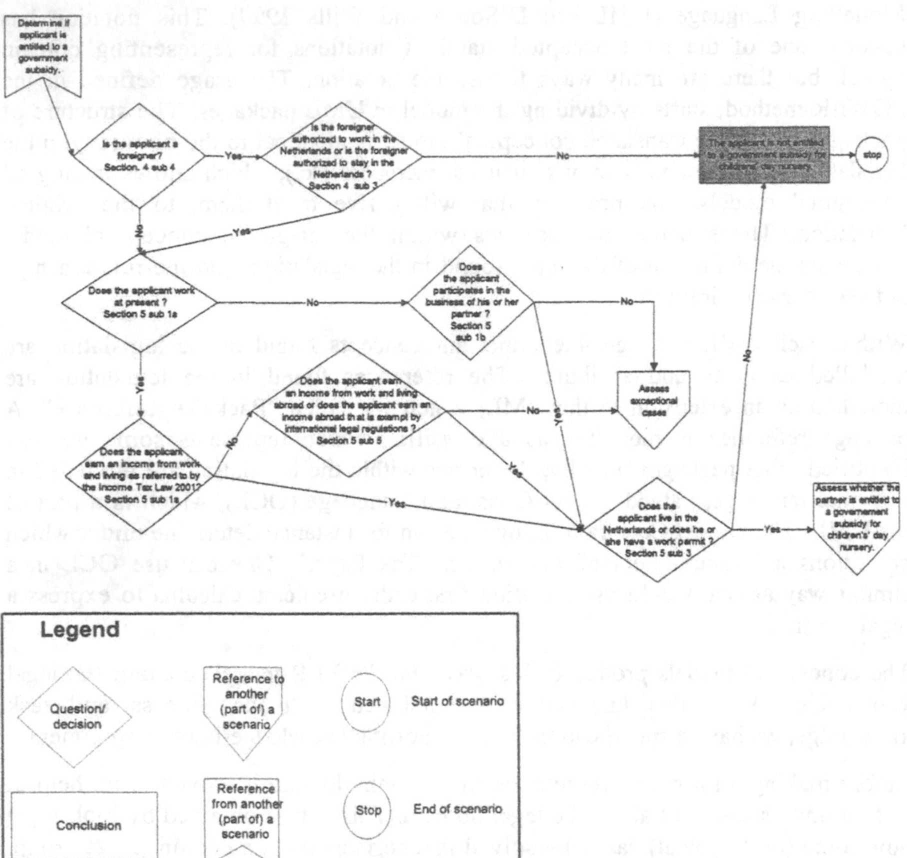

Figure 1. Example of a (part of) a scenario called "determine entitlement to a government subsidy for day nursery"

Many approaches exist in which these very decision diagrams *are* the main knowledge representation (and interface from the modelling tool to the knowledge engineer). Examples of such tools are amongst others, Ruleburst, Knowledge Tools and Be-Informed Studio.

POWER scenarios provide a pure functional idea of how legal experts use legislation to solve certain cases: it does not provide a "system view" on how a decision support system would function. This is the distinction between a POWER scenario and a UML scenario, which is a story about how a system will be used. A UML scenario describes a prototypical sequence of interactions in a business-collaboration or the system context (D'Souza et al., 1999). The main difference between POWER scenarios and UML scenarios is that UML scenarios are used to define the boundary of a system, whereas POWER scenarios can be considered as a (global) specification of the knowledge intensive process (which could be supported by a system). However different, UML scenarios and POWER scenarios match when it comes to the goal of capturing the task flow. UML scenarios are used to capture the ideal task flow as perceived by end users. POWER scenarios provide us with the means for discovering the implicit tasks and task flow within legal domains.

The idea of using these scenarios as the basis for knowledge-based systems design may be tempting, but essential to the POWER approach is that we base our knowledge models on the legal sources rather than on the experts' interpretation of these sources. As we found out the experts' interpretations may be incomplete or even conflict with these knowledge sources (i.e. in conflict with what is the law!). Furthermore a serious handicap of procedural representations is their limitations they put on the implementation. The order of the different reasoning steps represented in the scenarios may very well be not the most efficient one. Also when designing a user dialogue for a knowledge-based system one may want to choose a different order for posing questions then you would derive form such scenarios.

5. Conclusions

The POWER-method has shown to be a very useful approach for modelling normative systems. These systems are described in laws and other regulations including regulations that are used outside the government e.g. insurance policies. The POWER-method offers a structural design method for improving regulatory processes. One of its strong advantages is the support for detecting anomalies in legislation in an early stage of design (preferably even before the law becomes effective). This makes the Power-method a powerful tool for both legislation drafters, law-enforcement organizations and other organizations that are responsible for the design and/or execution of large bodies of regulations.

We experienced that despite these clear benefits implementation proved to be far from easy. In fact the implementation phase still continues. The transfer from knowledge from research projects such as the POWER programme into the regular processes of huge organisations as public administrations cost lots of energy and is time consuming. Changing people's way of working, demands a change of mind-set that not everyone can cope with. Another problem also not specific to the POWER-approach is the lack of managers with an information science back-ground in public administrations. Usually the managers are recruited with a completely different skill set. Therefore these managers simply don't understand the relationships between the features of the design processes (including methods, tools, staff and infrastructure) and the quality of the public administrations primary processes. Implementation of approaches such as the POWER-approach should therefore also be considered as an organisational change programme, demanding all kind of actions including educating the managers. I learned that learning at an individual level can be hard sometimes, but learning at corporate level is much harder.

References

1. Van Engers, T.M., Kordelaar, P., 1999, POWER: Programme for an Ontology based Working Environment for modeling and use of Regulations and legislation. Proceedings of the ISMICK'99.
2. Van Engers, T.M., Kordelaar, P.J.M., den Hartog, J., Glassée, E., 2000, POWER: Programme for an Ontology based Working Environment for modeling and use of Regulations and legislation. In Proceeding of the 11th workshop on Database and Expert Systems Applications (IEEE) Eds. Tjoa, Wagner and Al-Zobaidie, Greenwich London, ISBN 0-7695-0680-1, pp. 327-334.
3. Van Engers, T.M., Gerrits, G., Boekenoogen, M.R., Glassée E., Kordelaar, P.,2001, *POWER: Using UML/OCL for Modeling Legislation – an application report*. Proceedings of the ICAIL 2001, St. Louis.
4. Van Engers, T.M., Glassée, E., 2001, Facilitating the Legislation Process using a shared Conceptual Model. In: IEEE Intelligent Systems January 2001, p. 50- 57.
5. Van Engers, T.M., Van Driel, L., Boekenoogen, M., 2002, The effect of formal representations formats on the quality of legal decision-making, in Legal Knowledge and Information Systems (Bench-Capon, Daskalopulu, Winkels eds.), IOS Press Amsterdam, ISBN 1 58603 299 2, p 63-71.
6. Van Engers, T.M., Boekenoogen, M.R., 2003, Improving Legal Quality: an application report, in proceeding of ICAIL2003.
7. Van Engers, T.M., Legal engineering: A knowledge engineering approach to improving legal quality. In J. Padget, R. Neira, and J.L. De León, editors, *eGovernment and eDemocracy: Progress and Challenges*, pages 189-206. Instituto Politéchnico Nacional Centro de Investigacion en Computación, 2004. ISBN 970-36-0152-9.
8. Glassée, E., Van Engers, T.M., Jacobs, A., 2003 POWER: An Integrated Method for Legislation and Regulations from their Design to their Use in E-government Services and Law Enforcement, in Digital Legislation (ed Moens), die Keure, Brugge, ISBN 90 5958 039 7, p175-204
9. Preece, Shingal, 1994, Foundation and Application of Knowledge Base Verification, International Journal of Intelligent Systems, 9, 683 – 701
10. D'Souza D.F. and Wills A.C., 1999, Objects, components and frameworks with UML: the Catalysis approach, Addison-Wesley, ISBN 0-201-31012-0.
11. Spreeuwenberg, S., Van Engers, T.M., Gerrits, R.,2001, The Role of Verification in Improving the Quality of Legal Decision-Making, in Legal Knowledge and Information Systems, IOS press, ISSN 0922-6389.
12. Vanthienen, J., Mues C., Wets, G., 1997, Inter-Tabular Verification in an Interactive Environment, Proceedings Eurovav 97, 155 – 165
13. Voermans, W., 2000, Computer-assisted legislative drafting in the Netherlands: the LEDA-system, A National Conference on Legislative Drafting in the Global Village

BEST APPLICATION PAPER

Case-Based Reasoning Investigation of Therapy Inefficacy

Rainer Schmidt[1)], Olga Vorobieva[1+2)]

[1)] Institute for Medical Informatics and Biometry, University of Rostock, D-18055 Rostock, Germany
[2)] Sechenov Institute of Evolutionary Physiology and Biochemistry, St.Petersburg, Russia

Abstract. In this paper, we present ISOR, a Case-Based Reasoning system for long-term therapy support in the endocrine domain and in psychiatry. ISOR performs typical therapeutic tasks, such as computing initial therapies, initial dose recommendations, and dose updates. Apart from these tasks ISOR deals especially with situations where therapies become ineffective. Causes for inefficacy have to be found and better therapy recommendations should be computed. In addition to the typical Case-Based Reasoning knowledge, namely former already solved cases, ISOR uses further knowledge forms, especially medical histories of query patients themselves and prototypical cases (prototypes). Furthermore, the knowledge base consists of therapies, conflicts, instructions etc. So, retrieval does not only provide former similar cases but different forms and steps of retrieval are performed, while adaptation occurs as an interactive dialog with the user. Since therapy inefficacy can be caused by various circumstances, we propose searching for former similar cases to get ideas about probable reasons that subsequently should be carefully investigated. We show that ISOR is able to successfully support such investigations.

1 Introduction

In medical practice, therapies prescribed according to a certain diagnosis sometimes do not give desired results. Sometimes therapies are effective for some time but suddenly stop helping any more. There are many different reasons. A diagnosis might be erroneous, the state of a patient might have changed completely or the state might have changed just slightly but with important implications for an existing therapy. Furthermore, a patient might have caught an additional disease, some other complication might have occurred, or a patient might have changed his/her lifestyle (e.g. started a diet) etc.

For long-term therapy support in the endocrine domain and in psychiatry, we have developed a Case-Based Reasoning system, named ISOR, that not only performs typical therapeutic tasks but also especially deals with situations where therapies become ineffective. Therefore, it first attempts to find causes for inefficacy and subsequently computes new therapy recommendations that should perform better than those administered before.

ISOR is a medical Case-Based Reasoning system that deals with the following tasks:

- choose appropriate (initial) therapies,
- compute doses for chosen therapies,
- update dose recommendations according to laboratory test results,
- establish new doses of prescribed medicine according to changes in a patient's medical status or lifestyle,
- find out probable reasons why administered therapies are not as efficient as they should,
- test obtained reasons for inefficacy and make sure that they are the real cause, and
- suggest recommendations to avoid inefficacy of prescribed therapies.

ISOR deals with long-term diseases, e.g. psychiatric diseases, and with diseases even lasting for a lifetime, e.g. endocrine malfunctions.

For psychiatric diseases some Case-Based Reasoning systems have been developed, which deal with specific diseases or problems, e.g. with Alzheimer's disease [1] or with eating disorders [2]. Since we do not want to discuss various psychiatric problems but intend to illustrate ISOR by understandable examples, in this paper we focus mainly on some endocrine and psychiatric disorders, namely on hypothyroidism and depressive symptoms. Inefficacy of pharmacological therapy for depression is a widely known problem (e.g. [3, 4, 5, 6, 7]). There are many approaches to solve this problem. Guidelines and algorithms have been created (e.g. [8, 9, 10]). ISOR gives reference to a psychopharmacology algorithm [10] that is available on the website htp://mhc.com/Algorithms/Depression.

The paper is organized as follows. Firstly, we introduce typical therapeutic tasks, subsequently we present the architecture of ISOR and finally we illustrate its work by examples.

2. Methods: Typical Therapeutic Tasks

As a consequence of our experiences with ICONS [11], a system for antibiotic therapy advice, and with therapy support programs for hypothyroidism [12], we believe that four tasks exist for medicinal therapies. The first one means computing an initial therapy, secondly an initial dose has to be determined, later on dose updates may be necessary, and finally interactions with further diseases, complications, and especially with already administered therapies have to be considered.

In the following we illustrate the four tasks by our programs that deal with therapy support for hypothyroid patients. The antibiotics therapy adviser ICONS deals only with two of these tasks: computing initial therapies and initial doses.

2.1 Computing an initial therapy

Probably, the most important task for therapies is the computation of initial therapies. The main task of ICONS is to compute promising antibiotic therapies even before the pathogen that caused the infection is determined in the laboratory. However, for hypothyroidism ISOR does not compute initial therapies but only initial doses, because for hypothyroidism only one therapy is available: it is thyroid hormone, usually in form of levothyroxine.

2.2 Computing an initial dose

In ICONS the determination of initial doses is a rather simple task. For every antibiotic a specific calculation function is available and has to be applied.

For hypothyroidism the determination of initial doses (figure 1) is more complicated. Firstly, a couple of prototypes exist. These are recommendations that have been defined by expert commissions [13]. Though we are not sure whether they are officially accepted, we call them guidelines. The assignment of a patient to a fitting guideline is obvious because of the way the guidelines have been defined. With the help of these guidelines a range for good doses can be calculated.

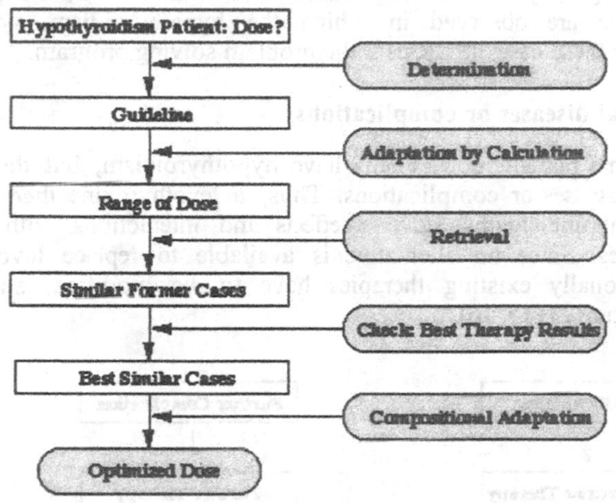

Fig. 1. Determination of an initial levothyroxine dose

To compute a dose with best expected impact, we retrieve similar cases whose initial doses are within the calculated ranges. Since cases are described by few attributes and since our case base is rather small, we use Tversky's sequential measure of dissimilarity [14]. On the basis of those retrieved cases that had best therapy results an average initial therapy is calculated. Best therapy results can be determined by values of a blood test after two weeks of treatment with the initial dose. The opposite idea to consider cases with bad therapy results does not work here, because bad results can also be caused by various other reasons.

To compute optimal dose recommendations, we apply two forms of adaptation. First, a calculation of ranges according to guidelines and patients attribute values. Secondly, we use compositional adaptation. That means, we take only similar cases with best therapy results into account and calculate the average dose for these cases, which has to be adapted to the query patient by another calculation.

2.3 Updating the dose in a patient's lifetime

For monitoring a hypothyroidism patient, three basic laboratory blood tests (TSH, FT3, FT4) have to be undertaken. Usually the results of these tests correspond to each other. Otherwise, it indicates a more complicated thyroid condition and additional tests are necessary. If the results of the basic tests show that the patients thyroid hormone level is normal, it means that the current levothyroxine dose is OK. If the tests indicate that the thyroid hormone level is too low, the current dose has to be increased by 25 or 50 μg, if it is high, the dose has to be decreased by 25 or 50 μg [15, 16]. So, for monitoring, adaptation means calculating according to some rules, which are based on guidelines. Since an overdose of levothyroxine may cause serious complications for a patient, a doctor cannot simply consider test results and symptoms that indicate a dose increase but additionally he/she has to investigate reasons why the current dose is not appropriate any more. In ISOR this situation is described as a problem of therapy inefficiency. In most cases the solution is obvious, e.g. puberty, pregnancy etc. These situations are covered by adaptation rules. Sometimes cases are observed in which the hypothyroidism syndromes are unexplained. For these cases ISOR uses the problem solving program.

2.4 Additional diseases or complications

It often occurs that patients do not only have hypothyroidism, but they suffer from further chronic diseases or complications. Thus, a levothyroxine therapy has to be checked for contraindications, adverse effects and interactions with additionally existing therapies. Since no alternative is available to replace levothyroxine, if necessary additionally existing therapies have to be modified, substituted, or compensated (figure 2) [15, 16].

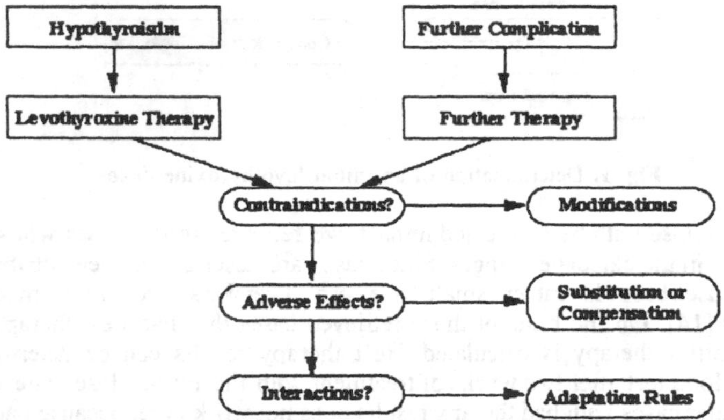

Fig. 2. Levothyroxine therapy and additionally existing therapies

ISOR performs three tests. The first one checks if another existing therapy is contraindicated to hypothyroidism. This holds only for very few therapies, namely for specific diets like soybean infant formula, which is the most popular food for babies who do not get enough mother's milk but it prevents the effect of levothyroxine. Such diets have to be modified. Since no exact knowledge is available to explain how to accomplish this, our program just issues a warning saying that a modification is necessary.

The second test considers adverse effects. There are two ways to deal with them. A further existing therapy has either to be substituted or it has to be compensated by another drug. Such knowledge is available, and we have implemented corresponding rules for substitutional and compensational adaptation.

The third test checks for interactions between both therapies. We have implemented some adaptation rules, which mainly attempt to avoid the interactions. For example, if a patient has heartburn problems that are treated with an antacid, a rule for this situation states that levothyroxine should be administered at least four hours after or before an antacid. However, if no adaptation rule can solve such an interaction problem, the same substitution rules as for adverse effects are applied.

3 System architecture

ISOR is designed to solve typical problems, especially inefficacy of prescribed therapies that can arise in different medical domains. Therefore most algorithms and functions are domain independent. Another goal is to cope with situations where important patient data is missing and/or where theoretical domain knowledge is controversial.

ISOR does not generate solutions itself. Its task is to help users by providing all available information and to support them to find optimal solutions. Users shall be doctors, maybe together with a patient.

Technically, ISOR is implemented in Delphi 7, the format for the case and knowledge bases is Paradox 7, and retrieval is performed by SQL.

In addition to the typical Case-Based Reasoning knowledge, namely former already solved cases, ISOR uses further knowledge components, namely medical histories of query patients themselves and prototypical cases (prototypes). Furthermore, ISOR's knowledge base consists of therapies, conflicts, instructions etc. The architecture is shown in figure 3.

In this section we explain the components and in the next chapter we present examples to show how the main knowledge components work together.

3.1 Medical case histories

Ma and Knight [17] have introduced a concept of case history in Case-Based Reasoning. Such an approach is very useful when we deal with chronic patients, because often the same complications occur again, former successful solutions can be helpful again, while former unsuccessful solutions should be avoided.

The case history is written in the patient's individual base as a sequence of records. A patient's base contains his/her whole medical history, all medical information that is available: diseases, complications, therapies, circumstances of his/her life etc. Each record describes an episode in a patient's medical history. Episodes often characterise a specific problem. Since the case base is problem oriented, it contains just episodes and the same patient can be mentioned in the case base a few times, even concerning different problems.

Information from the patient's individual base can be useful for a current situation, because for patients with chronic diseases very similar problems often occur again. If a similar situation is found in the patient's history, it is up to the user to decide whether to start retrieval in the general case base or not.

In endocrinology, case histories are designed according to a standard scheme, one record per visit. Every record contains the results of laboratory tests and of an interrogatory about symptoms, complaints and physiological conditions of a patient.

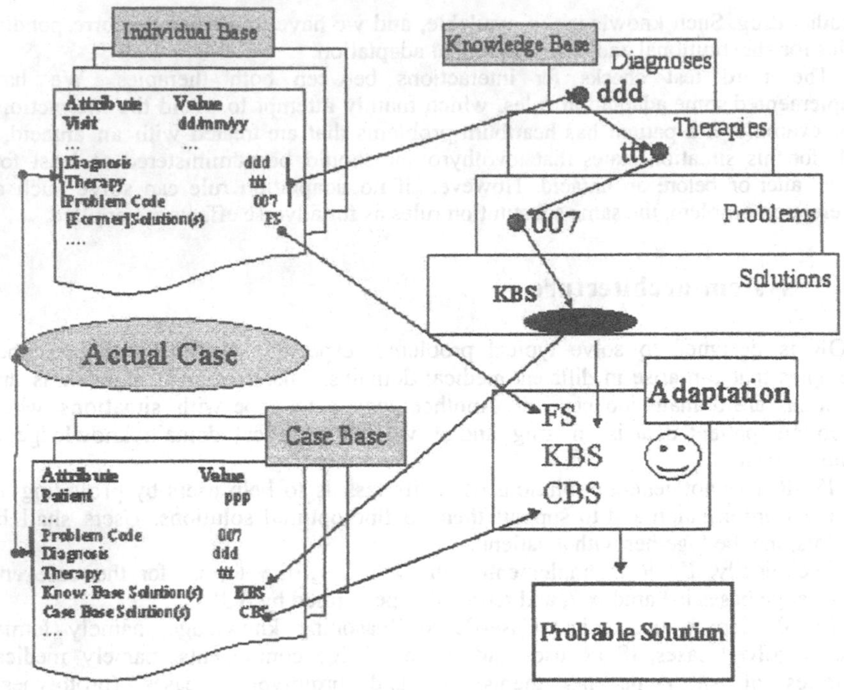

Fig. 3. System architecture

Therefore the retrieval of former similar situations from the individual base of an endocrine patient is easy to organise.

For psychiatric patients, case histories are often unsystematic and they can be structured in various forms. A general formalisation of psychiatric cases and their histories is not achieved yet. The design of case histories is problem dependent.

In both domains, we first search in the query patient's history for similar problems and for similar diagnoses.

3.2 Knowledge base, case base, and prototypes

The knowledge base contains information about problems and their solutions that are possible according to the domain theory. It has a tree structure and it consists of lists of diagnoses, corresponding therapies, conflicts, instructions, and medical problems (including solutions) that can arise from specific therapies. The knowledge base also contains links to guidelines, algorithms and references to correspondent publications [8, 9, 10].

The case base is problem oriented. Thus a case in the case base is just a part of a patient's history, namely an episode that describes a specific problem that usually has a solution too. So, the case base represents decisions of doctors (diagnosis, therapies) for specific problems, and their generalisations and their theoretical foundations (see the examples). A solution is called "case solution", abbreviated "CS". Every case solution has (usually two) generalisations, which are formulated by doctors. The first one is expressed in terms of the knowledge base and it is used as a keyword for searching in the knowledge base. Such a generalisation is called "knowledge base solution", abbreviated "KBS". The second generalisation of a solution is expressed in common words and it is mainly used for dialogues. It is called "prompt solution", abbreviated "PS".

Former cases (attribute value pairs) in the case base are indexed by keywords. Each case contains keywords that have been explicitly placed by an expert. For retrieval three main keys are used: a code of the problem, a diagnosis, and a therapy. Further keys such as age, sex etc. can be used optionally.

Prototypes (generalized cases) play a particular role. Prototypes help to select a proper solution from the list of probable or available solutions. A prototype may help to point out a reason of inefficacy of a therapy or it may support the doctor's choice of a drug.

3.3 Retrieval, adaptation, and dialogue

For retrieval keywords are used. Since our system is problem oriented, the first one is a code that implies a specific problem. The second keyword is the diagnosis and the other ones are retrieved from the knowledge base.

Adaptation takes place as a dialogue between the doctor, the patient, and the system. The system presents different solutions, versions of them, and asks questions to manifest them. The doctor answers and selects suggestions, while the patient himself or herself suggests possible solutions that can be considered by the doctor and by the system.

We differentiate between two steps of adaptation. The first one occurs as a dialogue between ISOR and a user. Usually, doctors are the users. However, sometimes even a patient may take part in this dialogue. The goal of these dialogues is to select probable solutions from all information sources mentioned in sections 3.1 and 3.2. Pieces of information are retrieved by the use of keywords. Specific menus support the retrieval process. The first step of adaptation can be regarded as partly user based: ISOR presents lists of probable solutions and menus of keywords, the user selects the most adequate ones. The second adaptation means proving obtained solutions. This proving is rule based and it includes further dialogues, laboratory test results, and consultations with medical experts. While the procedures supporting the first adaptation step are domain independent, the adaptation rules of the second step are mainly domain dependent.

4 Examples

By three examples we illustrate how ISOR works. The first and the second one are from the endocrine domain, the third one deals with a psychiatric problem.

4.1 Hypothyroidism

4.1.1 Inefficacy of Levothyroxine therapy

Every morning a mother gives her 10 year-old boy not only the prescribed Levothyroxine dose but also vitamin pills. These pills have not been prescribed but they are healthy and have lately been advertised on TV. Part of this medication is Sodium Hydrocarbonate (cooking soda) that causes problems with Levothyroxine.

Individual base. The same problem, inefficacy of Levothyroxine therapy, is retrieved from the patient's history. The solution of the former problem was that the boy did not take the drug regularly. This time it must be a different cause, because the mother controls the intake.

Knowledge base. It has a tree structure that is organised according to keys. One main key is *therapy* and the keyword is *Levothyroxine*. Another keyword is *instructions*. These instructions are represented in form of rules that concern the intake of Levothyroxine. For Levothyroxine a rather long list of instructions exists. Since the idea is that the boy may break an instruction, this list is sorted according to the observed frequency of offences against them in the case base.

Concerning these instructions a couple of questions are asked, e.g. whether the boy takes Sodium Hydrocarbonate together with Levothyroxine. Since the mother is not aware of the fact that Sodium Hydrocarbonate is contained in the vitamin pills, she gives a negative answer and no possible solution can be established by the knowledge base. However, *soda* is generated as one keyword for retrieval in the case base.

So, the following solutions are retrieved from the knowledge base, the third one does not fit for the boy.

Knowledge base solution 1: Sodium Hydrocarbon
Knowledge base solution 2: Soy
Knowledge base solution 3: Estrogene

Case base. Using the keyword *soda* eight cases with the following seven solutions are retrieved (case solution 4 occurs twice).

Case solution 1: Aspirin Upsa
Case solution 2: Cooking Soda
Case solution 3: Soluble juice
Case solution 4: Alka Seltzer
Case solution 5: "Invite"
Case solution 6: Vitamin "Teddy"
Case solution 7: Lime Pills"

Thus we get a list of drugs and beverages that contain sodium Hydrocarbonate, all of them belong to the generalised solution "soluble" (figure 4).

Solution. The boy admits to take Levothyroxine together with an instantiation of the generalised solution "soluble", namely soluble vitamin.

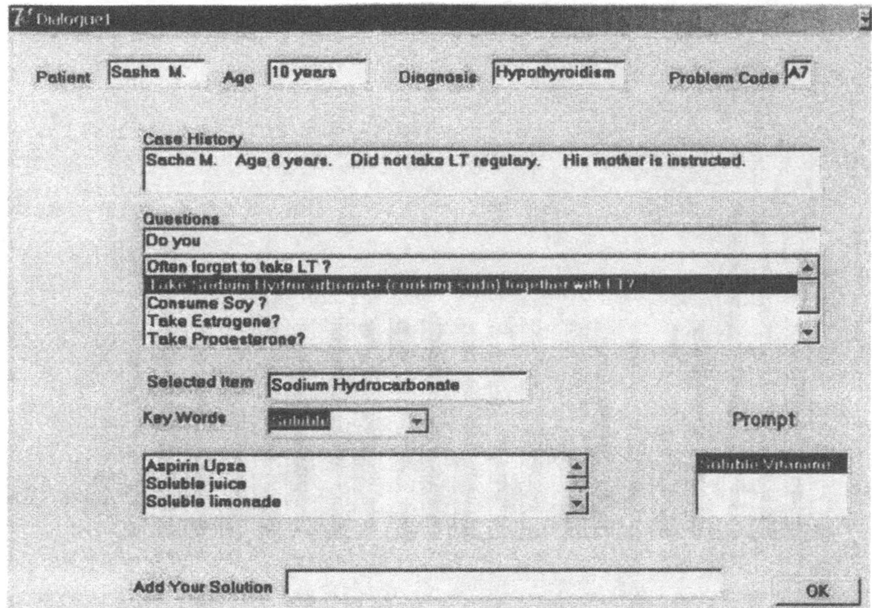

Fig. 4. Dialog for the first example

Recommendation. The boy is told to take vitamin four hours later than Levothyroxine. Additionally, further interactions between vitamin and Levothyroxine must be checked, because it might be necessary to adjust the Levothyroxine dose.

4.1.2 Improving the efficacy by dose updates

Figure 5 shows an example of a case study. We compared the decisions of an experienced doctor with the recommendations of ISOR. The decisions are based on basic laboratory tests and on lists of observed symptoms. Intervals between two visits are approximately six months. In this example there are three deviations between the doctor's and ISOR's decisions, usually there are less. At the second visit (v2), according to laboratory results the Levothyroxine should be increased. ISOR recommended a too high increase. The applied adaptation rule was not precise enough. So, we modified it. At visit 10 (v10) the doctor decided to try to decrease the dose. The doctor's reasons were not included in our knowledge base and since his attempt was not successful, we did not alter any adaptation rule. At visit 21 (v21) the doctor increased the dose because of some minor symptoms of hypothyroidism, which were not included in ISOR's list of hypothyroidism symptoms. Since the doctor's decision was probably right (visit 22), we added these symptoms to the list of hypothyroidism symptoms of ISOR.

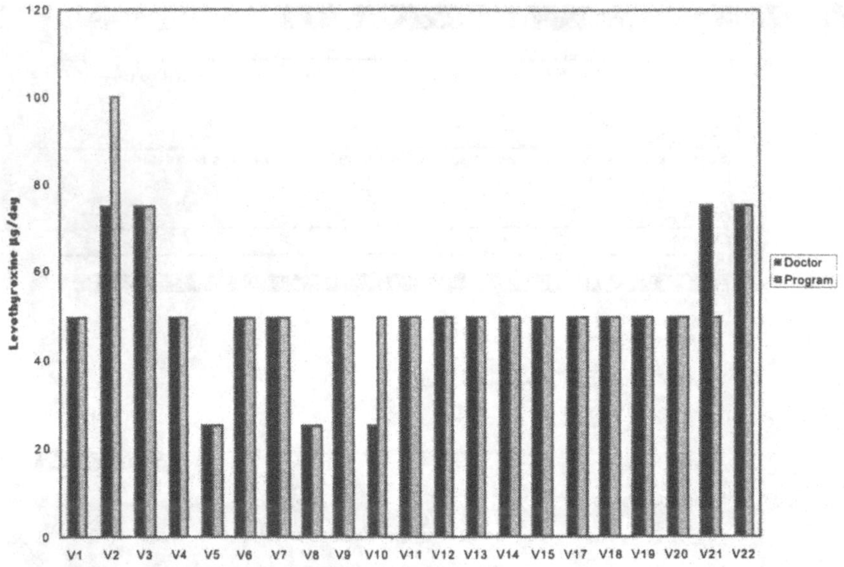

Figure 5. Dose updates recommended by our program compared with doctor's decision. V1 means the first visit, V2 the second visit etc.

4.2 Inefficacy of psychiatric drugs

Originally, ISOR was developed for the endocrine domain, especially for hypothyroidism, but later on it has been generalised. Now it can solve the same types of problems in different medical domains. Now we present an example from psychiatry.

A man, 55 years of age, has been treated for depression for 15 years. Symptoms of depression appeared after he was cruelly beaten near his house. Since he did not see any connection between his depression and the violence, he did not tell it to his doctor. At first, the antidepressant Tofranil for intake in the morning and the sedative Tisercin for better sleep at bedtime were prescribed. Later on, during another depression stage the antidepressant Fluoxetine helped. Now, his problem is that neither Fluoxetine, nor any other proposed antidepressant helps any more.

Retrieval. Keywords are used to retrieve information from all data sources. Since optional keywords about a patient's feeling (e.g. *feeling worse*) are used for retrieval of the patient's medical history, even biographical events of a patient can be retrieved.

Individual base. Since the problem of inefficacy of an antidepressant never arose in the patient's past, no solution can be found. However, indirect information was retrieved. The keyword *feeling better* provided a trip to Switzerland, while the result of the keyword *feeling worse* provided a trip to Israel, where the latest very severe depression began.

Feeling better: A trip to Switzerland

Feeling worse: A trip to Israel

The knowledge base contains information about depression, anxiety and other psychiatric diseases, possible complications and references to their theoretical grounds [18, 19, 20, 21, 22]. References to similar problems are retrieved, the most remarkable one is a link to the algorithm for psychopharmacology of depression [10, 23]. Though the idea of the algorithm is to solve the problem of non-response to an antidepressant, it does not really fit here, because it does not cover the situation that a therapy helped for some time and then stopped having an effect.

Case base. Eleven cases with similar depression problems are retrieved. Three of them are characterised by the general idea *depression is secondary to anxiety resulting from a psychical trauma*.

Case solution 1: A severe stress during the World War 2 (a woman)

Case solution 2: A bad experience in a Jail (a young man)

Case solution 3: Sexual assault in childhood (a woman)

The other cases have solutions that are generalised to *changes in therapy*.

Adaptation. ISOR displays retrieved information pieces. In this case, two strategies are offered. The first one suggests trying some other therapy. This strategy is supported by the majority of the retrieved cases and partly by theoretical recommendations. The second strategy means to check the diagnosis. This strategy is supported by three retrieved cases and by the patient's medical history. The choice between both strategies is up to the user. In this example the doctor chooses to attempt the second strategy at first. The doctor is especially led by the patient's medical history, because Switzerland is usually associated with a safe life (especially in comparison to life in Russia), while living in Israel is considered as unsafe. Furthermore, this strategy is supported by the general situation that some sedative drugs (e.g. Tisercin at the beginning) had helped for some time.

ISOR offers a list of questions for the favoured strategy and as a result the doctor concludes that in this case depression is in fact only second to anxiety. The man is permanently afraid of possible violence and anxiety is based on strong fear that occurred long ago.

Explaining remarks. Diagnosing anxiety needs good medical skills, because patients try to suppress traumatic events from their memory [24]. In this example depression even served as a mechanism of suppression. The accepted case-based solution spared the patient unnecessary experiments with other psychopharmacological drugs.

So, the first problem is solved, a new diagnosis is ascertained.

The next problem is prescription of a therapy. According to the domain theory and to our knowledge base anxiety implies Neuroleptics [22, 25]. Many of them are available but a good choice is not trivial.

Individual base. From the patient's history those sedatives (Neuroleptics) are retrieved that he took in his lifetime and that had positive effects on his psychical condition: Tisercin and Paxil, which is a drug that has both sedative and antidepressive effects.

Prototype. Among those prototypes that have been defined by doctors (based on their long experience with cases) the prototypical solution Paxil is retrieved.

Adaptation. Before described, every drug must be checked for conflicts with the patient's additional diseases and already existing therapy. Though the query patient has already taken Paxil in the past, our system checks all possible conflicts. If necessary, adaptation has to be performed. In this case no conflicts are discovered and Paxil is prescribed.

5 Conclusion

We have presented a CBR system that helps doctors to solve medical problems, particularly to investigate causes of inefficacy of therapies. It includes different knowledge containers, namely a case base, a knowledge base, prototypes, and individual bases of patients that reflect their medical histories. Information retrieved from these containers is arranged in form of dialogues.

The case base plays a central role in the dialogue forming process. It serves as a kind of filter when the knowledge base suggests too many possible solutions for the problem (as in the first example). In this situation the most typical cases are retrieved from the case base. When a solution from the knowledge base is not convincing or when it is hardly adaptable, the case base may provide better alternatives (as in the third example).

Generalisations, keywords and references to other knowledge components belong to the case base. The adaptation program uses them to create dialogues. In the part that concerns the case base and the dialogues ISOR can be considered as domain independent.

The design of the case base and our implementation allow solving problems from different medical domains. Specific, domain dependant features are attributed mostly to the individual base, because every domain requires a special design of case histories. The knowledge base in ISOR is domain-oriented, but all algorithms and functions are completely domain independent.

Acknowledgement
We thank Dr. Monika Mix, Children's Hospital of the University Clinic of Rostock, and Prof. Nikolai Nikolaenko, Sechenov Institute of Evolutionary Physiology and Biochemistry in St.Petersburg, for their data and for their help and time during our consultations.

References

1. Marling, C., Whitehouse, P.: Case-Based Reasoning in the care of Alzheimer's disease patients. In: Aha, D.W., Watson, I. (eds.): Case-Based Reasoning Research and Development, Springer Berlin (2001) 702-715
2. Bichindaritz, I.: A case-based assistant for clinical psychiatry expertise. Journal of the American Medical Informatics Association, Symposium Supplement (1994) 673-677
3. Hirschfeld, R.M., et al.: Partial response and nonresponse to antidepressant therapy: current approaches and treatment options. J Clin Psychiatry 63 (9) (2002) 826-37
4. Barbee, J.G., Jamhour, N.J.: Lamotrigine as an augmentation agent in treatment-resistant depression. J Clin Psychiatry 63 (8) (2002) 737-41
5. Lam, R.W., Wan, D.D., Cohen, N.L., Kennedy, S.H.: Combining antidepressants for treatment-resistant depression: a review. J Clin Psychiatry 63 (8) (2002) 685-93.
6. Keitner, G.I., Posternak, M.A., Ryan, C.E.: How many subjects with major depressive disorder meet eligibility requirements of an antidepressant efficacy trial? J Clin Psychiatry 64 (9) (2003) 1091-3

7. Cuffel, B.J., et al.: Remission, residual symptoms, and nonresponse in the usual treatment of major depression in managed clinical practice. J Clin Psychiatry 64 (4) (2003) 397-402
8. Alacorn, R.D., Glover, S., Boyer, W., Balon, R.: Proposing an algorithm for the pharmacological treatment of posttraumatic stress disorder. Ann Clin Psychiatry 12 (4) (2000) 239-246
9. Expert Consensus Guideline Series Treatment of Posttraumatic Stress Dosorder. J Clin Psychiatry 60 (suppl 16) (2000) 1-76.
10. Osser, D.N., Patterson, R.D.: Algorithms for the pharmacotherapy of depression, parts one and two. Directions in Psychiatry 18 (1998) 303-334
11. Schmidt, R., Gierl, L.: Case-based Reasoning for Antibiotics Therapy Advice: An Investigation of Retrieval Algorithms and Prototypes. Artificial Intelligence in Medicine 23 (2) (2001) 171-186
12. Vorobieva, O., Gierl, L., Schmidt, R.: Case-based Adaptation in Medicine - Focusing on Hypothyroidism. In: Lees, B. (ed.): UK-Workshop on Case-based Reasoning (2002) 61-68
13. Working group for paediatric endocrinology of the German society for endocrinology and of the German society for children and youth medicine (1998) 1-15
14. Tversky, A.: Features of similarity. Psychological review 84 (1977) 327-352
15. Hampel, R.: Diagnostik und Therapie von Schilddrüsenfunktionsstörungen. UNI-MED Bremen (2000)
16. DeGroot, L.J.: Thyroid Physiology and Hypothyroidsm. In: Besser GM, Turner M, editors. Clinical endocrinilogy. Wolfe, London (1994) Chapter 15.
17. Ma, J., Knight, B. A.: Framework for Historical Case-Based Reasoning. 5th International Conference on Case-Based Reasoning, Springer Berlin (2003) 246-260
18. Davidson, R.J.: Cerebral asymmetry and affective disorders: A developmentalperspective. In: Cicchetti, D., Toth, S.L. (eds.) Internalizing and externalizing expressions of dysfunction. Rochester Symp. on Developmental Psychopathology 2, Hillsdale (1991) 123-133
19. Flor-Henry, P.: Cerebral Basis of Psychopathology.John Wright. PSG.Inc. Boston, Bristol, London (1983)
20. Leonhard, K.: The Classification of the Endogenous Psychoses. John Wiley & Sons, New York (1979)
21. Tucker, D.M., Liotti, M.: Neuropsychological mechanisms of anxiety and depression. In: Boller, F., Grafman, J. (eds.): Handbook of Neuropsychology, Vol. 3. Elsevier, Amsterdam (1989) 443-456
22. Gelder, M.G., Lopez-Ibor, U., Andeasen, N.C. (eds.): New Oxford Textbook of Psychiatry. Oxford University Press, Oxford (2000)
23. htp://mhc.com/Algorithms/Depression
24. Stein, M.B.: Attending to anxiety disorders in primary care. J Clin Psychiatry 64 (suppl 15) (2003) 35-39
25. Kalinowsky, L., Hippius, H.: Pharmacolological, convulsive and other somatic treatments in psychiatry. Grunee&Stratton, New York London (1969).

SESSION 1:

APPLIED AI IN INFORMATION PROCESSING

Hybrid search algorithm applied to the colour quantisation problem

Lars Nolle and Gerald Schaefer

School of Computing and Informatics, Nottingham Trent University
Nottingham, United Kingdom
{lars.nolle,gerald.schaefer}@ntu.ac.uk

Abstract. We apply a variant of Simulated Annealing (SA) as a standard black-box optimisation algorithm to the colour quantisation problem. The main advantage of black-box optimisation algorithms is that they do not require any domain specific knowledge yet are able to provide a near optimal solution. To further improve the performance of the algorithm we combine the SA technique with a standard k-means clustering technique. We evaluate the effectiveness of our approach by comparing its performance with several specialised colour quantisation algorithms. The results obtained show that our hybrid SA algorithm clearly outperforms standard quantisation algorithms and provides images with superior image quality.
Keywords: black box optimisation, simulated annealing, colour quantisation, k-means clustering, stacked hybrid search algorithm

1 Introduction

Colour quantisation is a common image processing technique that allows the representation of true colour images using only a small number of colours and is useful for displaying images on limited hardware such as mobile devices, for image compression, and for other applications such as image retrieval [12]. True colour images typically use 24 bits per pixel which results in an overall gamut of 2^{24} i.e. more than 16.8 million different colours. Colour quantisation uses a colour palette that contains only a small number of colours (usually between 8 and 256) and pixel data are then stored as indices to this palette. Clearly the choice of the colours that make up the palette has a crucial influence on the image quality of the quantised image However, the selection of the optimal colour palette is known to be an np-hard problem [4]. In the image processing literature many different algorithms have been introduced that aim to find a palette that allows for good image quality of the quantised image [4, 3, 2].

In this paper we apply a variant of Simulated Annealing (SA) as a standard black-box optimisation algorithm to the colour quantisation problem. The main advantage of black-box optimisation algorithms is that they do not require any domain specific knowledge yet are able to provide a near optimal solution. We evaluate the effectiveness of our approach by comparing its performance to the results obtained by several purpose built colour quantisation algorithms [4, 3,

2]. The results obtained show that even without any domain specific knowledge our SA based algorithm is able to outperform standard quantisation algorithms and hence to provide palettised images with superior image quality. Although SA is able to always find good solutions, the presence of variation in the results gained from different runs suggests that these solutions were only near optimal. Therefore, in a second step we combine SA with a standard clustering algorithm, k-means, which is guaranteed to find a local minimum. The resulting hybrid algorithm is shown to further improve the effectiveness of the search and hence the image quality of the quantised images.

The rest of the paper is organised as follows: Section 2 provides the background for optimisation based on Simulated Annealing. Section 3 explains our colour quantisation algorithm. Section 4 provides experimental results based on a set of standard test images while 5 concludes the paper.

2 Simulated annealing

Simulated annealing (SA) was first introduced as a general optimisation method by Kirkpatrick *et al.* [6], based on the work of Metropolis *et al.* [8]. It simulates the annealing of metal, in which the metal is heated-up to a temperature near its melting point and then slowly cooled down. This allows the particles to move towards a minimum energy state, with a more uniform crystalline structure. The process therefore permits some control over the microstructure.

Simulated annealing is a variation of the hill-climbing algorithm. Both start from a randomly selected point within the search space of all the possible solutions. Each point in the search space has a measurable error value, E, associated with it, which indicates the quality of the solution. From the current point in search space, new trial solutions are selected for testing from the neighborhood of the current solution. This is usually done by moving a small step in a random direction. In this application, small and equally distributed random numbers from the interval $[-s_{max}, s_{max}]$ are added to each component of the current solution vector, where s_{max} is called the 'maximum step width'. The values for s_{max} need to be chosen from the interval between 0 and the upper limit of the search space dimension. The decrease in error values is ΔE. If ΔE is negative, i.e. the error of a trial solution is less than the error of the current one, the trial solution is accepted as the current solution.

Unlike hill-climbing SA does not automatically reject a new candidate solution if ΔE is positive. Instead it becomes the current solution with probability $p(T)$ which is usually determined using

$$p(T) = e^{-\Delta E/T} \qquad (1)$$

where T is referred to as 'temperature', an abstract control parameter for the cooling schedule. For a given temperature and positive values of ΔE the probability function shown in Equation 1 has a defined upper limit of one, and tends towards zero for large positive values of ΔE. That means, in a practical computer application, the probability $p(T)$ has to be calculated for each candidate solution and to be compared with an equally distributed random number from the interval [0, 1]. If the probability $p(T)$ is greater than the random number the candidate solution is accepted as the current solution, otherwise it is rejected.

The algorithm starts with a high temperature i.e. with a high transition probability. The temperature is then reduced towards zero, usually in steps, according to a cooling schedule such as

$$T_{n+1} = \alpha T_n \tag{2}$$

where T_n is the temperature at step n and α is the cooling coefficient (usually between 0.8 and 0.99).

During each step the temperature must be held constant for an appropriate number of iterations in order to allow the algorithm to settle into a 'thermal equilibrium' i.e. a balanced state. If the number of iterations is too small the algorithm is likely to converge to a local minimum.

Step width adapting simulated annealing (SWASA) [9] overcomes the problems associated with constant values for s_{max} by using a scaling function [11] to adapt the maximum step width to the current iteration by

$$s_{max}(n) = \frac{2s_0}{1 + e^{\beta n/n_{max}}} \tag{3}$$

where $s_{max}(n)$ is the maximum step width at iteration n, s_0 is the initial maximum step width, n_{max} the maximum number of iterations and β is an adaptation constant.

3 Hybrid Simulated Annealing for colour quantisation

In this paper we apply the SWASA algorithm described in Section 2 as a black box optimisation algorithm to the colour quantisation problem. For colour quantisation the objective is to minimise the total error introduced through the application of a colour palette. The colour palette C for an image I, a codebook of k colour vectors, should then be chosen so as to minimise the error function

$$\text{error}(C, I) = \frac{1}{\sum_{j=1}^{k} l_j} \sum_{i=1}^{k} \sum_{j=1}^{l_i} ||C_i - I_j|| + p(C, I) \tag{4}$$

with

$$p(C, I) = \sum_{i=1}^{k} \delta a_i, \quad a_i = \begin{cases} 1 & \text{if } l_i = 0 \\ 0 & \text{otherwise} \end{cases} \tag{5}$$

where l_i is the number of pixels I_j represented by colour C_i of the palette, $||.||$ is the Euclidean distance in RGB space, and δ is a constant ($\delta = 10$ in our experiments). The objective function error(C, I) used is hence a combination of the mean Euclidean distance and a penalty function. The penalty function $p(C, I)$ was integrated in order to avoid unused palette colours by adding a constant penalty value to the error for each entry in the codebook that is not used in the resulting picture.

As can be seen from Equation 4 the objective function is highly non-linear, i.e. it has a high degree of epistasis [1]. Past experience [10] has shown that for this kind of optimisation problems simulated annealing outperforms other generic optimisation algorithms like genetic algorithms [5].

For our colour quantisation algorithm we employ a population based version of the SWASA algorithm with a population size of 10. The start temperature was chosen to be 100 and the cooling coefficient was set to 0.9. The temperature was kept constant over 20 iterations and the maximum number of iterations was set to 10000.

Figure 1 shows a typical run of the SA method applied to colour quantisation. The solid line represents the average quantisation error over time (iterations) while the dashed line represents the best solution of each iteration.

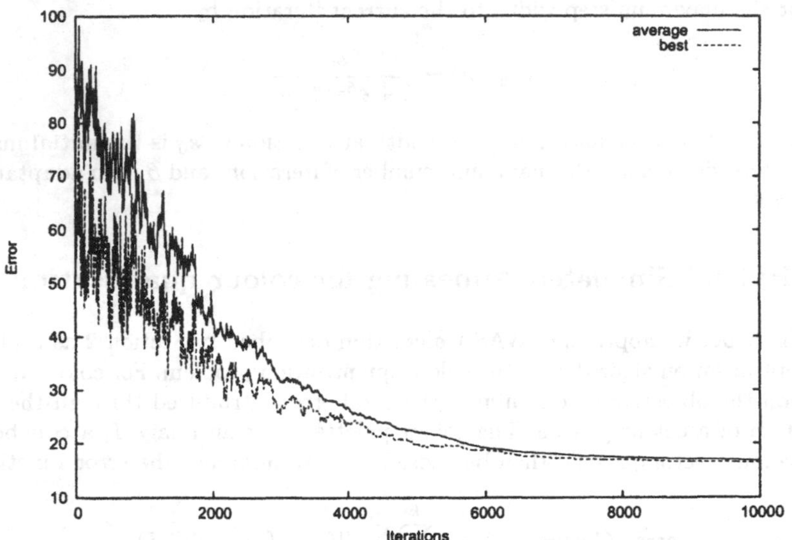

Fig. 1. Typical run of SA optimisation for colour quantisation.

As can be seen from Figure 1 there is always a variation in error values within the population which indicates that although Simulated annealing is able to find good solutions, i.e. solutions from within the region around the global optimum, it rarely exploits that region completely. Therefore, in a second step, we combine the SA approach with a standard k-means clustering algorithm [7] to provide a stacked hybrid optimisation method. K-means clustering is guaranteed to converge towards the local clustering minimum by iteratively carrying out the following two steps:

- Each input vector should be mapped to its closest codeword by a nearest neighbour search.
- The input vectors assigned in each class (i.e. for each codeword) are best represented by the centroid of the vectors in that class.

In this hybridised algorithm the SA component is hence responsible for identifying the region in the search space that will contain the global optimum while the k-means component will then descend into the minimum present in that region.

4 Experimental results

In order to evaluate our new method for colour quantisation we have taken a set of six standard images commonly used in the colour quantisation literature (*Lenna, Peppers, Mandrill, Sailboat, Airplane, and Pool* - see Figure 2) and applied our optimisation scheme to generate quantised images with a palette of 16 colours.

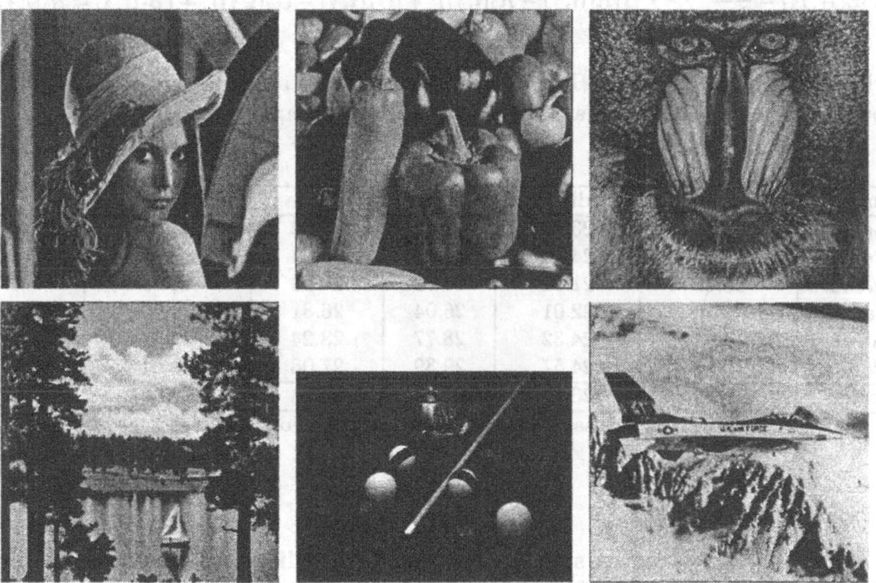

Fig. 2. The six test images used in the experiments: (*Lenna, Peppers, Mandrill, Sailboat, Pool, and Airplane.* (from left to right, top to bottom).

To put the results we obtain into context we have also implemented four popular colour quantisation algorithms to generate corresponding quantised images with palette size 16. The algorithms we have tested were:

- Popularity algorithm [4]: Following a uniform quantisation to 5 bits per channel the n colours that are represented most often form the colour palette.
- Median cut quantisation [4]: An iterative algorithm that repeatedly splits (by a plane through the median point) colour cells into sub-cells..
- Octree quantisation [3]: The colour space is represented as an octree where sub-branches are successively merged to form the palette.
- Neuquant [2]: A one-dimensional self-organising Kohonen neural network is applied to generate the colour map.

For all algorithms, pixels in the quantised images were assigned to their nearest neighbours in the colour palette to provide the best possible image quality.

The results are listed in Table 1, expressed in terms of peak-signal-to-noise-ratio (PSNR) defined as

$$\text{PSNR}(I_1, I_2) = 10 \log_{10} \frac{255^2}{MSE(I_1, I_2)} \tag{6}$$

with MSE (the mean-squared error) given as

$$\text{MSE}(I_1, I_2) = \frac{1}{3nm} \sum_{i=1}^{n} \sum_{j=1}^{m} \left((R_1(i,j) - R_2(i,j))^2 + (G_1(i,j) - G_2(i,j))^2 + (B_1(i,j) - B_2(i,j))^2 \right) \tag{7}$$

where $R(i,j)$, $G(i,j)$, and $B(i,j)$ are the red, green, and blue pixel values at location (i,j) and n and m are the dimensions of the images.

Image	Popularity alg.	Median cut	Octree	Neuquant	Sim. Annealing	Hybrid SA
Lenna	22.24	23.79	27.45	27.82	27.79	**29.70**
Peppers	18.56	24.10	25.80	26.04	26.16	**27.17**
Mandrill	18.00	21.52	24.21	24.59	24.46	**25.37**
Sailboat	8.73	22.01	26.04	26.81	26.69	**27.95**
Airplane	15.91	24.32	28.77	28.24	29.43	**32.04**
Pool	19.87	24.57	29.39	27.08	29.84	**31.57**
mean	17.22	23.39	26.94	26.73	27.40	**28.97**

Table 1. Quantisation results, given in terms of PSNR [dB].

From Table 1 we can see standard Simulated Annealing performs better than all purpose built quantisers for three of the six images and slightly worse for the other three. Overall a mean PSNR of 27.40 dB is achieved which is significantly better than the 26.94 and 26.73 dB obtained by Octree and Neuquant, the two next best algorithms.

As is evident from Table 1 the hybrid optimisation technique introduced in this paper was able to clearly further improve the performance and provide the best image quality for all images with a mean PSNR of 28.97 dB i.e. an improvement of 1.57 dB over the standard SA approach.

An example of the performance of the different algorithms is provided in Figure 3 which shows part of the *Pool* image together with the same part extracted from the images colour quantised by all algorithms. It is clear that the popularity algorithm performs poorly on this image and assigns virtually all of the colours in the palette to green and achromatic colours. Median cut is better but still provides fairly poor colour reproduction; most of the colours in the quantised image are fairly different from the original. The same holds true for the images produced by Neuquant. Here the most obvious artefact is the absence of an appropriate red colour in the colour palette. A far better result is achieved by the Octree algorithm, although here also the red is not very accurate and the colour of the cue is greenish instead of brown. Clearly the best image quality is maintained by applying our hybrid Simulated annealing technique. Although the colour palette has only 16 entries all colours of the original image are accurately presented including the red ball and the colour of the billiard cue.

Fig. 3. Part of original *Pool* image (top-left) and corresponding images quantised with (from left to right, top to bottom): Popularity algorithm, Median cut, Octree quantisation, Neuquant, and our hybrid Simulated annealing approach.

5 Conclusions

In this work we have applied a hybrid Simulated Annealing algorithm to the colour quantisation problem. A standard Simulated Annealing approach was combined with a standard k-means clustering technique. Experimental results obtained on a set of standard test images have demonstrated that this approach can not only be effectively employed but is even able to outperform standard purpose built colour quantisation algorithms.

References

1. Y. Davidor. Epistasis variance: Suitability of a representation to genetic algorithms. *Complex Systems*, 4:369–383, 1990.
2. A.H. Dekker. Kohonen neural networks for optimal colour quantization. *Network: Computation in Neural Systems*, 5:351–367, 1994.
3. M. Gervautz and W. Purgathofer. A simple method for color quantization: Octree quantization. In A.S. Glassner, editor, *Graphics Gems*, pages 287–293. 1990.
4. P. S. Heckbert. Color image quantization for frame buffer display. *ACM Computer Graphics (ACM SIGGRAPH '82 Proceedings)*, 16(3):297–307, 1982.
5. J.H. Holland. *Adaptation in Natural and Artificial Systems*. University of Mitchigan Press, 1975.
6. S. Kirkpatrick, C.D. Gelatt, and M.P. Vecchi. Optimization by simulated annealing. *Science*, 220(4598):671–680, May 1983.
7. Y. Linde, A. Buzo, and R.M. Gray. An algorithm for vector quanitzer design. *IEEE Trans. Communications*, 28:84–95, 1980.
8. A. Metropolis, W. Rosenbluth, M.N. Rosenbluth, H. Teller, and E. Teller. Equation of state calculations by fast computing machines. *Journal of Chemical Physics*, 21(6):1087–1092, 1953.
9. L. Nolle. On the effect of step width selection schemes on the performance of stochastic local search strategies. In *18th European Simulation Multi-Conference*, pages 149–153, 2004.
10. L. Nolle, D.A. Armstrong, A.A. Hopgood, and J.A. Ware. Simulated annealing and genetic algorithms applied to finishing mill optimisation for hot rolling of wide steel strip. *International Journal of Knowledge-Based Intelligent Engineering Systems*, 6(2):104–111, 2002.
11. L. Nolle, A. Goodyear, A.A. Hopgood, P.D. Picton, and N. Braithwaite. On step width adaptation in simulated annealing for continuous parameter optimisation. In *Computational Intelligence - Theory and Applications*, volume 2206 of *Lecture Notes in Computer Science*, pages 589–598. Springer, 2001.
12. G. Schaefer, G. Qiu, and G. Finlayson. Retrieval of palettised colour images. In *Storage and Retrieval for Image and Video Databases VIII*, volume 3972 of *Proceedings of SPIE*, pages 483–493, 2000.

The Knowledge Bazaar

Brian Craker[1] and Frans Coenen[2]
[1] Becoms Ltd, 69 Little Woodcote, Carshalton, Surrey SM5 4DD
Email: b.craker@knowledgebazaar.org
[2] Department of Computer Science, The University of Liverpool, Liverpool, L69 3BX. Email: frans@csc.liv.ac.uk

Abstract

The concept of the Knowledge Bazaar as a paradigm for the development of Expert Systems, whereby knowledge bases are created dynamically using knowledge supplied by self appointed Internet communities is proposed. The idea espouses the creation of individual Knowledge Bazaars, operating in specific domains, but all operating through a generic Knowledge Bazaar XML Web application. Issues addressed include the provision of the service, XML rule representations and rule integrity. The concept is illustrated with a demonstration gardening Knowledge Bazaar that is currently operational.
Keywords: Knowledge Bazaar, WWW Rule Based Systems, XML.

1. Introduction

In this paper we describe an application of expert system technology founded on the idea of, what we have called, the *knowledge bazaar* (as opposed to a more traditional *cathedral* approach). The terms bazaar and cathedral (popularised in Raymond 99) are used here to distinguish between the traditional centralised approach to software development and an alternative, de-centralised, approach facilitated by the Internet. Use of the Internet to permit access to Expert System technology is not new, there are many examples. However, these all operate in a limited and very different manner to the Knowledge Bazaar concept as proposed here, in that they only allow users to pose queries. There are a number of reasons for the current limitations on the use of Expert Systems across the Internet, which are mostly concerned with security and (to a lesser extent) transmission speed.

The philosophical underpinning behind the knowledge bazaar is the observation that knowledge can be accumulated, not from a limited number of experts or expert sources, but dynamically from Internet users as they solve problems and offer advice. Consequently expert systems developed using the bazaar approach will be able to evolve. The knowledge contained in such expert systems might then be considered to be akin to the shared knowledge found in a (market) bazaar --- another reason for the use of the term.

It is suggested in this paper that the Knowledge Bazaar concept is an efficient, effective and immensely powerful way of harnessing the combined knowledge of global communities of Internet users to develop and maintain expert systems. To illustrate the idea the authors have developed a generic Knowledge Bazaar XML Web Service. This generic Knowledge Bazaar facilitates communication and interaction with particular Knowledge Bazaars which, like traditional Expert Systems, operate in a specific domain (e.g. law, medicine, etc.). The Knowledge Bazaar communication model is illustrated in Figure 1. Note that, in the current demonstration system both the generic Knowledge bazaar and all specific Knowledge Bazaars are hosted on a single server. A gardening Knowledge Bazaar[1] has also been developed to illustrate both the principle and the operation of the Knowledge Bazaar concept.

The generic Knowledge Bazaar provides the interface to allow Bazaar users to submit queries to specific Bazaars, which are either:

Answered immediately if the answer is available in the system's knowledge base, or (If the answer is not available) posted to await an answer from members of a self appointed, on-line, community with respect to the domain.

In the second case, when an answer is provided, the Bazaar will update its knowledge base and post the answer to the user who originally posted the query. In this manner the knowledge (expertise) contained in individual Knowledge Bazaars will evolve with time.

In the remainder of this paper the background to the Knowledge bazaar concept is presented in further detail in Section 2. Design considerations are discussed extensively in Section 3 which includes much consideration of the available technology. In sub-sections 3.1, 3.2, 3.3 and 3.4 special consideration is given to: service-client communication, implementation of the Knowledge bazaar web service, the adopted XML rule representation, and rule integrity. The operation of the generic Knowledge Bazaar is considered in further detail in Section 4, and that of the demonstration gardening Knowledge Bazaar in section 5. The overall approach is evaluated in Section 6, and some final conclusions drawn in Section 7.

2. Background

The terms bazaar and cathedral in the context of software development were first popularised by Raymond. Raymond describes the cathedral approach as the traditional "monolithic, highly planned, top-down style" of software development; while the Bazaar approach, by contrast, involves a "chaotic, evolutionary, market-driven model" (Raymond 99). The Bazaar approach is evident in the open-source software movement e.g. the development of the Linux Operating System. Advocates of the Bazaar approach argue that it is more cost effective and produces a higher quality product than traditional "cathedral" type developments. Critics (for example Bezroukov 99) suggest that things are much more complex, i.e. it is quality rather than quantity that is important. However, Bezroukov does

[1] Available at www.knowledgebazaar.org

acknowledge that by removing geographic boundaries the Internet increases the quality of the pool of expertise. The Knowledge Bazaar is thus the application of Raymond's ideas on Bazaar development to knowledge gathering for Expert Systems.

Expert Systems have had a presence on the WWW for many years. Grove discusses a number of these (Grove 2000) --- one example is Acquired Intelligences' "Whale Watcher"[2]. As noted in the introduction, what most of these systems have in common is that the interaction is limited to querying. In the case of Whale Watcher the user is simply taken down a decision tree structure using a sequence of queries. Most of the current Expert Systems accessible over the internet tend to be very small scale (Adams 2001). It is suggested here that the Knowledge Bazaar approach will serve to significantly improve on the current Expert System presence on the WWW.

Many of the current WWW Expert Systems are written using the JESS (Java Expert System shell) rule engine which is designed to easily integrate with Java applications, which in turn makes JESS well suited to integrating Expert Systems with Internet applications. The XML markup language has also facilitated the provision of Expert System style WWW services. For example agent based systems that: extract rules from HTML pages (Shan 2003), or exchange rules between knowledge bases (Sedbrook 1998). Unsurprisingly XML has also been used to represent rules; in this respect it is argued that XML offers advantages of "interoperability, editability and searchability" (Friedman-Hill 2003).

There is also a significant amount of current research directed at the generic representations of knowledge on the WWW. Given the above the Knowledge Bazaar concept has been implemented as a XML WWW service using JESS as the expert system shell.

3. Design Considerations

The operation of any specific Knowledge Bazaar is facilitated through a Generic Knowledge Bazaar XML WWW Service. This allows remote users to interact with a domain specific Knowledge Bazaar (see Figure 1). Currently the Knowledge Bazaar system is implemented as a basic XHTML Internet site, with all interaction facilitated using forms (thus avoiding the need for natural language processing).

The XML WWW service is based on SOAP (Simple Object Access Protocol) with J2EE used to handle server side client support. The programming language used to implement the generic web service is, of course, independent of that used for individual Knowledge Bazaars, however since JESS was used as the Expert System shell it made sense to use Java for the WWW service.

---

[2] Available at http://www.aiinc.ca/demos/whale.shtml

The Interface to the web service is defined using the Web Service Definition Language (WSDL). WSDL is one of the essential building blocks for Web Services (Schmelzer et al. 2002). It is an official World Wide Web Consortium (W3C) standard which defines an XML grammar for Web Service definition. It describes both the operations of a Web Service and the format of the messages that are sent and received by it. A client uses the WSDL document to determine how to invoke the Web Service. WSDL provides a hierarchical definition. At the top level, the service is broken down into a number of port definitions. Each port represents the availability of a particular binding at a particular web address or endpoint. A binding corresponds to the implementation of a port using a specific protocol. Although SOAP was used to implement the Knowledge Bazaar service, the WSDL structure also allow for other protocols e.g. CORBA.

It is also worth noting here that the WSDL document could be published in a UDDI registry to allow for automatic service discovery. For the demonstration system described here this was deemed unnecessary. The WSDL document does however form the basis for the development of both the service and client parts of the prototype.

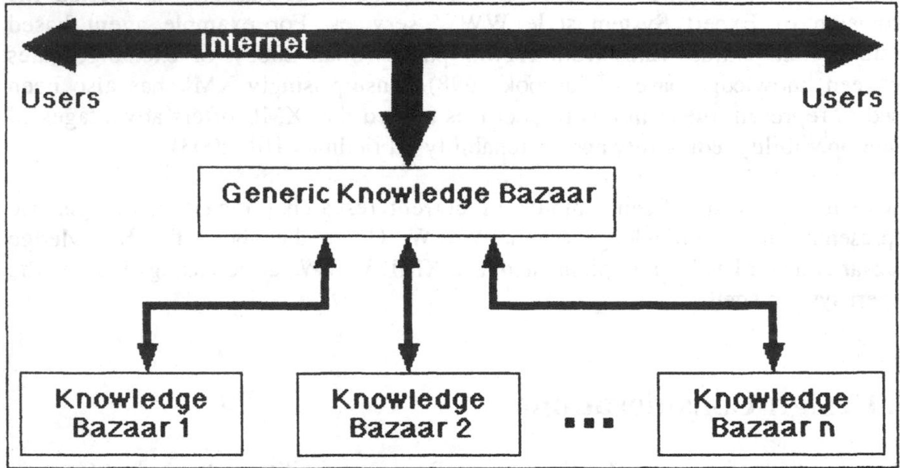

Figure 1: The Knowledge Bazaar communications model

3.1. Service-client communications

As noted above the WSDL document describes the interface in terms of XML. In the context of the Knowledge Bazaar concept the WSDL document declares that the communication between service and client should use the Simple Object Access Protocol (SOAP). This Remote Procedure Call (RPC) protocol is also an XML text based representation – each message consists of an XML document. This contains Envelope, Header and Body elements based upon the information described in the WSDL. The use of open text based protocols has many advantages for Web Services. For example they allow interoperability irrespective of whether different technologies are used at either end, and they allow easy passage through firewalls.

For both client and server it was necessary to handle the transmission protocol for the SOAP messages and convert the contents from the XML message structures to Java type representations. It was also necessary to ensure that messages were converted into function calls and any "fault messages" were converted into exceptions. There are a number of possible approaches by which this may be achieved, with different vendors producing different SOAP interfacing packages. For example the Web Service Development Pack (WSDP) package provided by Sun, includes the SOAP with Attachments API for Java (SAAJ) that provides the "javax.xml.soap" Java package that in turn allows SOAP messages to be constructed directly.

An alternative to SAAI, and arguably a better choice for simple applications such as the Knowledge Bazaar concept, is to use an implementation of the Java API for XML-based Remote Procedure Calls (or JAX-RPC). The JAX-RPC API hides the complexity of the underlying calls to SOAP. There is no need to generate or parse SOAP messages and the JAX-RPC runtime system handles the translation between SOAP messages and API calls. JAX-RPC is a common standard, but there are different implementations available such as: Glue, Axis and the Sun WSDP implementation. There are also different ways to create a JAX-RPC application, but all involve using the WSDL file to generate files which perform the necessary translations between XML and Java.

For the service endpoint, the process involves running the WSCompile tool that forms part of an JAX-RPC implementation, during the software development phase (via the J2EE Application Server GUI or the command line). This tool processes the WSDL file and generates the interface and related Java classes associated with the complex types used in the interface. Skeleton interface implementation classes are also generated for each port endpoint. The developer then needs to flesh out the skeleton files with the functionality that the service should implement. When the Web Service is deployed additional JAX-RPC files are generated for the runtime environment.

For the client side of the interface, the link between the WSDL file and code generation is not so clear. Since the WSDL file is under the control of the Service provider, it may not be possible to use it directly. It is also necessary to acknowledge that the file could change without notice. Using a tool to generate static stubs would place an over-reliance on implementation specific classes. To address these concerns different methods for producing Web Service Clients have been developed. Generated files are obviously needed at run-time, however the point in time at which the interfaces to the Java code are generated can change.

For simple applications where the service and client are produced by the same organisation and the WSDL file is relatively static, the recommended solution is for the tool to generate static stubs offline and use these to access the service. The two alternative approaches are to use a Dynamic Proxy or a Dynamic Invocation Interface (DII). For Dynamic Proxy, the client makes the RPC call through a class that is created at runtime. The client code does not rely on an implementation-specific class but the WSCompile tool is still required. For DII, there is no need to use an offline tool. All necessary files are generated at runtime directly from the WSDL file, rather than at the service endpoint. A client can therefore make a call even if the signature of the remote procedure is unknown at compilation time. For the demonstration gardening Knowledge bazaar it was decided to use the more powerful DII dynamic approach.

The chosen J2EE platform proved to be far from robust (e.g. incorrect generation of interface files if the name of an operation starts with an uppercase letter in the WSDL file --- although this should be perfectly acceptable). The level of support for XML schema types (e.g. string length restrictions) was also very limited, leading to the need to simplify the interface. "Workaround" solutions were found and implemented. However, with hindsight, the authors suggest that an alternative JAX-RPC implementations from a different organisations might have been better.

3.2. The Knowledge Bazaar XML Web Service Implementation

From the above the generic Knowledge Bazaar service was implemented using the JAX-RPC files generated from the WSDL. The additional functionality required for the service was provided by a combination of Java software and calls to an executing instance of the JESS Expert System Shell. The initialisation of JESS is performed using a batch file which creates structures, queries and local subroutines using the JESS language.

The Knowledge bazaar service is in effect half implemented in Java and half in JESS. JESS provides a very flexible interface. It is possible for the developer to choose where best to implement any routine – either internally within JESS or externally in Java using low level calls to JESS. Implementation within JESS is slightly less efficient, since subroutine calls need to be parsed. JESS is implemented in Java so it is more efficient if the JESS Java API is called directly from Java wherever possible. One advantage of using JESS code is however that it is "thread-safe". The allocation of user IDs is therefore best performed within JESS functions so that there is no chance that two users will be assigned the same value.

3.3. XML Rule Representation

Previous work has established that representing knowledge rules using XML has advantages in terms of 'interoperability, editability and searchability' (Friedman-Hill 2003); against the disadvantage of larger storage requirement. A number of projects are currently attempting to define standard, XML based, domain independent rule languages - for example the RuleML project (Wagner et al. 2004). It is clear that there are significant interoperability advantages from the development of an industrial standard in this area. These projects however are very general and still at an early stage of progress. Whatever the case only a small subset of such a standard would be applicable to a knowledge bazaar application.

With respect to the work described here a very simple XML structure, sufficient to implement the Knowledge Bazaar concept, was developed. Of course, if one of the current XML rule languages does develop into an industry standard, it will be easy to later transform rules generated within a Knowledge Bazaar into a RuleML (or another) structure using the XSLT XML conversion language. With respect to the Knowledge Bazaar system a very simple binary structure, which would allow simple object-operation-property tuples (propositions) to be expressed, was considered to be a sufficient representation. The syntax is presented in Table 1.

```
<Kbrule>
        <Object> … </Object>
        <Operation> … </Operation>
        <Property> … </Property>
</Kbrule>
```

Table 1: Knowledge Bazaar XML Rule Structure

Thus to express the fact that a Cox is a variety of apple, the following XML would be used:

```
<Kbrule>
        <Object>Cox</Object>
        <Operation>is_a_variety_of</Operation>
        <Property>Apple</Property>
</Kbrule>
```

(See Section 5 for further detail concerning the above example rule.)

The XML structure given in Table 1 allowed Knowledge Bazaars to effectively represent most simple facts. However, to take a greater advantage of the reasoning power of Expert Systems, it was felt necessary to also be able to express relationships between facts. Using the above structure this can be achieved by allowing the object and property elements to represent facts rather than nodes. The operation element can then be used to express the relationship between two facts. The gardening Knowledge Bazaar demonstrator therefore includes two special operations: `IMPLIES` and `NOT IMPLIES`. When the generic knowledge bazaar receives rule data with these operation values it will treat the object and property values as encoded facts rather than atoms and insert appropriate rules in to the Expert System.

The above also allowed the authors to keep the interface, between client and server, simple. It is anticipated that, with respect to potential future Knowledge Bazaar applications, a more complex grammar may very well be required to allow more complex rules to be expressed.

3.4. Rule Integrity

An important feature of the system is that it ensures both security and integrity of the knowledge contained in individual bazaars. If a user inadvertently, mistakenly or maliciously enters false information this is removed quickly. At the same time the system ensures that trusted information is harder to remove, and guards against inadvertent or malicious removal.

It is acknowledge that, no matter how well accepted information is now, it can become redundant through the passage of time. For some knowledge domains, e.g. IT support, the rate of obsolescence can be high. For the gardening Knowledge Bazaar demonstrator, most information is expected to remain constant; although factors such as new discoveries, plant breeding advances, global warming etc. may at some point mean that even here previously correct information might need to be replaced. Since the authors wished to fully adhere to the Bazaar principles for all aspects of the system, it was decided to use feedback from peer review, to guide the automatic integrity maintenance mechanism built into the system. To this end, users of the Knowledge Bazaars are encouraged to provide feedback as to whether previously supplied advice had proved accurate or false via a form driven interface. It is equally important that good as well as negative feedback is supplied. Currently only (trusted) registered users are permitted to contribute knowledge to the bazaar (though everyone can post queries). Associated with every user is a quality metric which is maintained by the system (not unlike the mechanism operated with e-bay). In addition there is a quality metric associated with every piece of knowledge contained within the system. The initial quality associated with the knowledge is based upon the current quality value of the user who supplies the information.

As users report feedback (or supply knowledge which conflicts or agrees), these quality values are adjusted. Negative feedback causes the quality of a rule to diminish, whereas positive feedback causes it to increase. If the quality of a rule diminishes below a threshold then it will be removed from the system and the quality of the original contributor reduced. Conversely, users that contribute information that is reported as correct by other users (not themselves) have their quality values increased. This process is illustrated shown in the Figure 2.

To date it has been found that the above simple mechanism ensures that errors can be corrected, but that when knowledge has proved useful to many people, it becomes harder to remove - so reducing the possibility of abuse. Information supplied by users who have contributed lots of useful information in the past is, at least initially, harder to remove than that supplied by new users or poorly performing contributors.

4. Generic Knowledge Bazaar Operation

The generic, knowledge domain independent, knowledge bazaar offers facilities for users to contribute knowledge either on their own initiative (unsolicited) or in response to requests from other users (solicited). Users can also request advice or provide feedback as to the validity of content. The generic Knowledge Bazaar services these requests through communication with the appropriate domain specific Knowledge Bazaar (as illustrated in Figure 1).

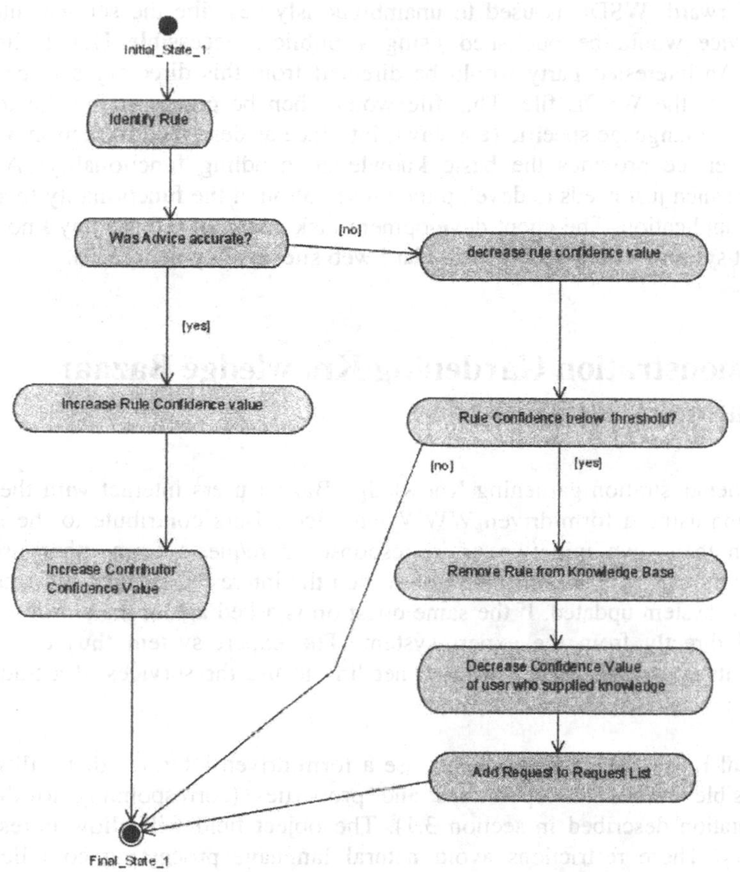

Figure 2: Knowledge Bazaar Rule Integrity Mechanism

In the case of the Generic Bazaar Service, three ports were identified as useful for the service:

- A User Data port (to handle user registration and logon verification).
- A Knowledge Bazaar port (to handle the Knowledge Bazaar processing for normal users).
- A Supervisory port (to allow the client operator to access performance data and to perform maintenance operations).

(Note that a client could choose to handle user registration locally or may have no need for the supervisory functionality. However the port separation ensures that the core bazaar functionality is isolated and clearly identified.)

The generic knowledge bazaar interface has been designed using industry standard Web Service technologies which ensure the development of a client is relatively straightforward. WSDL is used to unambiguously describe the service interface. The service would be published using a publicly accessible UDDI directory service. An interested party would be directed from this directory service to the location of the WSDL file. This file would then be processed by the tools to generate the language specific (e.g. Java) interface as described in section 3.1. The generic service provides the basic knowledge handling functionality. A client developer then just needs to develop the presentation of the functionality to suit the specific application. The client development task does not require any knowledge of expert systems. It just requires standard web site development skills.

5. Demonstration Gardening Knowledge Bazaar Operation

For the demonstration gardening Knowledge Bazaar users interact with the client application using a form-driven WWW interface. Users contribute to the system either on their own initiative or in response to requests from other users. If someone provides an answer to a request then the interested party is informed and the expert system updated. If the same question is asked again, the answer will be obtained directly from the expert system. The expert system thus continually expands its knowledge base - without needing to use the services of a traditional expert.

Individual Knowledge Bazaar clients use a form driven interface that will restrict the possible entries for operations and properties (corresponding to the rule representation described in section 3.1). The object field will allow unrestricted text entry. These restrictions avoid natural language processing complications. With respect to the gardening knowledge bazaar Table 2 shows the values that are permitted:

For queries, the user will be asked to supply an Object and an Operation and the associated Property will be sought.

For knowledge contribution, a simple interface allows users to enter facts in the form of object-operation-property tuples. It is anticipated that in the future a more complex interface will allow a user to specify two complete facts (as object, operation, property tuples) and state if one fact implies, or does not imply, the other fact.

For Knowledge Bazaar applications, it might be that some form of Fat Client Peer to Peer architecture could offer some advantages. If instead of storing all knowledge centrally it was distributed across many machines then it might be possible to mitigate the storage costs and processing delays that could arise for large knowledge bases. However, in the interest of ease of access and simplicity of design, the authors opted for a thin client application as the most appropriate choice.

The demonstration gardening Knowledge Bazaar is currently available at http://www.knowledgebazaar.org, interested readers are invited to interact with the system to obtain a better appreciation of its operation.

Operation	Property
Is a variety of	No restriction
Flowers in	Summer, spring, winter,
Has longevity	Annual, perennial, biannual
Has fragrance	Low, medium, high
Has sun requirement	Low, medium, high, easy
Has temperature requirement	Low, medium, high, easy
Has frost tolerance	Low, medium, high
Has water requirement	Low, medium, high
Has soil ph requirement	Acid, alkaline, easy

Table 2: Gardening Knowledge Bazaar Rule Restrictions

6. Evaluation

At time of writing (May 2005) the gardening Knowledge bazaar demonstrator had been in full operation for several months only. Feedback from a survey conducted by the company, where some fifty participants were asked to interact with the demonstrator, indicates that the basic Knowledge Bazaar concept has been well received. The majority of respondents gave a very positive reaction to the knowledge bazaar concept. Over half (i.e. more than 25 of the respondents) agreed that they would use such a system as a source of information with only 3% disagreeing (the rest were undecided). Even more people (65%) said they would be prepared to contribute their knowledge to such a system with only 6% disagreeing. The basic Knowledge Bazaar concept is further supported by the observation that online communities have proliferated over the last few years, indicating that Internet users are happy to provide answers to problems/questions (for example using "message boards").

With respect to rule integrity half of the respondents believed that Peer review would be sufficient to ensure the quality of the knowledge base. The reaction to the form driven interface designed to support Knowledge Bazaar applications was also interesting in that most respondents regarded a Natural Language Processing (NLP) interface as a low-priority enhancement rather than a necessity.

The authors always considered the threat of abuse to be the greatest challenge to the Knowledge Bazaar concept in that the soliciting of knowledge would allow users to post objectionable content as queries. The Survey participants were asked for their views on the best way to tackle this. Most (47%) thought that some kind of filter mechanism should be introduced despite the time and cost implications. Peer review was however thought to be sufficient by a large minority (35%). The option of requiring personal details for membership was less popular (18%), reflecting the objections that many people also have to registering with "message board" Internet sites.

The positive results obtained from the survey were further supported by the authors' intuition that experts systems developed using the Knowledge Bazaar approach more accurately reflect the way in which knowledge is applied. The authors believe that the traditional approach to building Expert Systems, which assumes knowledge can be detached from its social context, is flawed. Even during the "golden age" of Expert Systems, Bobrow was already advocating the need for "Community knowledge bases that integrate expertise from many different sources" (Bobrow 1986). This view is supported by Wenger (1998) who argues that knowledge, and the process of learning, involves much more than information gathering or technology. Wenger suggests a number of components to learning that are embraced by *communities of practice*. Wenger's ideas about communities of practice with respect to knowledge elicitation strongly support the Knowledge Bazaar concept as proposed here.

7. Conclusions

In this paper the idea of the Knowledge Bazaar approach to building expert systems has been introduced. The term "Knowledge Bazaar" has been proposed to describe the concept of a body of knowledge that evolves dynamically using the contributions, supplied across the Internet, of self-selected individuals. To illustrate the concept a gardening Knowledge Bazaar demonstrator has been developed which has been well received. The feedback indicates that the concept has great potential for harnessing the knowledge available across the Internet so as to build genuinely useful knowledge based systems and applications.

References

1. Adams, J (2001). *The feasibility of distributed web based expert systems.* Proc. IEEE Systems, Man, and Cybernetics Conference.
2. Bezroukov, N. (1999). A Second Look at the *Cathedral and* the Bazaar. First Monday Journal, Vol 4, num 12 (Available from http://firstmonday.org/issues/issue4_12/bezroukov/index.html).
3. Bobrow et al (1986). *Expert Systems: Peril and Promise*. Communications of the ACM. Vol 29, Num 9.

4. Friedman-Hill, E (2003). *JESS in Action – Rule-Based Systems in Java.* Manning Publications.
5. Grove, R. (2000). *Internet Based Expert Systems.* Expert Systems, Vol. 17 No.3.
6. Raymond, E. (1999). The Cathedral and the Bazaar: Musings on Linux and Open Source by an Accidental Revolutionary. O'Reilly.
7. Schmelzer, R., Vandersypen, T., Bloomberg, J., Siddalingaiah, M., Hunting, S., Qualls, M., Darby, C., Houlding, D. and Kennedy, D. (2002). *XML and Web Services Unleashed.* SAMS Publishing.
8. Sedbrook, T (2001). Integrating e-business XML business forms and rule-based agent technologies. Expert Systems, Vol.18, No.5.
9. Shan, F et al (2003). A programmable agent for knowledge discovery on the Web. Expert Systems, Vol. 20, No. 2.
10. Wagner, G., Antoniou, G., Tabet, S. and Boley, H. (2004). *The Abstract Syntax of RuleML - Towards a General Web Rule Language Framework.* Proc. Web Intelligence 2004: 628-631
11. Wenger, E. (1998). Communities of Practice – Learning, Meaning and Identity. Cambridge University Press.

Generating Feedback Reports for Adults Taking Basic Skills Tests

Ehud Reiter and Sandra Williams
Dept of Computing Science, University of Aberdeen
{ ereiter,swilliam}@csd.abdn.ac.uk

Lesley Crichton
Cambridge Training and Development Ltd
lesleyc@ctad.co.uk

Abstract

SkillSum is an Artificial Intelligence (AI) and Natural Language Generation (NLG) system that produces short feedback reports for people who are taking online tests which check their basic literacy and numeracy skills. In this paper, we describe the SkillSum system and application, focusing on three challenges which we believe are important ones for many systems which try to generate feedback reports from Web-based tests: choosing content based on very limited data, generating appropriate texts for people with varied levels of literacy and knowledge, and integrating the web-based system with existing assessment and support procedures.

1. Introduction

There are a growing number of short assessment tests available on the Web, which people can use to assess their health, education, entitlement to benefits, and so forth. Users fill out a form (typically multiple-choice questions), and submit this to a server, which returns to them a numerical score and a fixed text explaining the score. For example, someone using the nicotine addiction test on www.healthcalculators.org will be told whether he or she has a low, medium, or high level of nicotine addiction, together with some explanatory text. Such tests are popular because people can use them at any time, and in complete privacy; we expect that their use will continue to grow, and indeed they will be regarded as essential tools of life in the 21st century.

Currently people using such tests get limited feedback, typically just a level (as in the nicotine addiction example) accompanied by a fixed explanatory text and often a suggestion to contact a professional doctor, lawyer, tutor, etc in order to learn more. The goal of our research is to try to develop a system which produces more detailed and personalised feedback, using Natural Language Generation (NLG) technology, in the belief that better feedback will make such tests more useful and effective.

This paper discusses SkillSum, an NLG system which generates short feedback reports for adults who have just completed a screening test of their basic literacy or numeracy skills. We focus on the following issues, which we believe are relevant to feedback-report-generation applications in general, not just SkillSum:

- Selecting content based on very limited data.
- Generating texts which are easy to read, for people with varied levels of reading ability.
- Integrating report-generation systems into the overall assessment process.

Overall, generating high-quality feedback reports from the results of short tests is more difficult than we first expected; but we believe that it is possible, and that this technology could be both commercially important and beneficial to society.

2. Background

2.1 Natural Language Generation

Natural Language Generation (NLG) systems automatically generate texts in English and other human languages, typically based on some non-linguistic input data, using AI and NLP techniques (Reiter and Dale, 2000). For example, the STOP system (Reiter, Robertson, Osman 2003) generates personalised smoking-cessation leaflets based on a smoker's responses to a questionnaire about her smoking habits, beliefs, and so forth; and the ILEX system (O'Donnell *et al*, 2001) generates descriptions of museum exhibits based on a knowledge base that contains information about items in the museum.

This paper focuses on SkillSum as an application, not on technical NLG issues. For general information on NLG, see Reiter and Dale (2000).

2.2 Basic Skills Assessments

Poor adult literacy and numeracy is a major problem in the UK. The Moser study (Moser et al, 1999) reported that one in five adults in the UK is not functionally literate; for example, if given the alphabetical index to the Yellow Pages, they cannot locate the page reference for plumbers. One in four adults is not functionally numerate; for example, they cannot calculate how much change to expect from £2 when buying a 68p loaf of bread and two 45p tins of soup. Such people have difficulty finding and keeping jobs, and also have a lower quality of life; poor literacy and numeracy are also a major cause of low productivity in the UK economy as a whole. Recognising these problems, the UK government launched the *Skills for Life* strategy, and is committed to raising the basic skills of 1,500,000 adults in England by 2007; similar initiatives are in place in Scotland, Wales and Northern Ireland. Information and Communication Technology (ICT) is seen as a key element in these efforts.

The first step in improving an individual's basic skills is for that person to acknowledge that he or she may have a problem, and to come forward to have their existing level of literacy and numeracy assessed to give a clear picture of his or her strengths, weaknesses and learning needs. Proper assessment requires the individual to complete a detailed assessment instrument, such as Cambridge Training and Development's *Target Skills: Initial Assessment* (http://www.targetskills.net). Such assessments must be taken in a formal setting, with the results analysed and explained by a basic skills tutor. They require a substantial time commitment on the part of the student, who must come to a scheduled session which may last several hours.

As many people may initially be reluctant to make this time commitment, there is increasing interest in short *screener* tests, which can be completed quickly and give a general indication of the student's abilities. These can quickly tell students who are concerned about their skills whether they have any problems, and hence whether they should consider enrolling in a class to improve their skills (a detailed assessment test is usually administered as part of such classes). Screener tests are also useful for organisations such as UK Further Education (FE) colleges (similar to American community colleges), which need to determine which incoming students should be asked to attend skills classes.

Screener tests should be as easy to take as possible, which means that they should be short, and also that ideally people should be able to take them anywhere (not just in a classroom) with minimal support from human tutors. Screener tests are already being put on the web, which makes them available anywhere there is Internet access. But if they are going to be used with minimal support from human tutors, they also need to be able to present their results to users in an easy-to-understand and meaningful fashion. This is the goal of SkillSum: to automatically generate a personalised report summarising how well someone did on a basic skills screener, which encourages this person (if appropriate) to agree to more detailed assessment, to accept basic skills support as part of another course, or to sign up for a discrete literacy or numeracy course.

2.3 Related Work

Some existing web-based educational assessment tools, such as iAchieve at home (http://www.iachieve.com.au) (which is intended for children, not adults) provide limited feedback reports. For example iAchieve reports tell students how many questions they got wrong, explain how this performance compares to other children at the same grade level, and also give (fixed) explanations of how questions should be answered. There are also a number of commercial systems which help teachers write reports on their pupils, such as ReportMaster (http://www.learnsoftware.co.uk/report.htm).

We are not aware of any online assessment tools that use NLG technology to generate feedback reports. The Criterion system (Burstein, Chodorow, Leacock 2003) uses sophisticated NL Understanding techniques to analyse writing samples (which students can submit on the web) and identify problems in how a student writes, but it does not use NLG to communicate its analysis to the student.

3. SkillSum

SkillSum's goal is to develop an NLG system which automatically generates useful and understandable feedback reports for people who are taking a short online screening test of their basic skills. It is a collaborative project between the University of Aberdeen and Cambridge Training and Development. It builds on an earlier PhD project at Aberdeen [Williams 2004] which made an initial attempt at building such a system. Essentially the PhD project focused mostly on theoretical issues involved in generating texts for low-literacy readers, and did not seriously try to build a real application. The goal of SkillSum is to explore application issues as well as theoretical issues, and to build a system which is robust and realistic enough to enable us to evaluate whether we can indeed automatically generate useful and helpful feedback texts for real people who are concerned about their basic skills.

An example output (with the name of the student changed) from the current version of SkillSum is shown in Fig. 1. This report is generated from the student's response to 27 assessment questions (mostly multiple choice). A typical question is shown in Fig. 3, together with some background information about the student (Fig. 2).

3.1 Knowledge Acquisition

SkillSum reports are based on knowledge acquisition (KA) activities with domain experts (basic skills tutors) (Williams and Reiter, 2005a) and on pilot experiments. Essentially we asked tutors to write some example reports; analysed these to determine what information tutors were trying to communicate to students and also how they thought this information should be expressed; and then implemented a simplified version of these rules in the software. We then showed reports produced by our software to both tutors and students taking basic skills courses, and revised the reports based on this feedback. This follows the general KA for NLG methodology described by Reiter, Sripada, and Robertson (2003).

One of the most important findings of our KA activities was that reports should be short. Some initial versions of SkillSum generated much longer and more detailed reports, but our pilot experiments showed that users wanted short and simple reports, perhaps with details available on another page (e.g. the more information link in Fig. 1); this may reflect the fact that reading a long report requires considerable effort from people with limited literacy.

Our experiments and KA sessions also suggested that

- reports should focus on diagnosis (what the student can and cannot do) and advice (what the student should do to improve his/her skills)
- reports should be relevant to the student's interests and objectives
- reports should not used specialised terminology

While these points may seem obvious in retrospect, in fact some early versions of SkillSum included background information about basic skills, did not try to tailor the reports to students skills and interests, and used terminology that was meaningful to tutors but not to students.

3.2 Implementation

SkillSum is implemented as a web-based system using J2EE (Java); the NLG system is a server-side system which gets input from web forms and databases, and produces an HTML web page as its output. The system divides the task of generation texts into three stages (document planning, microplanning, and realisation), following the architecture of Reiter and Dale (2000).

The *Document Planner* decides what information should be communicated in the text, and how the text should be organised rhetorically. Conceptually it is based on rules acquired by our KA activities, such as:

> IF the student has said he/she is not confident about his/her English skills (even if their level is in fact OK for the student's intended course)
>
> THEN add a message that he/she should consider taking an English course to improve his/her confidence

The "*But an English class...*" sentence in Figure 1 is based on this rule.

The output of the document planner is a tree whose leaves are messages, and whose internal nodes communicate discourse (rhetorical) relations that relate messages and groups of messages (Williams, 2004).

Three representations of messages were used in different versions of SkillSum. Initially we represented messages as deep syntactic structures, similar to those used by RealPro (Lavoie and Rambow, 1997). However, as we modified the system based on KA activities and pilots, in many cases we simply encoded messages as strings, as that was quicker and also considerably easier for people who had limited linguistic expertise. The current version of SkillSum uses an intermediate representation, essentially strings annotated with choices that must be made by the microplanner. An example of such an annotated string is

> "your [English] skills $HEDGE are$ $okay$ for your XX $class$"

Square brackets ([]) indicate optional fragments which the microplanner can delete if it wishes, and dollar brackets ($$) indicate words which can be replaced by a synonym if the microplanner wishes. There are also some flags; for example HEDGE means that a word can be hedged if the microplanner wishes. For example, if the microplanner processes the above string and decides to include optional fragments, include hedges where possible, and replace $class$ by its synonym "*course*", then the result is one of the sentences in Figure 1, namely:

> *Your English skills seem to be okay for your Art, Design and Media course.*

The *Microplanner* (second NLG module) makes choices on how to express content and structure. Content-expression choices basically are the choices involved in processing annotated structures such as the above; this is currently done using a set of rules suggested by tutors. Structure-expression choices include deciding on the order of messages, on the placement of sentence and paragraph breaks, and on the choice of cue phrases such as "*But*" and "*however*". Structure-expression choices are made using a constraint-based approach which has been described in detail elsewhere (Williams and Reiter, 2005b).

The *Realiser* (final NLG module) generates actual texts based on the decisions made by the Document Planner and Microplanner. The most complex part of the SkillSum realiser is a (much) simplified and cut-down version of RealPro (Lavoie and Rambow, 1997), which is used to convert deep-syntactic messages (if these are present) into text. Otherwise, the SkillSum realiser just addresses capitalisation, punctuation, and HTML issues.

3.3 Evaluation

As mentioned in Section 3.1, we have conducted a number of pilot evaluations of SkillSum. These evaluations involved showing SkillSum reports (or several variations of SkillSum reports) to students who are already enrolled in skills courses, and asking them to do various activities with the reports (such as commenting on them, giving preferences between versions, reading them aloud, and answering comprehension questions). We have conducted 7 of these pilots so far: 6 small ones involving 5-20 people, and one larger one involving 60 people. These evaluations were mostly viewed as knowledge acquisition exercises to improve our system. At our most recent evaluation (in June 2005) we asked 15 students to express a preference between SkillSum reports and the simple reports currently generated by CTAD's software (which just give a score and level, see Figure 4). 13 of the 15 preferred SkillSum reports (significant at $p < .01$ using binomial test), which is encouraging and suggests the system is working reasonably well (we did not see such a clear preference with early versions of SkillSum).

We will conduct a larger final evaluation of SkillSum in September 2005. During this evaluation, we will ask 200 students who are just entering an FE college to take the SkillSum screener test. These students will be divided into three groups:

- *Baseline*: will receive simple reports generated by CTAD's current software. An example baseline report is shown in Figure 4.
- *SkillSum-control*: will receive reports generated by SkillSum using a microplanning choice model which is based on the most common choices observed in two corpora (British National Corpus (BNC) and RST Discourse Treebank Corpus (Carlson 2002)).
- *SkillSum-ER*: will receive reports generated by SkillSum using a microplanning choice model which is based on our KA activities, and which we believe encodes appropriate expression choices for readers with limited literacy.

We will ask students to self-assess their current skill levels and interest in doing a skills course, both before and after they take the test and read the report. We will measure changes in self-assessment accuracy and interest in doing courses in the three groups. We will also ask some of the students comprehension questions about reports, and to read reports aloud; we will measure correctness and time taken to respond to comprehension question, and the time taken and errors made in reading reports aloud. Last but not least, we will ask students to express a preference between different versions of their report, and ask them for general qualitative comments and feedback.

English Skills

Thank you for doing this test.

You answered 19 questions correctly. More information.

You made some mistakes on the questions about writing.

But you got most of the questions right where you had to read.

Your English skills seem to be okay for your Art, Design and Media course.

But an English class might help you, because you said you do not feel very confident with your reading.

Click here to find courses at ABC FE College.

Figure 1: Example report produced by SkillSum

Course subject: Art, Design and Media

Course type and level: BTEC Introductory Diploma, Level 1

Are you receiving help with your English? no

Do you think your English skills are good enough for your course or job? no, not quite

How often do you read/write? a few times a year

Figure 2: Responses to background questions for Figure 1 student

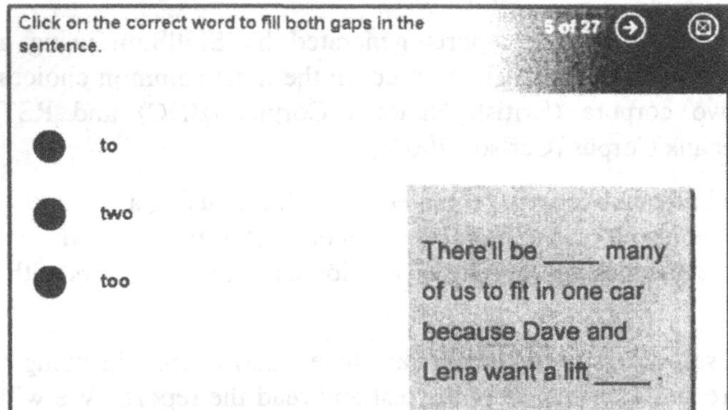

Figure 3: Example SkillSum assessment question

Thank you for doing this test. You scored 19. You are OK at level 1 literacy but may need help at level 2. Talk to your tutor or supervisor

Figure 4: Baseline report for Figure 1 student

4. Main challenges

In this section we discuss three general issues which are important in SkillSum and which we believe will be important in most (perhaps all) systems which attempt to generate feedback reports from SkillSum-like data.

4.1 Choosing Content from Limited Data

One of the main challenges in building a system like SkillSum is deciding what to tell people, especially as our data is very limited. In early versions of the system, we experimented with giving people detailed analyses of how good they are in specific areas such as grammar and punctuation; this was done by associating questions with specific skills. We even at one point discussed detailed diagnosis of incorrect responses; for example, we wanted to tell people not just that they had problems adding and subtracting, but that the problems were due to not being able to carry and borrow. However, basic skills experts we worked with were concerned about this because it was based on very limited data. For example, there are only 3 questions on grammar in the SkillSum literacy test, which is a very small amount data for telling people that their grammar skills are good or bad. Also, different people use different techniques; for example, some people do not carry when adding. Finally, pilot experiments showed that users (understandably!) became annoyed if we told them that they were poor at something which they thought they were good at; and also that people did not interpret words such as "*grammar*" and "*punctuation*" as we expected (for example, some people thought grammar mistakes included punctuation errors).

In other words, the diagnostic inferences we were making about people's skills were not robust, because they were based on very limited data. Communication of these inferences was also error-prone, since people interpreted words in unexpected ways. Finally, the cost of an incorrect inference was high, because incorrectly telling someone they were bad at something could annoy them or diminish their self-confidence, and incorrectly telling someone they were good at something might reduce their interest in getting help. Hence we decided to only give very high-level diagnostic summaries, accompanied (in the latest versions of SkillSum) by a list of the specific questions they got wrong.

We also initially wanted to give people detailed motivational information, explaining why improving their literacy and numeracy would benefit them, given their personal circumstances. We based this on a questionnaire which asked people about possible motivations, such as improving job prospects or helping children with their homework. But again we had major problems because these questions were vague, and hence did not provide much information; and also sometimes people again interpreted questions differently from what we expected. And again getting things wrong could anger people. For example, we originally thought we could say something like "*if you improve your English, you can help your children write reports for school*" if the user had ticked "helping children with homework" as one of his or her motivations; but in fact it is impossible to say this without knowing a lot about the current skills of the user and the user's children, and also the skills being taught by the children's school. Furthermore, the above phrase might anger someone who thought she was already helping her children to some degree, and just wished she could do a bit more.

The current version of SkillSum, which is targeted towards students attending Further Education colleges, bases its motivational information on the requirements of the specific course that the person wishes to take. For example, it might tell someone that their English skills appear to be adequate for a Level 1 BTEC (British Technical Education Council) Diploma course in Art, Design and Media at ABC FE College. In the text shown in Figure 1, for example, the student's score on the literacy assessment is above the threshold required for a Level 1 BTEC Introductory Diploma course; hence SkillSum tells her this ("*Your English skills seem to be okay for your Art, Design and Media course.*"). However, the student stated that she did not think her skills were adequate and that she is not receiving help with English, so SkillSum tells her that an English course might help her (indeed, her score indicates that she may have some problems with literacy). On the other hand, if the student had scored below the threshold, SkillSum would tell her that she might need help to bring her English skills up to the level required for her course.

Basing motivation information on the requirements of a course is not ideal because improving skills in order to complete a course is only one type of motivation, and may be less important than intrinsic motivations such as improving self-confidence and self-esteem (Kotler, Roberto, Lee 2002). It also means SkillSum must have detailed knowledge of the requirements of various courses. But from the data perspective, intended course is reliable and easily obtainable data, which is associated with specific literacy and numeracy constraints on students who wish to take the course; whereas most motivations we considered were difficult to obtain reliably, and also difficult to map to specific literacy and numeracy requirements.

The fact that the cost of mistakes is high (because it can annoy and/or demotivate people) certainly makes choosing content in SkillSum considerably more difficult. In contrast, the cost of making mistakes was much lower in the STOP system (also developed at Aberdeen) (Reiter, Robertson, Osman 2003), which generated personalised smoking-cessation leaflets. STOP had to choose which bits of encouragement and advice to include in its leaflets, and did this by analysing questionnaire data to attempt to identify the most useful encouragement and advice; but in general making a mistake in this regard and choosing less-than-ideal advice did not anger people, it just meant that the leaflets were a bit less useful than they might have been.

In short, it is difficult to choose content when the data is limited (and noisy), and the cost of a mistake is high; we suspect this is one of the main challenges for many systems which generate feedback reports based on short assessments. This is one area where human tutors, who have face-to-face dialogues with students and also have extensive knowledge of skills and motivations, do a better job than computer systems, and probably will continue to do so for the foreseeable future. But nonetheless SkillSum shows that it is possible to give more information than just a skill level and associated generic information which is not at all personalised; and we believe that further research will reveal other techniques for suggesting useful content in such contexts. One idea we would like to explore in the future is making the system more interactive, so that users can to some degree tell SkillSum what they want to know. Our experiments certainly show that students vary greatly in what information they want; some in fact want quite detailed analyses of their performance, while others just want reassurance that they are not "thick".

4.2 Producing Texts for Low-Literacy Readers

SkillSum originated in a PhD project which focused on generating texts which could be easily read by people with poor literacy skills, and this remains one of the challenges of building the system. While this is especially important in SkillSum as most SkillSum users are people with below-average literacy, in fact any system which generates texts for the general public needs to make sure its texts are accessible to people with poor literacy. Unfortunately, 20% of UK adults have a "reading age" of 10 or less (in other words, they cannot read at the level expected of 11 year old children), and 6% of UK adults have a reading age of 6 or less (Moser, 1999). Similar percentages of adults in the US have poor literacy. The situation is a bit better in some other European countries such as Sweden and The Netherlands, but even in these countries about 10% of adults have problems with literacy (Carey, Low, Hansbro 1997).

We have described this aspect of SkillSum elsewhere (Williams and Reiter, 2005b), so we will only give a brief summary here. Basically we focus on microplanning choices, including lexical choice, aggregation (how many messages are realised in each sentence), sentence ordering, and choice of discourse cue phrases. For these choices, we have developed a set of rules (based on pilot experiments and KA with tutors) which we believe are appropriate for low-skill readers, and we experimentally compare texts generated with these rules to texts generated with rules which are based on the most common choices in a corpus.

We continue to actively work on lexical (word) choice in particular. In general, psychological research (Rayner and Pollatsek, 1989; Perfetti 1994) suggests that people find easiest to read those words which they are most familiar with (that is, the words they have used and encountered the most). The simplest way to estimate familiarity is to use frequency in a standard corpus such as the BNC. Unfortunately BNC frequency is not always a good predictor of word familiarity, in part because the BNC includes texts (such as academic research papers) which most English speakers never encounter. Another issue is ambiguity; common words tend to have many meanings, and it is not clear when this is acceptable, and when it is preferable to use rarer words which have fewer meanings and hence are less ambiguous. Skills tutors have also pointed out to us that the ease of reading a word can depend on its visual properties, such as how difficult a word is to sound out from its spelling, and indeed what the overall visual shape of a word is.

Another issue is individual variation. It is clear from our pilot experiments, and indeed from work we have done in other projects (Reiter and Sripada, 2002) that there major differences between individuals that affect lexical choice. These include

- *Variations in meaning*: For example, as mentioned in Section 4.1, different people interpret "*grammar*" in different ways.
- *Variations in connotations*: For example, "*teacher*" is a very common word, but it has bad connotations for students who disliked school; for such students it is better to use an alternative word such as "*tutor*".
- *Variations in language use and exposure*: For example, someone who has learned English as a second language may be more comfortable with semi-technical terms such as "*punctuation*" than a native English speaker who never tried to learn another language.

In fact, a general problem with our approach is that we use the same microplanning choice model for all poor readers, but poor readers are very diverse, and have "spiky" ability profiles (good in some areas, poor in others) (young children, in contrast, tend to have more uniform profiles, with similar performance in all areas). In future research we would like to explore using more specialised choice models, indeed perhaps using choice models which are tailored for specific individuals.

Finally, one point that has emerged very clearly in our pilot experiments with SkillSum is that content and structural choices are very important for readability. As above, we had originally thought of readability in terms of microplanning choices which affected how information is expressed, but not what information is communicated in a text. However, as is perhaps obvious in retrospect, our pilots showed that the length of a text (which is determined by its information content) is also very important; poor readers need short texts that don't overstrain their abilities. Also, poor readers need text that they perceive as being worth reading, otherwise they may not make the effort required to read them. Since people typically start reading a document from the beginning, this means that texts intended for poor readers should start with useful information; hence for example the content-free "*Thank you for doing this test*" sentence in the report shown in Fig. 1 should perhaps be at the end of the report, not the beginning.

4.3 Integration

Our initial vision of SkillSum was that it would be a stand-alone system, which people could access from home or community sites (such as libraries), without needing any support from human tutors or administrators. SkillSum might encourage users to sign up for a formal assessment, but this would be its only link with the existing assessment process.

We have changed our opinion in this respect, and now see SkillSum as an add-on to the existing assessment process, not something which is separate from it. Our current vision is that SkillSum will be deployed at FE colleges and other organisations (large employers, military, etc) that already test people's skills, and be used to provide extra feedback to people who the organisation has already decided to assess, and also to allow other people (who the organisation has not yet decided to assess) to get some information about their skills. In both cases, SkillSum is integrated into the current assessment process of the host organisation, and is seen as a tool for that organisation as much as a tool for the individuals being assessed.

Partially this is due to standard issues: all IT systems are of course more likely to be used if they integrate well with existing processes, and AI systems which may make incorrect inferences (in our case because of sparse data) are often deployed in contexts where human experts are "in the loop". Also, we had decided in any case to focus SkillSum on specific groups, such as students entering a particular FE course, rather than poor readers in general. Such a focus makes it much easier to generate motivational information, as described above. Also, focusing on specific groups reduces variation in subject's ability profiles, which makes it easier both to specify appropriate NLG choices, and to experimentally determine if our choices do indeed make texts more readable (Williams and Reiter, 2005b). In any case, once we had decided to focus SkillSum on groups instead of the general public, which made it much more natural to think of deploying SkillSum within an organisation instead of as a general tool for everyone.

Integration in this sense means that we should support tutors as well as students. We have experimented with generating separate reports intended for tutors, which are much longer and more detailed than reports for students, and which freely use technical vocabulary which students would not know. Another idea we would like to explore is giving tutors some control over the reports produced for their students.

A related point is that if SkillSum is targeted towards specific groups, we need to allow tutors (or developers) to encode the information needed by that group. For example, we will need to tell the system what courses students might undertake, and what level of literacy and numeracy is needed by students in the course. Also, as assessment tests are often adapted for specific groups (for example, a numeracy assessment for Hairdressing might focus on skills needed for Hairdressing, such as dealing with money), we need a mechanism for telling SkillSum about specific tests, and how they should be interpreted.

5. Future Work

There are a number of topics we would like to investigate in future work. Firstly, we would like to further explore individual variations in language use. It is clear that people are very different in their linguistic preferences, linguistic abilities, and linguistic history (what language they have seen and used), and we believe that a system like SkillSum could do a much better job at generating easy-to-read texts if it could adapt texts according to the recipient's linguistic preferences, ability, and history. We would like to empirically explore to what degree people do indeed have different preferences, etc; and empirically measure the impact of adapting texts to an individual's personal use of language.

Secondly, we would like to further explore motivational issues, again probably emphasising individual differences. People have very different motivations for enrolling in skills courses, and SkillSum would probably be considerably more effective if it had a better idea of what a user's motivations were; our STOP system for generating smoking-cessation letters (Reiter, Robertson, Osman 2003) would probably similarly have been more effective if it had a better understanding of users' motivations. Our experiences in both projects suggest that a coarse model of motivation (such as "I want to help my children", or "I want to be healthier") may not be very effective (see Section 4.1). We would like to develop techniques for obtaining a more detailed understanding of motivation, and see if this improved SkillSum's effectiveness.

Last but not least, we would like to make SkillSum more interactive, and also incorporate multimedia (audio and graphics) as well as written text. In theory an interactive version of SkillSum could give users control over what information they see (Section 4.1); audio might be a good media for communicating information to people with limited literacy but good oral English; and graphics might make the system more appealing and friendly to some users.

6. Conclusion

Making it easier for people to assess their literacy and numeracy skills, and indeed other things (such as their health), would be beneficial to society and valuable commercially. We have addressed this problem by trying to build a system which produces a feedback report which is short and easy to read, but nonetheless is more useful than existing "you scored N and are at level X" reports.

SkillSum was harder to build than we at first anticipated, largely because of the fact that we had very limited data about people to work with, and the fact that people are so variable in terms of their skills, motivations, and ability to read. We believe developing techniques for reasoning about people's skills, motivations, etc based on limited data is one of the major research challenges for this class of AI system. However, we also believe that in the longer term more data will in any case be available about individuals, because people are likely to accumulate large amounts of digital data about themselves (Fitzgibbon and Reiter, 2003). Hence while SkillSum-like systems will probably never have as much data about their users as they would like, we suspect that they will have much more data in 10 years time than they do today, because they will be able to access (if permission is given, of course!) large data sets that people have accumulated about themselves. In other words, we believe the long-term prospects of this type of system are very good.

Acknowledgements

Our thanks to the many people who have helped us in SkillSum, including in particular the tutors and students who have participated in our experiments. SkillSum is supported by the ESRC/EPSRC/DTI PACCIT programme under grant ESRC RES-328-25-0026.

References

1. J Burstein, M Chodorow, C Leacock (2003) CriterionSM Online Essay Evaluation: An *Application for Automated Evaluation of Student Essays. In Proceedings* of IAAI 2003, pages 3-10
2. S Carey, S Law, J Hansbro (1997). *Adult Literacy in Britain*. Office of (UK) National Statistics.

3. L Carlson, D Marcu, and M Okurowski (2002). Building a Discourse-Tagged Corpus in the Framework of Rhetorical Structure Theory. In *Current Directions in Discourse and Dialogue*, J. van Kuppevelt and R. Smith eds., Kluwer Academic Publishers.

4. Fitzgibbon and E. Reiter (2003). *Memories for life: Managing information over a human lifetime*. Grand Challenge proposal, published by UK Computing Research Committee (UKCRC).

5. P Kotler, N Roberto, N Lee (2002). *Social Marketing: Improving the Quality of Life (2nd Ed)*. Sage.

6. B Lavoie and O Rainbow (1997). A Fast and Portable Realizer for Text Generation Systems. In *Proceedings of ANLP-1997*, pages 265-268

7. C Moser et al (1999) *Improving Literacy and Numeracy: A Fresh Start*. Available at http://www.lifelonglearning.co.uk/mosergroup/

8. M O'Donnell, C Mellish, J Oberlander, A Knott (2001) ILEX: An architecture for a dynamic hypertext generation system. *Journal of Natural Language Engineering*, 7:225-250.

9. C Perfetti (1994). Psycholinguistics and Reading Ability. In M Gernsbacher (ed), *Handbook of Psycholinguistics*. Academic Press.

10. K Rayner and A Pollatsek (1989). *The Psychology of Reading*. Prentice Hall.

11. E Reiter and R Dale (2000). *Building Natural Language Generation Systems*. Cambridge University Press.

12. E Reiter, R Robertson, and L Osman (2003). Lessons from a Failure: Generating Tailored Smoking Cessation Letters. *Artificial Intelligence* **144**:41-58.

13. E Reiter and S Sripada (2002). Human Variation and Lexical Choice. *Computational Linguistics* **28**:545-553

14. E Reiter, S Sripada, and R Robertson (2003). Acquiring Correct Knowledge for Natural Language Generation. *Journal of Artificial Intelligence Research* **18**:491-516.

15. S Williams (2004). *Natural Language Generation of Discourse Relations for Different Reading Levels*. PhD thesis, Dept of Computing Science, University of Aberdeen.

16. S Williams and E Reiter (2005a). Deriving content selection rules from a corpus of non-naturally occurring documents for a novel NLG application. In *Proceedings of Corpus Linguistics 2005 workshop on using Corpora for NLG*, pages 41-48.

17. S Williams and E Reiter (2005b). Generating readable texts for readers with low basic skills. In *Proceedings of the 2005 European Natural Language Generation Workshop*, pages 140-147.

A Neural Network Approach to Predicting Stock Exchange Movements using External Factors

Niall O'Connor and Michael G. Madden
National University of Ireland, Galway
Galway, Ireland.
niallaoconnor@gmail.com, michael.madden@nuigalway.ie
www.it.nuigalway.ie/m_madden

Abstract

The aim of this study is to evaluate the effectiveness of using external indicators, such as commodity prices and currency exchange rates, in predicting movements in the Dow Jones Industrial Average index. The performance of each technique is evaluated using different domain specific metrics. A comprehensive evaluation procedure is described, involving the use of trading simulations to assess the practical value of predictive models, and comparison with simple benchmarks that respond to underlying market growth. In the experiments presented here, basing trading decisions on a neural network trained on a range of external indicators resulted in a return on investment of 23.5% per annum, during a period when the DJIA index grew by 13.03% per annum. A substantial dataset has been compiled and is available to other researchers interested in analysing financial time series.

1. Introduction

The Dow Jones Industrial Average (DJIA) index was launched in 1896 with 12 stocks, and is now the world's most often-quoted stock exchange index, based on a price-weighted average of 30 significant companies traded on the New York Stock exchange (NYSE) and Nasdaq. The index is used as a general indication of how the market reacts to different information. Financial institutions offer mutual funds based on this index, enabling investors to capitalise on market growth. Several researchers in the past have applied machine learning techniques such as neural networks in attempts to model predict movements in the DJIA and other stock exchange indices. A common approach involves the use of technical indicators which are derived from the DJIA time series itself, such as moving averages and relative strength indices. This relies on past events in the time series repeating themselves to produce reliable predictions. Although machine learning studies using technical indicators, such as those of Yao & Tan [1] and Rodrígues et al. [4], have claimed successful returns, the key limitation of these approaches is that such models do not capture the *cause* of the movements in the market.

The earnings of companies are affected by both internal influences such as product development and external influences such as the cost of energy and the currency exchange rates with foreign markets. The external factors tend to affect the majority of companies in the same way; for example, a rise in energy costs results in a decline in profitability and thus an adverse effect on the value and share price of companies other than energy suppliers. Thus, we hypothesise that such factors will have an observable effect overall on the Dow Jones index, and consideration of them should improve one's ability to predict movements in the index.

Accordingly, this work seeks to identify some prominent external indicators of the Dow Jones index, and use neural networks to model the effect these indicators have on the index. If an effective model is created it will be possible to predict, to some extent, future movements in the index based on current and past data, thus capitalising on the prior knowledge.

Clearly, there is an enormous range of other factors that would not be accounted for by this approach, but an effective model should perform better than random and better than the baseline growth in the index over the testing period. For that reason, this work places emphasis on the evaluation of model performance. Model predictions are used to drive a trading strategy so that the profitability of models may be assessed. Models are also evaluated relative to simple benchmarks.

The contributions of this work are:

- As described in Section 3, a substantial dataset has been compiled with daily values of the DJIA, derived technical indicators, and external indicators. It is available by email from the second author for use by the research community.
- A profit-based evaluation procedure for financial prediction systems is proposed, based on simulations with a simple trading strategy. As discussed in Section 4, this is more meaningful than evaluating systems based on the error between predicted and actual values, as is sometimes done.
- A neural network approach is shown to be successful in predicting movements of the DJIA in Section 5, provided that external factors are considered. These results may be used as a baseline against which to compare other prediction techniques in the future.

2. Related Research

Many of the papers published in this domain are based entirely on analysing the stock market index time series itself, along with derived quantities, without reference to external indicators. For example, Rodrígues et al. [4] develop a rather simple model based entirely on the time series of the Madrid Stock Market General Index. The previous nine days of the index were used as inputs and a buy/sell signal was the output. The research concluded that the neural network trading model was superior to a strategy of simply buying and holding stocks for a bear market (period of decline) and stable market (period of neither growth nor decline), but for a bull market (period of growth) the model performed poorly when compared with the buy-hold strategy for that period. It is difficult to determine if the model created was effective; it stands to reason that a buy-hold strategy cannot be profitable for a period of market decline or stagnation, which implies that a different benchmark against which to compare against might have been more appropriate.

Likewise, in the work of Yao & Tan [1], the effectiveness of a time series model based on the FOREX (foreign currency exchange market) with no external input parameters was evaluated. The paper discusses the concept of market efficiency, which is the time taken for asset prices to react to new information in the market. It is claimed by the Efficient Market Hypothesis that in an efficient market, prices react essentially instantaneously, so that traders cannot capitalise on new information and asset prices reflect all information available to the market. The neural network model created by Yao & Tan performed well for most foreign exchange markets except the Japanese Yen/US Dollar exchange. Better results were seen when moving average technical indicators were incorporated into the model, except again in the Yen/Dollar market. Yao & Tan suggest that technical analysis is not suitable for this market as it is highly efficient and the use of technical indicators would be widely adopted by traders in this market.

Other related research includes neural network approaches to forecasting trends in the Kuala Lumpur Stock Exchange [13], and the Taiwan stock index [9], an approach using genetic programming [2], and a combined genetic algorithm and neural network system for trading of individual stocks [10, 11]. In each of these, forecasting is based solely on the past movements of the time series of interest.

This paper considers the Dow Jones index, which is an average of significant companies in the New York Stock Exchange, which in turn is the largest stock exchange in the world handling volumes of over 1 million trades per day, so it should be highly efficient. The efficiency of the Dow Jones makes it unlikely to be a profitable candidate for technical analysis, resulting in a need for our approach considering external factors.

Hellström and Holmström [12] provide a good introductory tutorial on stock market prediction using both technical and external fundamental indicators. In predicting movements of the USD/GBP exchange rate, Anastasakis and Mort [14] use other exchange rates as fundamental indicators of the USD/GBP, and show how the addition of external information to the model results in a marked improvement in the root mean squared error (RMSE). However, as will be noted in Section 4, low RMSE is not necessarily correlated with correct predictions of the direction of market movement. Lendasse et al. [15] describe an approach to forecasting movements in the Belgian Bel-20 stock market index, with inputs including external factors such as security prices, exchange rates and interest rates. Using a Radial Basis Function neural network, they achieve a directional success of 57.2% on the test data.

Using fundamental and technical analyses is not the only approach to this problem. An interesting study was conducted by Lavrenko et al. [3], predicting trends in stock prices of companies based on news articles relating to these companies. Starting with a time series of the company's stock value, trends are extracted using piecewise linear regression, to re-describe the time series as a sequence of trends. Each trend is assigned a label according to its slope. The time-stamped news articles are aligned with the trends, with a news article being considered to be associated with a trend if its time-stamp occurs within a certain timeframe before the trend occurs. It is possible that a single news article can affect more than one trend. A language model is built relating the typical language used in a news with the trend it is associated with. For instance, a news story corresponding to an upward trend might have words such as "merger" or "higher earnings" contained within it. A Bayesian classification model is created to classify future trends from new news articles. At first glance the results from this approach are quite impressive: over a period of 40 days trading on Yahoo.com stock, a net profit of $19,000 was generated from a principal of $10,000. However, 570 trades were made over the 40 days, which by any standard is a large number of trades; this amounts to an average of $50 profit per transaction or a 0.5% return on investment per transaction. The market simulation did not take into account transaction cost, which for such a large number of trades may have had a significant negative impact on profits. While the Yahoo.com stock represents one significant positive result, when tested over other time periods the mean return was -$9,300 (loss).

3. Dataset Compilation

For the purposes of this work, a dataset has been compiled containing daily opening and closing values of the DJIA index, and corresponding values for a range of external indicators. (Note that one day's closing value of the index can be slightly different from the next day's opening value, due to the recent introduction of after hours trading between institutions' private exchanges.)

In choosing external indicators, an important consideration is of course whether an indicator is likely to have a significant influence on the movement of the index, so that indicators are selected that tend to have an impact on the earnings of the companies in the DJIA. As will be described in Section 5, the relevance of the chosen external indicators was determined experimentally by adding them as inputs to the neural network models and assessing whether they improved performance.

Two other criteria had to be satisfied: high frequency of observations and high availability of historic data. These criteria preclude the use of some external factors even though they may be significant. For instance, the Federal Reserve interest rate is announced quarterly, while the network is trained on daily data, so there is difficulty in representing such an occurrence. One cannot simply interpolate the value between announcements, as in a real-time system one will not know the future announcement. Conversely, a step-wise representation, where the value is constant at all other times except when a change is announced, would be problematic as announcements tend to cause short-term changes in the index. Furthermore, the rate change itself does not hugely affect the earnings of the companies, but rather than how traders view their investments. This factor was therefore not considered.

Even though different companies are dependant on different resources and markets, the earnings of all will be affected to varying degrees by external factors such as the value of oil or foreign currency exchange rates.

To represent oil prices, the daily spot values of WTI Cushing Crude Oil were included in the dataset because it is a common oil type internationally traded and a large volume of historic data is available for it. The choice of currency exchange rates was made by selecting the largest US trading partners with the largest volume of historic data available: US Dollar/Canadian Dollar, US Dollar/Japanese Yen and US Dollar/Pound Sterling.

The dataset was formed from figures taken from three sources:

1. Yahoo.com Finance Section [5] for the daily spot values of DJIA

2. US Energy Information Administration [6] for data on the daily price of WTI Cushing Crude Oil
3. OANDA.com[7] for currency exchange rates

Since the data was taken from multiple sources, the representation of non-trading days differed. The data from Yahoo.com removed weekends and public holidays from their data store, while data from EIA did not and simply used the previous trading day's closing value for the subsequent non-trading days' entries. It was necessary to use a uniform representation across all data sources, therefore the Yahoo.com data streams was used as the standard form and all other sources were adjusted to conform to this standard. In some cases public holidays were on different days, as in the case of foreign currency markets being different to US public holidays. This gave rise to some "missing" values in the data, which were substituted with the previous trading days' values.

Since global currency markets close at different times there is the potential for "future" data being supplied unintentionally to the model. To guard against this, the only current-day element of the input vector is the opening value of the Dow Jones index; all other values are taken from the previous five days. This buffers models from the variations in the closing times of global markets.

The dataset also includes technical indicators derived from the DJIA spot values, specifically the daily gradient of the DJIA, calculated as (Closing–Opening)/Opening, and 10-day and 30-day moving averages of opening values.

The working dataset comprises 4818 data points beginning on 2 Jan 1986 and ending on 4 Feb 2005.

4. Model Construction and Evaluation

4.1. Evaluation Methodology

To determine the effectiveness of training and thus determine if the resulting model is effective for the desired application, four simple benchmark functions were evaluated over the test set. They estimate the current day's closing value as:

1. Average of previous 5 days' opening values
2. Average of previous 10 days' opening values
3. Average of previous 30 days' opening values
4. One day lag i.e. today's closing value is the same as yesterday's.

Each benchmark function was used to predict the current day's closing value and its effectiveness was measured by the error between the functions output and the actual closing value. The performance was computed in three ways:

1. Root Mean Squared Error (RMSE)
2. Error in Dow Jones Points (i.e. RMSE re-scaled to DJIA units)
3. Directional Success (i.e. how often a rise/fall was correctly predicted)

The following table lists the performance of each of the benchmarks described above when applied to the 500 days of test data (18 Dec 2002 to 13 Dec 2004):

	RMSE	DJ Points	Dir.Success
Benchmark 1 – **5 day moving Ave**	0.08143	48.04	51.9%
Benchmark 2 – **10 day moving Ave**	0.00913	53.88	50.3%
Benchmark 3 – **30 day moving Ave**	0.01620	95.59	49.8%
Benchmark 4 – **One day Lag**	0.00443	26.47	40.2%

Table 1: Performance of Benchmark Approaches to DJIA Prediction

RMSE is often optimised in neural network applications, although from an end-user's point of view it can be quite abstract. By using the Error in DJ Points, the progress of training can be viewed in the context of the application. However, it is hazardous to infer model application performance from either of these error measures. Directional success is an important metric as buy/sell decisions will be based on predictions that the index will rise/fall. Examining Benchmark 4, it is clearly has lower error than the other benchmarks yet it has poor directional success, indicating a lack of ability to generalise. There is an intuitive rationale for this: we would expect that a day's closing value would be close to the previous day's closing value, so that Benchmark 4 should have low RMSE, but the change could be a rise or fall with almost equal probability, so the previous day's closing value is not a good basis for trading decisions on the current day.

4.2. Trading Strategy

While the accuracy of a model may be measured using RMSE, Error in DJ Points or Directional Success, what is ultimately needed is a measure of the effectiveness of the model in relation to its use in driving decisions to buy/sell shares. A fourth application-specific measure of model performance is therefore introduced: Return on Investment (ROI). This is computed by basing trading decisions on the output of the model. A simple trading strategy is proposed here: *No Threshold All In/Out.*A ll trades are conducted at the start of business (i.e. at the opening value of the DJ), and the models predict its closing value. If the market is predicted to rise by any amount (no threshold) this signals a *buy*, while if it is predicted to fall this signals a *sell*.

We assume the existence of an idealised Index Tracking Fund that exactly mirrors the movements of the DJIA. (As discussed in the Conclusions, real-world tracking funds are not so precise.) We further assume that fractional amounts of the idealised fund may be traded, rather than just whole units. We start with an initial capital amount C_0 = \$10,000. Then, the first day that a *buy* signal is received from the model, an investment is made in the idealised fund using the full capital amount (all in). *Buy* signals on subsequent days are ignored (they are treated as *hold* instructions) until a *sell* signal is received, when all investment units currently held are sold, yielding a capital amount C_1. Because of the assumptions, this is computed simply as $C_1 = C_0\, D_S/D_B$ where D_B is the opening value of the DJIA index on the day of the *buy* and D_S is the corresponding value on the day of the *sell*.

Subsequent days' *sell* signals are again treated as non-trades, until another *buy* is received, and the process is repeated. The overall ROI over the investment period is the percentage gain in investment capital. While the test period spans 500 working days, for clarity ROI is expressed as an average per annum figure.

We may also account for transaction charges. While such charges vary between brokerage institutions, we assume a flat-rate charge of $8 per trade, which is typical of some reputable online trading services[1]. We do not deduct charges directly from the investment capital but assume they are accounted for separately. However, transaction charges are deducted at the end when computing ROI. Results for ROI are reported with and without transaction charges because of the potential variability of transaction charges, and because if a larger starting capital sum were used, flat-fee charges would be proportionately less significant.

The profits from the benchmark approaches using this strategy are shown below.

	ROI Per Annum	ROI Per Annum with Tr. Charges
Benchmark 1	6.90%	1.78%
Benchmark 2	3.49%	1.53%
Benchmark 3	5.9%	2.78%
Benchmark 4	-14.20%	-24.10%

Table 2: Performance of Benchmark Approaches in Terms of Return on Investment

These figures must be taken in the context of the market environment during the test period. The Dow Jones for this period saw growth with a daily market direction rise 52.8% of the time. Furthermore, if one was to invest on the first day of the test set and hold until the last day, one's investment would have grown 13.03% per annum. Using the trading strategy described, an oracle with perfect knowledge of the future would attain a maximum ROI of 234.81% per annum over this period, or 223.86% per annum when accounting for transaction costs.

Comparing the metrics of the benchmarks as presented in Tables 1 and 2, it clear that several metrics are needed to accurately determine the effectiveness of a model during training and ultimately for the desired application.

4.3. Neural Network Architecture & Parameters

As will be described in Section 5, a range of experiments have been conducted. In all cases, the aim was to predict the current day's closing DJIA index value, given that day's opening value and other inputs such as some previous days' opening values of the DJIA and moving averages over several previous days. Multi-layer feed-forward neural networks were used in all experiments, trained using the back-propagation with momentum algorithm. The training parameters lay within the following ranges:

1. Learning Rate, ? (0.001 – 0.2)
2. Momentum, μ (0.003 – 0.3)
3. Flat Spot elimination, c (0.1)

---

[1] http://personal.fidelity.com/accounts/services/content/brokerage_commission_index.shtml

In all cases, a range of different parameter settings and configurations of hidden nodes were evaluated, and the most successful ones are documented in Section 5.

For all experiments, networks were trained on 4000 days' data (11 Feb 1987 – 17 Dec 2002) and tested on 500 days' data (18 Dec 2002 – 13 Dec 2004). Remaining data points were unused.

5. Experiments & Results

A range of experiments were carried out, in each case using feed-forward neural networks to predict the current day's DJIA index closing value. In the first experiment, predictions were based on the current and previous 5 days' opening values, and in successive experiments additional inputs were added.

As stated earlier, all networks were trained on 4000 days' data, from 11 Feb 1987 to 17 Dec 2002 and tested on 500 days' data from 18 Dec 2002 to 13 Dec 2004. For each experiment, a range of different training parameters and numbers of hidden nodes were tried, and the best results are listed here.

For each experiment, error in predicting training and test set outputs are reported, in terms of both RMSE and DJ Points, along with the directional success and annual return on investment on the test set, with and without transaction charges.

5.1. Details of Experiments

Experiment 1 – Simple Time Series Experiment

Input Data: Current day's Dow Jones Opening Value
Previous 5 days' Dow Jones Opening Values

Network Architecture: 6-10-5-1 (115 Weights)

Training Parameters: ? = .01 ? .001, ? = .03 ? .003,c=0.1, 4000 epochs

Prediction Error:	RMSE	DJ Points
Training Set	0.04144	224.51
Test Set	0.0150	88.3

Directional Success on Test Set	53.30%
Annual ROI on Test Set	9.96%
Annual ROI inc. Transaction Charges	8.03%

Experiment 2 – Technical Indicators

Input Data: Current day's Dow Jones Opening Value
Previous 5 days' Dow Jones Opening Values
10-day Moving Average of Opening Values
30-day Moving Average of Opening Values

Network Architecture: 8-10-5-1 (135 weights)

Training Parameters: η = .01 ? .001, μ = .03 ? .003, c=0.1, 4000 epochs

Prediction Error:	RMSE	DJ Points
Training Set	0.0456	269.43
Test Set	0.0146	86.26

Directional Success on Test Set	53.74%
Annual ROI on Test Set	8.56%
Annual ROI inc. Transaction Charges	7.65%

Experiment 3- Transformation of Time Series

Input Data: Current day's Dow Jones Opening Value
Previous 5 days' Dow Jones Opening Values
Previous 5 days' Daily Gradients of Dow Jones

Network Architecture: 11-9-7-1 (169 weights)

Training Parameters: η = .01 ? .001, μ = .03 ? .003, c=0.1, 4000 epochs

Prediction Error:	RMSE	DJ Points
Training Set	0.0395	233.57
Test Set	0.0147	86.21

Directional Success on Test Set	52.70%
Annual ROI on Test Set	12.08%
Annual ROI inc. Transaction Charges	9.25%

Experiment 4 – Addition of Crude Oil Data

Input Data: Current day's Dow Jones Opening Value
Previous 5 days' Dow Jones Opening Values
Previous 5 days' WTI Cushing Crude Oil Price
(Price per Barrel)

Network Architecture: 11-9-7-1 (169 weights)

Training Parameters: η = .01 ? .001, μ = .03 ? .003, c=0.1, 4000 epochs

Prediction Error:	RMSE	DJ Points
Training Set	0.04086	241.14
Test Set	0.0150	88.486

Directional Success on Test Set	53.31%
Annual ROI on Test Set	18.44%
Annual ROI inc. Transaction Charges	12.53%

Experiment 5 - WTI Cushing Crude Oil and Currency Data

Input Data:
Current day's Dow Jones Opening Value
Previous 5 days' Dow Jones Opening Values
Previous 5 days' WTI Cushing Crude Oil Price
Previous 5 days of the USD/YEN exchange rate
Previous 5 days of the USD/GBP exchange rate
Previous 5 days of the USD/CAN exchange rate

Network Architecture: 26-39-20-1 (1814 Weights)

Training Parameters: η = .01 ? .001, μ = .03 ? .003, c=0.1, 4000 epochs

Prediction Error:	RMSE	DJ Points
Training Set	0.03416	211.0
Test Set	0.017087	88.8

Directional Success on Test Set	54.3%
Annual ROI on Test Set	20.52%
Annual ROI inc. Transaction Charges	18.28%

Experiment 6 – Currency Data, Crude Oil and Gradient of Dow Jones

Input Data:
Current day's Dow Jones Opening Value
Previous 5 days' Dow Jones Opening Values
Previous 5 days' Daily Dow Jones Gradients
Previous 5 days' WTI Cushing Crude Oil Price
Previous 5 days of the USD/YEN exchange rate
Previous 5 days of the USD/GBP exchange rate
Previous 5 days of the USD/CAN exchange rate

Network Architecture: 31-37-20-1 (1907 Weights)

Training Parameters: η = .01 ? .001, μ = .03 ? .003, c=0.1, 6000 epochs

Prediction Error:	RMSE	DJ Points
Training Set	0.03656	215.7
Test Set	0.0145	85.7

Directional Success on Test Set	55.1%
Annual ROI on Test Set	23.42%
Annual ROI inc. Transaction Charges	21.10%

5.2. Discussion

The purpose of Experiment 1 is to determine the performance of a neural network trained solely on the Dow Jones time series. While this shows profitability of 9.93% per annum, it is not greater the market growth (13.03% per annum over the test period, as stated in Section 4.3). This is to be expected, because of the efficient nature of the Dow Jones, and is comparable with the results of Yao & Tao [1], where similar experiments were performed on the Japanese Yen foreign exchange markets.

In Experiment 2, two derived indicators (10-day and 30-day moving averages of the DJ spot values) are added to the input data. In this case the profitability of the model falls significantly even though the directional success rises slightly. This highlights the importance of the profitability metric: while we would expect the profitability to rise with increased generalization ability as indicated by the directional success, this model appears to have got its predictions right on less profitable days than other models.

In Experiment 3, an alternative derived indicator, the gradient of the index in the past several days, is used. The results indicate that this is useful; yet the profit is not greater than market growth and the directional success is poorer than the previous two experiments.

In Experiment 4, crude oil prices are added to the input vector and it is clear that this external variable has had a positive effect on the generalization capabilities of the model. The profitability of the model increases relative to the earlier experiments.

In Experiment 5, the effect of the external variables can be seen clearly. The crude oil data and the currency exchange rates are all used. Greater generalization is seen with a return on investment of 20.52% per annum, which is significantly better than market growth.

In Experiment 6, the gradient of the Dow Jones is added to the input data, which has an interesting effect. In Experiment 3, when this was combined with the Dow Jones time series data only, significantly poorer results were seen. In contrast with this, in Experiment 6 it is added to the external variables of Experiment 5 with marked improvements in generalisation ability and profitability.

It is clear that by adding external indicators to the input vector, the overall performance in terms of profitability and directional success of the model has improved significantly. On the other hand, the accuracy in terms of Dow Jones Points of the best neural network model is poor, when compared to the benchmarks. The least accurate benchmark is Benchmark 3, with an average error of 95 Dow Jones points, while our model only achieves an accuracy of 99.7 Dow Jones points. While the generalization capabilities of the model allows profitable trades since the signal to buy and sell is still valid, the poor accuracy makes it difficult to refine the trading strategy to maximize profits. As well as pointing to the weakness of the trading strategy used, this also indicates a disparity between RMSE and profitability, which in turn indicates that a neural network architecture that directly optimised profitability (or a strongly related quantity) might be better for this application.

5.3. Comparison with Profitability of Benchmarks

Of the simple benchmarks that were presented in Section 4, the one that performed the best was Benchmark 3, with an annual return on investment of 5.92%. As was noted in Section 4, this is not as good as simply buying and holding for the duration of the test period.

Figure 1 is a graph of profits accumulated over the test period when using Benchmark 3, Buy/Hold and the neural network model of Experiment 6. As it shows, using a neural network trained with external variables as well as variables derived from the DJIA index itself is superior to the other approaches considered in this paper.

It may be seen that the neural network model achieves relatively profitable results without engaging in a very large number of trades (59 over 500 days). Most notably, it does not trade for almost 200 days in the latter part of the test period. The market in this period is generally relatively flat. An investment is made at the start of this period at the market's high point, and then held. Since the simple investment strategy does not support bear trades (sell and buy back at a lower price) it cannot profit from a declining market.

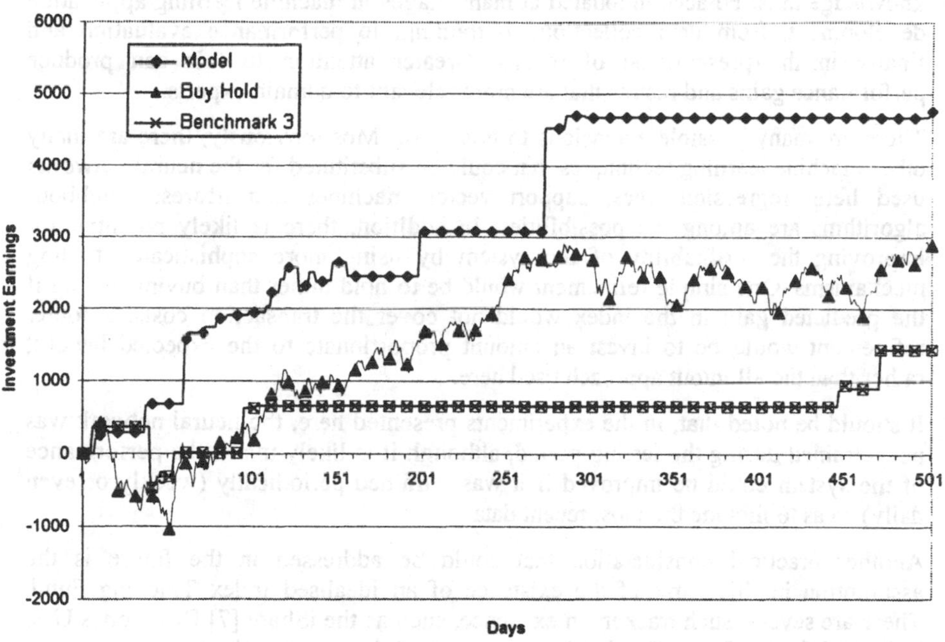

Figure 1: Comparison of Growth in Investment Earnings when Using Experiment 6 Model, Buy/Hold Strategy and Benchmark 3 Strategy

5. Conclusions

Even though, as observed in the Introduction, there is an enormous range of factors that are not accounted for by this approach, the analyses presented here demonstrate the benefit of considering some external factors when predicting stock exchange movements. While it is uncertain whether the addition of further external factors will result in further gains in profitability, it is clear from the analysis presented here that their use is warranted. In Experiment 6, they led to a return on investment of 23.4% per annum (excluding transaction charges) during a period when the DJIA index grew by 13.03% per annum. In Experiments 4 and 5, there was less benefit arising from including fewer external factors.

Conversely, Experiments 1 to 3 have demonstrated little benefit in the commonly-used strategy of predicting future movements based solely on past trends. Also, the analysis of the performance of neural networks and benchmark strategies show a disconnect between being able to predict the closing value of the index with low error and being able to translate this into a profitable trading strategy. This implies that analysts should avoid reporting results in terms of RMSE but should compute a return on investment using a method like the one described in this paper, if results are to be convincing. It also implies that a machine learning approaches to this problem would be more successful if they sought to optimise profitability, or a strongly related quantity, directly.

As this work demonstrates, the use of domain-specific metrics and domain knowledge must be accommodated at many stages in machine learning application development, from data collection, to training, to performance evaluation and finally in the presentation of results. Greater attention to this can produce performance gains and results that are more relevant to domain experts.

There are many possible extensions to this work. Most obviously, there are many other machine learning techniques that could be substituted for the neural networks used here; regression trees, support vector machines and nearest neighbour algorithms are among the possibilities. In addition, there is likely potential for improving the profitability of the system by using more sophisticated trading mechanisms. One simple refinement would be to hold rather than buying/selling if the predicted gain in the index would not cover the transaction costs. Another refinement would be to invest an amount proportionate to the expected benefit, rather than the all in/out approach used here.

It should be noted that, in the experiments presented here, the neural network was not retrained during the testing period, although it is likely that it the performance of the system could be improved if it was retrained periodically (weekly or even daily) so as to include the most recent data.

Another practical consideration that could be addressed in the future is the assumption in this work of the existence of an idealised Index Tracking Fund. There are several such trackers in existence, such as the iShare [7] Dow Jones U.S. Industrial Sector Index Fund. We have conducted some initial experiments using the predictions output by Experiment 6 model to trade in iShares. However, it was found that this fund does not track the Dow Jones perfectly and a significant time lag was observed. This affected the timing of the model, as the end-of-day closing price predicted by the model was not realised in the iShares fund until the following day. The solution is to train the system on iShares data. However, at present there is not sufficient historical data available on the fund to substitute it for the DJIA data used. As more fund data becomes available, this could be explored.

Finally, there are other forms of analysis that could be performed with the dataset that has been compiled as part of this work. It includes daily opening and closing values of the DJIA, some derived technical indicators, and external indicators including daily oil prices and currency exchange rates, all covering a period from 1986 to 2005.

References

1. Yao, J. & Tan, C.J.: "A Case Study on Using Neural Networks to Perform Technical Forecasting of FOREX", Neurocomputing, 2000.
2. Li, J. & Tsang, E.P.J.: "Improving Technical Analysis Predictions: An Application of Genetic Programming", Florida Artificial Intelligence Research Symposium, USA, 1999.
3. Lavrenko, V., Schmill, M., Lawrie, D. & Ogilvie, P.: "Mining of Concurrent Text and Time Series", Proc. 6th ACM SIGKDD International Conference on Knowledge Discovery and Data Mining, Workshop on Text Mining, 2000.
4. Fernández-Rodríguez, F., González-Martel, C., Sosviall-Rivero, S.: "On the Profitability of Technical Trading Rules based on Artificial Neural Networks: Evidence from the Madrid Stock Market", Economics Letters, 2000.
5. Historic Dow Jones Data, Yahoo Finance, http://finance.yahoo.com.
6. WTI Cushing Crude Oil data, US Dept. of Energy Information Administration, http://www.eia.doe.gov.
7. Foreign Currency Data, Oanda, The Currency Site, http://www.oanda.com/.
8. iShare Dow Jones ETF: http://www.ishare.com.
9. Chen, A.S., Leung, M.T. and Daouk, H.: "Application of Neural Networks to an Emerging Financial Market: Forecasting and Trading the Taiwan Stock Index", Computers & Operations Research, Vol. 30, No. 6, 2003.
10. Thawornwong, S., D. Enke, and C. Dagli, "Genetic Algorithms and Neural Networks for Stock Trading Prediction and Technical Signal Optimization", 33rd Annual Meeting of the Decision Sciences Institute in San Diego, 2002.
11. Thawornwong, S., D. Enke, and C.H. Dagli, "Using Neural Networks and Technical Analysis Indicators for Predicting Stock Trends", Intelligent Engineering Systems through Artificial Neural Networks, Vol. 11, 2001.
12. Hellström, T. & Holmström, K.: "Predicting the Stock Market", Technical Report IMa-TOM-1997-07, Mälardalen University, Sweden, 1997.
13. Yao, J., Tan, C.J. & Poh, H.L.: "Neural Networks for Technical Analysis: A Study on KLCI". International Journal of Theoretical and Applied Finance, Vol.2, No.2, 1999.
14. Anastasakis, L. and Mort, N.: "Neural Network-Based Prediction of the USD/GBP Exchange Rate: The Utilisation of Data Compression Techniques for Input Dimension Reduction", Technical Report, University of Sheffield, 2000.
15. Lendasse, A., de Bodt, E., Wertz, V. and Verleysen, M.: "Non-Linear Financial Time Series Forecasting – Application to the Bel 20 Stock Market Index", European Journal of Economic and Social Systems, Vol. 14, No. 1, 2000.

SESSION 2:

TECHNIQUES FOR APPLIED AI

A Fuzzy Rule-Based Approach for the Collaborative Formation of Design Structure Matrices

Kostas M. Saridakis and Argiris J. Dentsoras
Machine Design Lab.
Dept. of Mech. Eng. & Aeronautics,
University of Patras,
26500, Patras, GREECE

Abstract

Engineering design requires extensive decomposition and integration activities relying on a multidisciplinary basis. A design structure matrix (DSM) can be used as a representation and analysis tool in order to manage the design process under diverse perspectives. The design outcome is always subject to the abstract nature, the subjectivity and the low availability of the required design knowledge. This paper addresses the DSM as a communicating design tool among multiple designers. A fuzzy-logical inference mechanism permits the collaboration among designers on the qualitative definition of the interrelations among the design problem's entities or tasks and the resulting DSM may be then utilized for various tasks (partitioning, clustering, tearing etc.) depending on the problem under consideration. A DSM is deployed for the case of the parametric design of an oscillating conveyor where two (2) designers are collaboratively involved.

1 Introduction

Knowledge representation and manipulation in engineering design has been extensively researched during the last decades. The objective of the design process is the generation of solutions taking into account specifications usually stated under different formalisms. The multidisciplinary character of design requires the establishment of relations (functional, computational, topological, logical, temporal etc.) among design entities and across different engineering domains. These relations are always required, irrespective of the specific characteristics of the domain that the design problem pertains to. They represent complex associations among different design entities and their ensemble may be considered as the available design knowledge.

During the design process, intensive decision-making is addressed for multiple technical and managerial issues. The extensive decomposition of the problem, which usually takes place, adds complexity that requires utilization of formal methods for the representation and manipulation of the design knowledge. Design Structure

Matrix (DSM) was firstly introduced by Stewart [1] in early 60's. Two decades intervened before the scientific community started utilizing DSM-based approaches in a variety of contexts, including project planning and management, product development, organization design, systems engineering etc. Usually the relations among generic design elements (tasks, processes, components, parameters) can be represented through directed graphs (digraphs). DSM may be considered as a binary square-matrix representation of these digraphs. For example, the selection of a drive model (DP_1) for an oscillating conveyor is related - through a selection matrix - with the conveyor type (DP_2) and the conveying capacity (DP_3). This relation can be expressed in terms of a dependency matrix as follows.

*	(DP_1)	(DP_2)	(DP_3)
(DP_1)	*	1	1
(DP_2)	0	*	0
(DP_3)	0	0	*

Figure 1. A dependency matrix for the relations among three design parameters.

A design structure matrix defines how a row-element depends on a column element. According to a Boolean approach the dependency may be denoted with 1's and the non-dependency with 0's. In fig. 1, the DSM states that DP_1 depends on DP_2 and DP_3. DP_2 and DP_3 are independent design parameters. It is reasonable that all three DPs could be interdependent and all elements of the table full with 1's. However, in the specific design problem, it is clear that neither the conveying capacity nor the conveyor type should be defined depending on a previous selection of drive type.

Figure 2 shows the three possible configurations of DSM building blocks stated in graph and matrix representations for two design parameters. For all three configurations, the diagonal elements of the DSM that represent the dependency of a design parameter on itself are considered as blank and noted with an asterisk (*). In the parallel configuration, there is no dependency between DP_1 and DP_2 and 'zero' elements are considered in the DSM. In the sequential configuration, DP_2 depends on DP_1 and this dependency is noted with 'one' in the DSM matrix, while a 'zero' element is inserted in the corresponding DSM for the dependency '*DP_1 depends on DP_2*'. In the coupled configuration, the design parameters depend on each other and these dependencies are noted with 'one' elements.

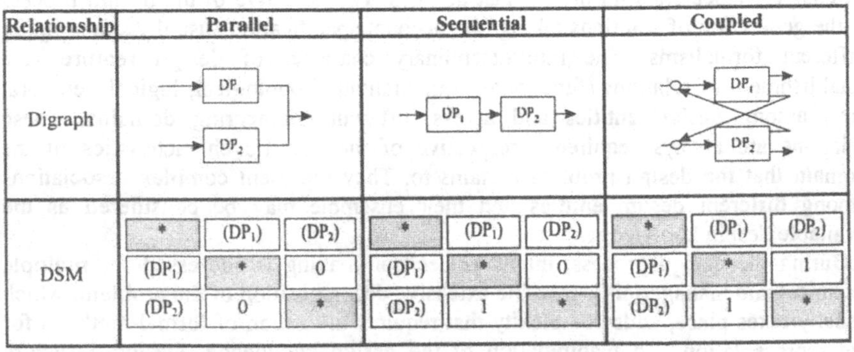

Figure 2. Possible configurations of DSM building blocks.

The iterations provided using coupled processes may enforce creative and efficient solutions. However, speed is sometimes more favourable than innovation while searching for a solution [2]. The cost in time that relies on the information exchange may be reduced by decoupling related design entities (parameters, tasks etc.) with a corresponding loss of efficiency or creativity.

During the last decades a lot of research has been done on DSM. Browning et al. [3] presented a review of numerous DSM-based applications classified according to a general taxonomy. As shown in figure 3, there are two main categories of DSMs: static and time-based. A static DSM is utilized for representing system elements (system parameters, product's components, groups in organizations) simultaneously and it usually integrates clustering algorithms. In a time-based DSM the configuration of the relations among its elements indicate flows of activities through time. The time-based DSMs are analyzed using sequencing algorithms extracting certain ordering of the process activities.

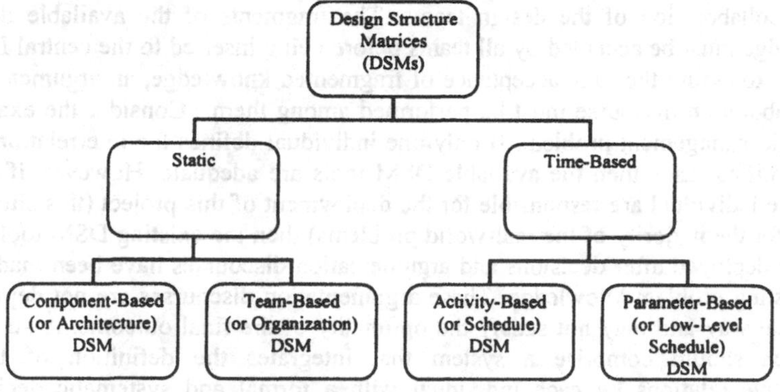

Figure 3. Classification of DSMs [3]

Smith et al. [4] pointed out DSM as an efficient process modelling tool and investigated its potential by comparing it to other modelling approaches for product development. The product development process modelling and analysis [5] was based on the computation of the lead time in a resource-constrained project network and was implemented through advanced simulation techniques. Other researchers identified design as a data-driven process with some portions of design knowledge being more important than others as far as the impact of the decision-making was concerned [6]. Dong et al. [7] proposed a requirement-driven DSM in the context of obtaining the design information flow pattern during early design stages by constructing DSMs from Design Matrices (DMs). Yasine et al. [8] addressed connectivity maps in order to capture the interrelation among multiple matrices. The perspective of combining knowledge-based systems with DSM modelling and analysis was discussed by Whitney et al. [9]. Yassine et al. proposed an information structure approach for the engineering design management introducing specific measures for analyzing the information dependencies [10].

Towards the direction of applying DSMs to various design problems, several tools have been proposed. Clarkson et al. [11] presented a tool relying on the assumption that a design process could be constructed from a predefined set of tasks. The design parameters were utilized as a basis for identifying (or signposting) the sequence of the tasks. DeMAID (Design Manager's Aid for Intelligent Decomposition) [12] uses coupling strengths for ordering of the design tasks, providing a hint about the removal or the temporal suspension of certain tasks or couplings. Its successor, DeMAID/GA [13] uses Gendes (GENetic DEsign Sequencer) [14], a tool for sequencing the design processes with a genetic algorithm, thus minimizing computational cost and time. Another DSM-tool, that uses genetic algorithm and the minimum description length (MDL) principle, is proposed by Yu et al. for partitioning the product architecture into an "optimal" set of modules or sub-systems [15].

Modelling in large problems usually demands a considerable amount of information that must be often delivered by diverse, multi-disciplinary and spatially dispersed design teams. The communication of design teams contribute to faster and more efficient modelling of the design process and, in this context, DSMs supported by web technologies became the research interest of researchers [16]. Sabbaghian et al. proposed a web-based system that utilizes a multi-tiered DSM configuration to present data collected from diverse sources [17].

Although the web-based technologies provide communication among diverse design teams by adding efficiency and speed to the modelling of large and complex design problems, their functionality is usually limited to coordination tasks and not to the collaboration of the design teams. The fragments of the available design knowledge must be accepted by all teams before being inserted to the central DSM. In order to assure the total acceptance of fragmented knowledge, an argumentation or collaboration discourse must be performed among them. Consider the example of a task management problem. If only one individual defines the interrelations for the identified tasks then the available DSM tools are adequate. However, if more than one individual are responsible for the deployment of this project (this situation stands for the majority of the real-world problems) then the existing DSM tools can only be deployed after decisions and argumentation discourses have been made for the existing problem knowledge. These argumentation discourses are not deployed in formal way and may not satisfy the optimality of the final outcome. A superior approach should comprise a system that integrates the definition of tasks' associative relations by each individual with a formal and systematic decision-making process.

The present paper addresses the collaboration issue among individual designers by using a fuzzy, rule-based approach. The DSM is modelled as a fuzzy inference system where each designer contributes a set of rules. Therefore the design knowledge is proposed independently by each designer and then submitted to a fuzzy aggregation process that extracts the final representation scheme. The efficiency of the proposed approach is tested through a tool developed in Matlab [18] and applied to a design problem from the domain of oscillating conveyors.

2 The proposed approach

In the following paragraphs, the proposed approach is described. The underlying features and functionalities are demonstrated through an example of a design of an oscillating conveyor. The efficiency and the perspectives are also discussed.

2.1 Fuzzy rule-based modelling of design structure matrices

The proposed method approaches design problem modelling through a Mamdani fuzzy rule inference system [19]. This system uses two inputs (line and column) and one output (fuzzyRelation) (see figure 4). The inputs are used for pointing an element inside the DSM and the output is used for determining its relation strength after performing rule firing. According to his/her beliefs, each designer may independently apply a set of rules to this fuzzy rule inference system thus capturing the interdependencies inside the DSM. The rule base that is ultimately used for reasoning is the base that consists of the sum of all independent rule sets proposed by all designers. For every designer, a specific opinion weight is predefined, that is inherited by the corresponding rule set. The current application uses fuzzy numbers [19] for the two input variables and five fuzzy sets [19] for the output variable (see figure 5). The output variable is structured with: a. two crisp fuzzy membership functions (singletons) '*norelation*' and '*identity*' that represent the boundary cases of *non-existence* of a relation and of the *identity* relation (diagonal elements) and b. three triangular membership functions ('*low*', '*medium*', '*high*') representing the strength of the relation. Other membership functions may be suggested depending on the design problem under consideration.

Assuming the element DSM(i , j) of ith line and j^{th} column of the matrix DSM, then three different designers could possibly apply the following rules:

Designer 1: If *line* is **i** and *column* is **j** then *fuzzyRelation* is **strong**
Designer 2: If *line* is **i** and *column* is **j** then *fuzzyRelation* is **low**
Designer 3: If *line* is **i** and *column* is **j** then *fuzzyRelation* is **medium**

All three rules are encapsulated in the rule base and the outcome is extracted according to a defined aggregation strategy. The reasoning scheme and the aggregation process are described in the next section. The architecture of the proposed representation and reasoning framework is depicted in figure 6.

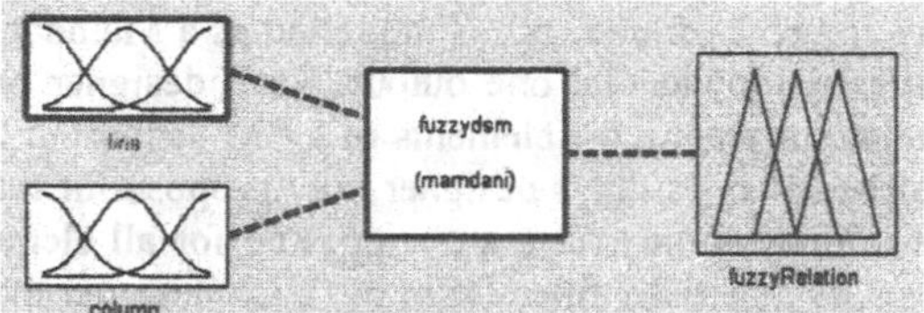

Figure 4. Fuzzy rule structure for DSM

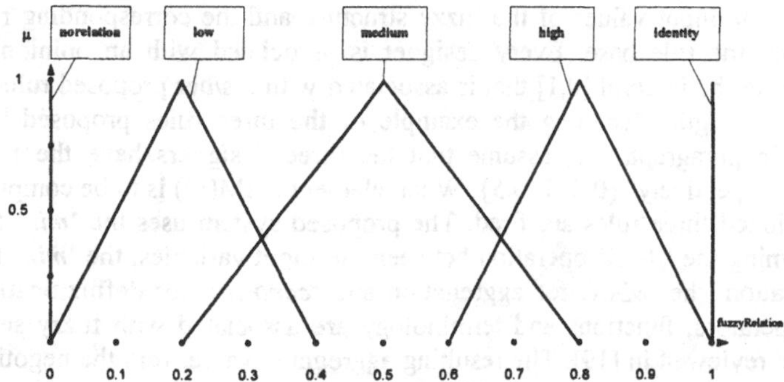

Figure 5. Representation of the DSM elements relation through fuzzy membership functions

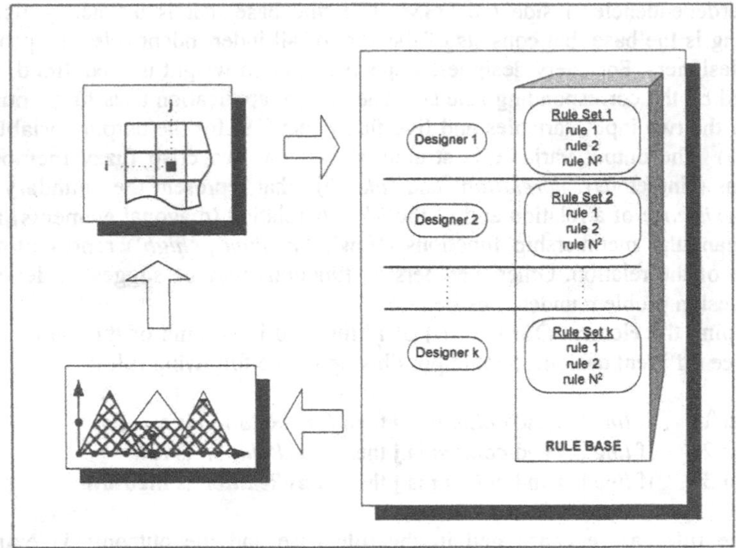

Figure 6. The proposed collaborative framework

2.2 The reasoning scheme

The collaborative inference framework is modelled as a Mamdani fuzzy inference system [18,19] with two inputs and one output. Each designer proposes rules for representing the relations among the elements of DSM according to his/her beliefs. The maximum number of rules that a designer may propose for a N*N DSM is N^2. However it is not imperative that rules are suggested for all elements. That means that the result is usually a partially filled DSM per each designer that is translated by the system in a rule set to be merged with other similar proposed rule-sets thus forming the final rule base.

The designers express their beliefs about strength of dependencies inside the DSM in qualitative number by choosing among five alternatives (*'norelation'*, *'low'*, *'medium'*, *'high'*, *'identity'*). An algorithm processes all the elements of the DSM by varying the input values of the fuzzy structure and the corresponding rules are 'fired' from the rule base. Every designer is associated with an opinion weight normalized to the interval [0,1] that is associated with his/her proposed rule-set as a rule firing strength. Recalling the example of the three rules proposed by three designers in paragraph 2.1, assume that the three designers have the following weighting respectively: {0.8, 1, 0.5}. When element DSM(i,j) is to be computed, the aforementioned three rules are fired. The proposed system uses the *'min'* function for performing the *'AND'* operation between the input variables, the *'min'* function for implication, the *'MAX'* for aggregation and *'centroid'* for deffuzification. The utilized operators, functions and terminology are associated with fuzzy set theory and can be reviewed in [19]. The resulting aggregated value from the negotiation of the designers is shown in figure 7. The three designers have defined for the specific DSM element (that represents a relation) three different fuzzy sets. The first designer identifies the relation as *'high'*, the second designer as *'low'* and the third designer as *'medium'*. The proposed fuzzy sets are cut at levels corresponding to the opinion weighting of the respective designers. For example, the fuzzy set proposed by the 3rd designer is considered up to a level of 0.5 that corresponds to his/her opinion weighting. The area that is formed by the fuzzy sets after the cutting is considered for defuzzification. The deffuzification is performed by finding the centroid of the formed area through the calculation of the following integral:

$$\text{centroid} = \frac{\int x \cdot \mu(x)}{\int \mu(x)}$$

where $\mu(x)$ is the value of the membership function for a value of x (figure 7). If for a specific x more than one fuzzy sets exist (multiple membership functions) then the fuzzy set with the highest value of membership function is considered (MAX operation).

The obtained aggregated value is registered to the main DSM. After all elements are computed by the fuzzy inference mechanism, the DSM is partitioned and teared (if needed) thus obtaining a final DSM without loops. The final DSM contains arithmetic values normalized to the interval [0, 1] that represent the relations, but can be easily adapted to obtain a fuzzy representation. For instance, if a relation in the final DSM is represented with the value 0.5 then this relation may be represented with the qualitative relation '*medium*'.

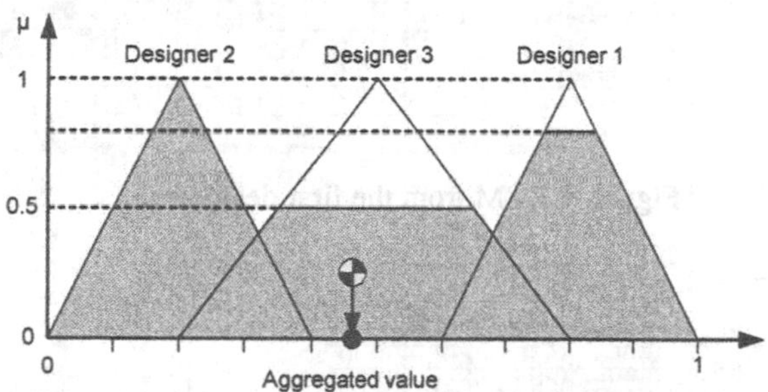

Figure 7. Aggregation of the rules defined by three designers

2.3 An example case: Oscillating conveyor design

An example of parametric design of oscillating conveyors is selected for demonstrating the functionalities and the features of the proposed framework. This parametric problem is analyzed into 33 design parameters and several associative relations, both computational and empirical [20]. The available design knowledge for the specific design problem is not strictly established and relies on an empirical basis. The existence of diverse problem representations enhances the consideration that no systematic way of representing and manipulating the design knowledge exists. Two designers contribute on forming of the DSMs of the problem and the two proposed individual DSMs are then aggregated in order to obtain the final DSM. The two designers consider different aspects about the representation and manipulation of the specific design problem. The approach may be extended for more designers.

The approach that is described in the next paragraphs demonstrates how the contradicting representation aspects can be combined in order to extract a unified scheme that is described by a fuzzy aggregated DSM.

The DSM proposed by the two designers may contain integer numbers (1,2,3,4,5) that correspond to the linguistic fuzzy sets. For example, if a relation is noted with 2, then the relation is '*low*'. A portion of the DSMs and the correspondence among quantitative and linguistic measures are shown in figures 8 and 9 for the two designers respectively.

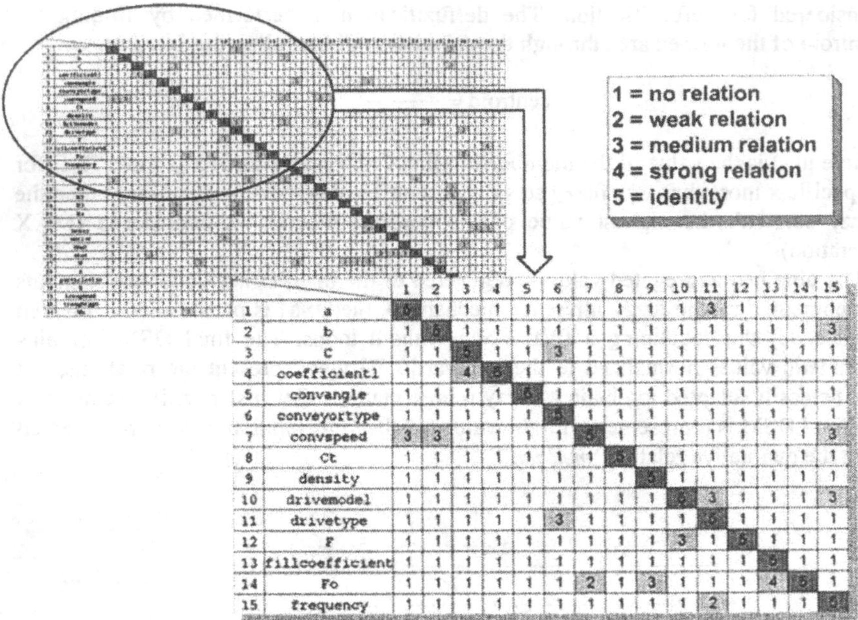

		1	2	3	4	5	6	7	8	9	10	11	12	13	14	15
1	a	5	1	1	1	1	1	1	1	1	1	3	1	1	1	1
2	b	1	5	1	1	1	1	1	1	1	1	1	1	1	1	3
3	c	1	1	5	1	1	3	1	1	1	1	1	1	1	1	1
4	coefficient1	1	1	4	5	1	1	1	1	1	1	1	1	1	1	1
5	convangle	1	1	1	1	5	1	1	1	1	1	1	1	1	1	1
6	conveyortype	1	1	1	1	1	5	1	1	1	1	1	1	1	1	1
7	convspeed	3	3	1	1	1	1	5	1	1	1	1	1	1	1	3
8	Ct	1	1	1	1	1	1	1	5	1	1	1	1	1	1	1
9	density	1	1	1	1	1	1	1	1	5	1	1	1	1	1	1
10	drivemodel	1	1	1	1	1	1	1	1	1	5	3	1	1	1	3
11	drivetype	1	1	1	1	1	3	1	1	1	1	5	1	1	1	1
12	F	1	1	1	1	1	1	1	1	1	3	1	5	1	1	1
13	fillcoefficient	1	1	1	1	1	1	1	1	1	1	1	1	5	1	1
14	Fo	1	1	1	1	1	1	2	1	3	1	1	1	4	5	1
15	frequency	1	1	1	1	1	1	1	1	1	1	2	1	1	1	5

Figure 8. DSM from the first designer

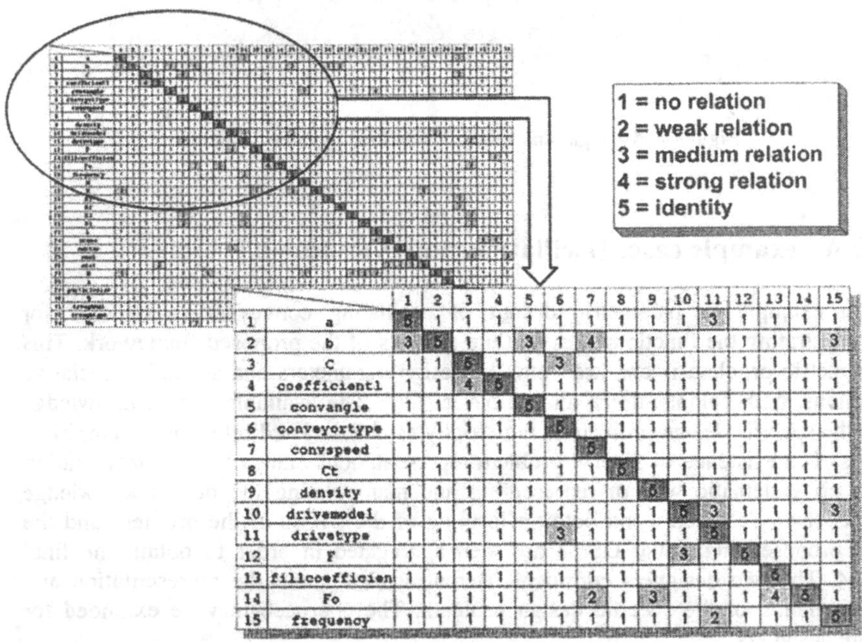

		1	2	3	4	5	6	7	8	9	10	11	12	13	14	15
1	a	5	1	1	1	1	1	1	1	1	1	3	1	1	1	1
2	b	3	5	1	1	3	1	4	1	1	1	1	1	1	1	3
3	c	1	1	5	1	1	3	1	1	1	1	1	1	1	1	1
4	coefficient1	1	1	4	5	1	1	1	1	1	1	1	1	1	1	1
5	convangle	1	1	1	1	5	1	1	1	1	1	1	1	1	1	1
6	conveyortype	1	1	1	1	1	5	1	1	1	1	1	1	1	1	1
7	convspeed	1	1	1	1	1	1	5	1	1	1	1	1	1	1	1
8	Ct	1	1	1	1	1	1	1	5	1	1	1	1	1	1	1
9	density	1	1	1	1	1	1	1	1	5	1	1	1	1	1	1
10	drivemodel	1	1	1	1	1	1	1	1	1	5	3	1	1	1	3
11	drivetype	1	1	1	1	1	3	1	1	1	1	5	1	1	1	1
12	F	1	1	1	1	1	1	1	1	1	3	1	5	1	1	1
13	fillcoefficien	1	1	1	1	1	1	1	1	1	1	1	1	5	1	1
14	Fo	1	1	1	1	1	1	2	1	3	1	1	1	4	5	1
15	frequency	1	1	1	1	1	1	1	1	1	1	2	1	1	1	5

Figure 9. DSM from the second designer

If no collaboration among designers took place then the proposed DSMs would have resulted to the independent digraphs of figure 10 after partitioning. Using the proposed collaborative framework, an aggregated DSM (see figure 11) is formed leading to a unique digraph. This matrix – after a normalization to the numerical

interval [0,1] - may be then submitted to partitioning and tearing processes. The final aggregated and partitioned DSM is shown in figure 12.

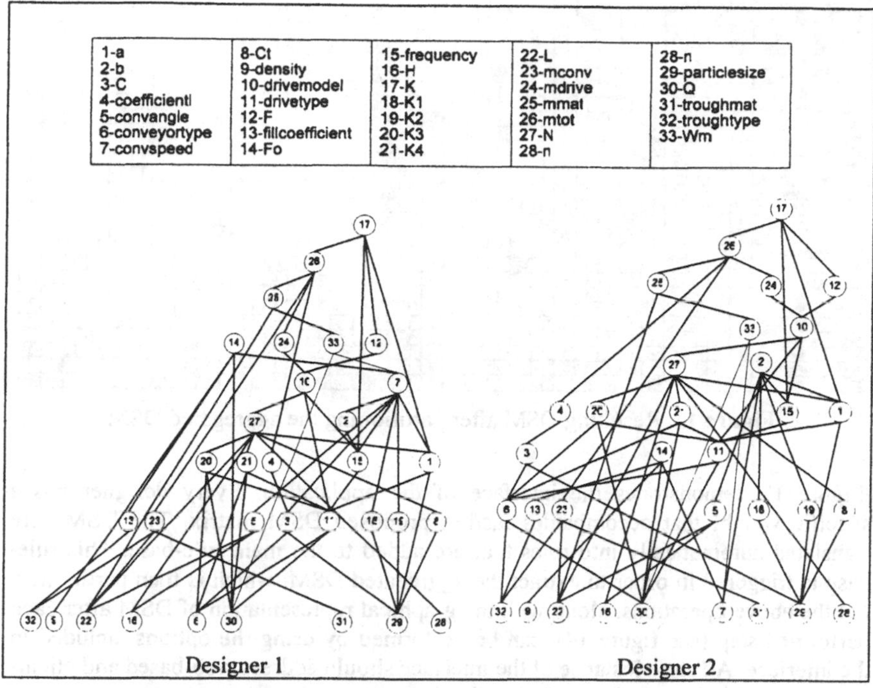

Figure 10. Individual resulting digraphs without collaboration

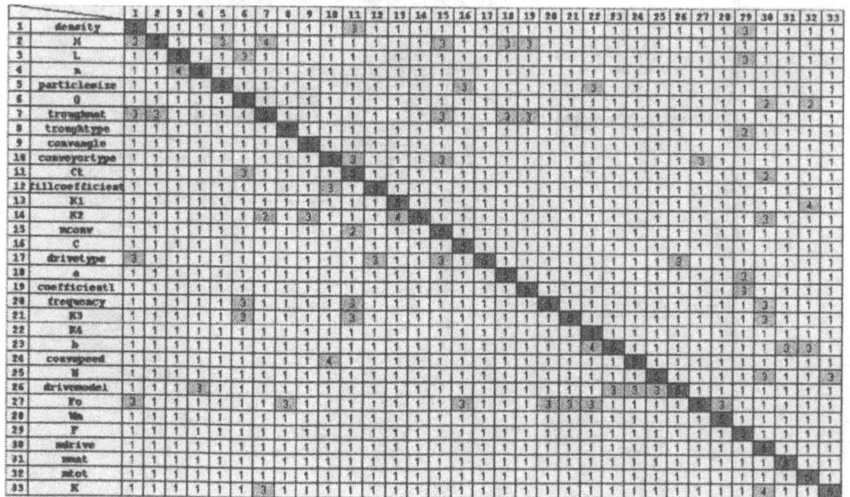

Figure 11.R esulting DSM after the aggregation of the DSMs proposed by the two designers

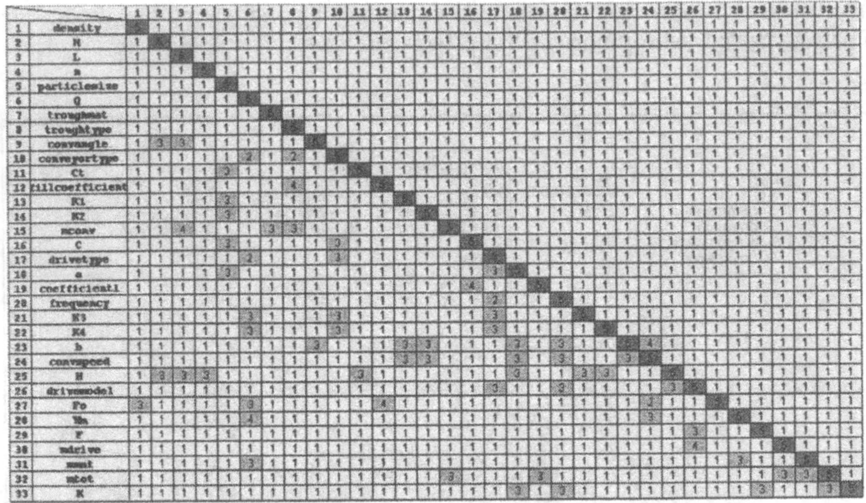

Figure 12. Resulting DSM after partitioning the aggregated DSM

Figure 13 demonstrates the interface of the application. Every designer has a specific weight that accompanies his/her proposed DSM matrix. The DSMs are translated automatically into rules that are added to the main rule-base. This rule-base is triggered in order to extract the aggregated DSM, which is then partitioned. All the above operations, along with the graphical representation of DSM after each performed step (see figure 14), can be performed by using the options included in the interface. A future instance of the interface should address web-based and client-server capabilities and advanced visualization tools.

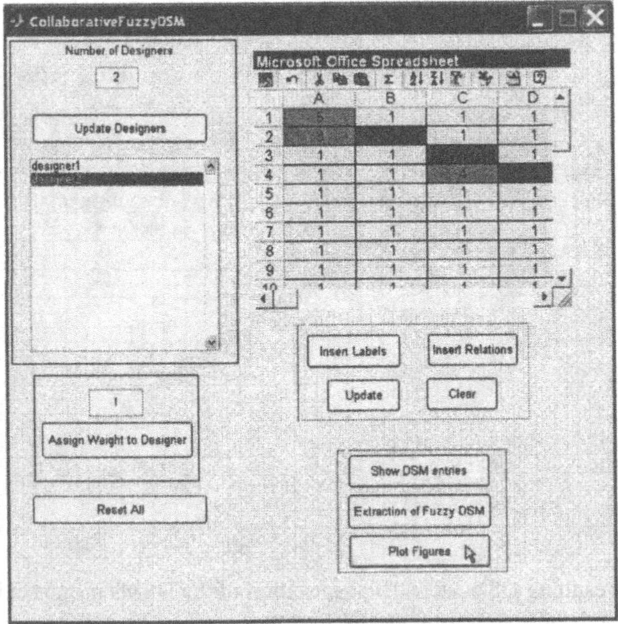

Figure 13. Snapshot of the interface for the collaborative fuzzy DSM framework

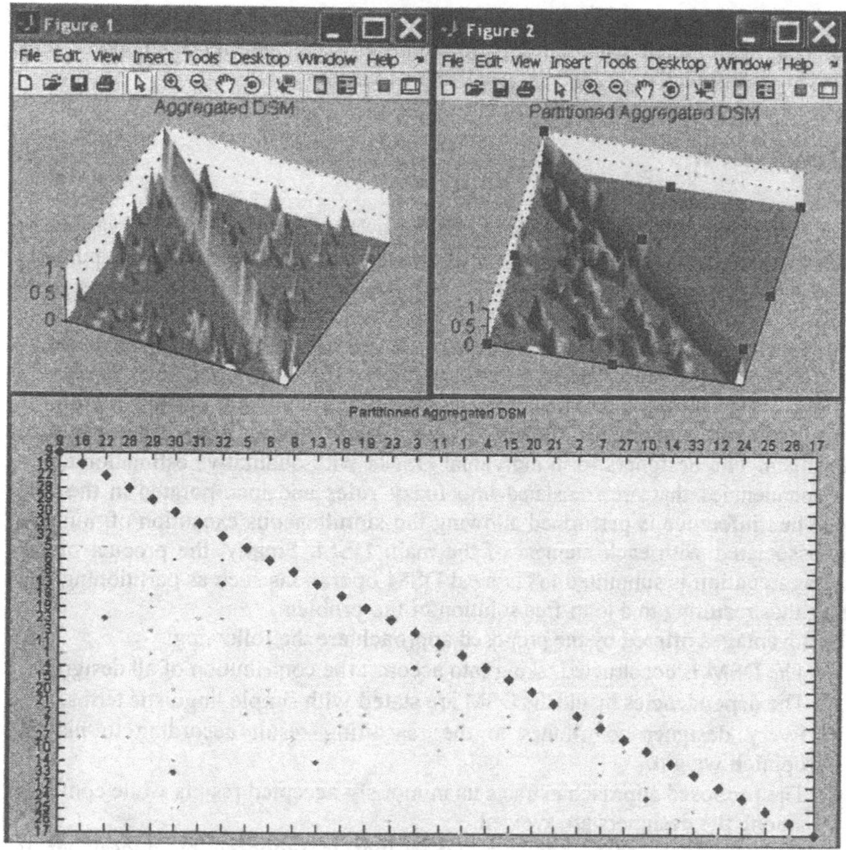

Figure 14. Snapshots of the constructed figures

As far as the oscillating conveyor problem is concerned, the formed DSM (figures 12,14) after partitioning still retains a closed-loop inside the matrix involving the elements 7 and 2 ('*convspeed*' and '*b*' respectively). Thus in order to deliver a loop-free DSM one dependency must be submitted to a 'tearing' procedure. It is proposed to tear the dependency with the lower strength, e.g. the dependency '*convspeed* depends on *b*'. If the strengths are the same then specific knowledge about the problem under consideration is required in order to proceed. Generally, tearing a dependency inside the DSM means that an approximation/estimation has been performed for the instantiation of one of the related elements.

For the considered design problem, the representation and the manipulation of knowledge with DSM deployment results to an efficient and systematic way that coincides – to some extent - with some existing approaches [20]. However if multiple designers have to collaborate for constructing a representation schemes for the design parameters and their associative relations, then there is no existing DSM-based approach that supports the collaboration with a reasoning framework. Instead, if several designers have contradicting opinions about a specific relation, then a decision must be made for the dominating opinion to be further used for the DSM. The proposed collaborative framework is capable of representing and manipulating the design knowledge in a fuzzy aggregated DSM that is extracted after taking into account the proposals from all designers according to a pre-defined opinion weighting. In the context of the presented example, the final fuzzy aggregated DSM captures a representation scheme that is extracted after performing systematic manipulation of the contradicting relations proposed by the two designers. The underlying aggregation scheme results in commonly accepted representations, thus preserving the objectivity of the derived design solutions.

3 Discussion

The increasing utilization of Design Structure Matrices (DSMs) in a variety of engineering problems highlights their sufficiency in representing and manipulating the available knowledge. Although some web-based instances of DSMs have been proposed for integrating concurrency among dispersed designers, none of these frameworks/systems incorporates schemes for defining relations with a collaborative way. The present paper proposes a framework for forming DSMs in design problems where multiple designers are collaboratively involved. For this reason the design problem is modelled through a main DSM and a fuzzy rule inference mechanism. The designers form individual DSMs with qualitative estimation about the dependencies that are translated into fuzzy rules and incorporated in the rule base. Then inference is performed allowing the simultaneous execution of multiple rules associated with each element of the main DSM. Finally, the product of the fuzzy aggregation is submitted to classical DSM operations such as partitioning and tearing thus resulting to a loop-free solution of the problem.

The advantages offered by the proposed approach are the following:

- The DSM is constructed taking into account the contribution of all designers.
- The dependencies inside the DSM are stated with simple linguistic terms.
- Every designer contributes to the reasoning result according to his/her opinion weight.
- The proposed approach extracts unanimously accepted results while conflicts among the designers are avoided.

As aforementioned, each individual DSM that is proposed by a designer is translated to a set of rules. The architecture of the proposed application is designed to support a main rule-base that accommodates individual rule-sets proposed by the designers. This could facilitate the development of a distributed web-based platform for collecting and aggregating the corresponding individual DSMs. At this point the issue of computational cost is raised considering large-scaled problems. A $N*N$ DSM may be translated to a set with N^2 rules that is multiplied by the number k of the designers resulting finally to a rule-base with (N^2*k) rules.

A test was conducted in order to estimate a mean time for each rule needed by the system to process the aggregation and partitioning procedures. For this test the dimension of the DSM (N) and the number of the designers k, varied in the intervals [10,50] and [1,10] respectively. The mean time needed for an Intel® Pentium® M 1.6 GHz processor for each rule was estimated **0,00686 sec,** which is significantly high. However this is the highest possible computational cost and it is present in the case that the designers have different preferences about all the dependencies of the design problem, which is not realistic. Usually the differentiations of the designers' choices are limited to a small number of DSM elements and only for these elements the corresponding rules must be taken account from all designers. Thus an algorithm could be deployed for checking similarities among proposed rule-sets and accepting only the rules that have not been submitted. Further reduction of the rules could be accomplished if the diagonal elements of the DSMs are not translated into rules in the proposed rule-sets. Instead they should be a priori taken as '*identity*' relation in the final aggregated DSM matrix.

Future work will be undertaken in order to improve the efficiency of the proposed method towards the following directions:

- Optimization of the rule-based reasoning algorithm in order to obtain faster solutions.
- Combination of traditional DSM partitioning and clustering techniques with more advanced methods (genetic algorithms, fuzzy aggregation).
- Incorporation of web technologies for the development of a communicating shared DSM platform.

References

1. Steward, Donald. Partitioning and Tearing Systems of Equations. SIAM Numerical Anal., ser. B, vol. 2, no. 2, pp. 345-365, 1965
2. Eppinger Steven D. Innovation at the Speed of Information, Harvard Business Review, vol. 79, no. 1, pp. 149-158, 2001
3. Browning Tyson R. Applying the Design Structure Matrix to System Decomposition and Integration Problems: A Review and New Directions. IEEE Transactions on Engineering Management, Vol. 48, No. 3, pp. 292-306, 2001
4. Smith Robert P., Morrow, Jeffery. Product Development Process Modeling. Design Studies, Vol. 20, pp. 237-261, 1999
5. Cho Soo-Haeng, Steven Eppinger. Product Development Process Modeling Using Advanced Simulation. Proceedings of the 13th International Conference on Design Theory and Methodology, Pittsburgh, Pennsylvania, USA, 2001
6. Nikolidakis E.A., Dentsoras A.J.. An Environment for the Efficient Analysis of Defining Relationships among Design Entities, 23rd SGAI Int. Conference on Innovative Techniques and Applications of Artificial Intelligence, Cambridge, UK, 2003
7. Dong Qi, Whitney Daniel. Designing a Requirement Driven Product Development Process. Proceedings of the 13th International Conference on Design Theory and Methodology, Pittsburgh, Pennsylvania, USA, 2001
8. Yassine Ali, Dan Whitney, Steve Daleiden, Jerry Lavine. Connectivity Maps: Modeling and Analyzing Relationships In Product Development Processes. Journal of Engineering Design, Volume 14, No 3, 2003
9. Whitney Daniel E., Dong Qi, Judson Jared, Mascoli Gregory. Introducing Knowledge-Based Engineering into an Interconnected Product Development Process. M.I.T. Center for Innovation in Product Development, Cambridge, MA, White Paper Jan. 27, 1999
10. Yassine Ali, Falkenburg A., Donald R., Chelst Ken. Engineering Design Management: An Information Structure Approach. International Journal of Production Research, vol. 37, no. 13. pp. 2957-2975, 1999
11. Clarkson Peter John, James Robert Hamilton. 'Signposting', A Parameter-driven Task-based Model of the Design Process. Research in Engineering Design, 12: 18-38, 2000
12. Rogers James L., Bloebaum, Christine. Ordering Design Tasks Based on Coupling Strengths, 5th AIAA/USAF/NASA/ISSMO Symposium on Multidisciplinary Analysis and Optimization, Panama City, Florida, AIAA paper No. 94-4326, 1994
13. Rogers James L. DeMAID/GA - An Enhanced Design Manager's Aid for Intelligent Decomposition. 6th AIAA/USAF/ NASA/ISSMO Symposium on Multidisciplinary Analysis and Optimization, Seattle, WA , AIAA paper No. 96-4157, 1996
14. McCulley C., Bloebaum Christine. A Genetic Tool for Optimal Design Sequencing in Complex Engineering Systems, Structural Optimization, Vol. 12, No. 2-3, pp. 186-201, 1996

15. Yu Tian-Li, Yassine Ali, David Goldberg. A Genetic Algorithm for Developing Modular Product Architectures. Proceedings of the ASME 2003 International Design Engineering Technical Conferences, 15th International Conference on Design Theory & Methodology, Chicago, Illinois, 2003
16. Rogers James L., Salas A.O., Weston R.P. A Web-Based Monitoring System for Multidisciplinary Design Projects. Proceedings of the Seventh AIAA/USAF/NASA /ISSMO Symposium on Multidisciplinary Analysis and Optimization, St. Louis, MO, 1998
17. Sabbaghian Nader, Eppinger Steven D., Murman, Earll. Product Development Process Capture & Display Using Web-Based Technologies. Proceedings of the IEEE International Conference on Systems, Man, and Cybernetics, San Diego, CA, pp. 2664-2669, 1998
18. MATLAB © The Mathworks Inc, version 7.0.1.24704
19. Kosko B. Neural Networks and Fuzzy Systems: A dynamical systems approach to machine intelligence. Prentice-Hall, Englewood Cliffs, 1992
20. Saridakis K.M., Dentsoras A.J. Computer-Aided Design of Oscillating Conveyors, XVI International Conference on Material Flow, Machines and Devices in Industry, Belgrade, Yugoslavia, 2000

Acknowledgements

The present research work has been done within the framework of the project 2991 funded by the Research Committee of the University of Patras, Greece.

University of Patras is a member of the EU-funded I*PROMS Network of Excellence.

Geometric Proportional Analogies In Topographic Maps: Theory and Application

Emma-Claire Mullally, Diarmuid P. O'Donoghue,
Department of Computer Science / National Centre for Geocomputation
National University of Ireland, Maynooth, Ireland.
{emmaclaire.mullally;diarmuid.odonoghue}@nuim.ie
www.cs.nuim.ie/~dod / www.nuim.ie/ncg

Amy J. Bohan, Mark T. Keane,
Department of Computer Science
University College Dublin, Ireland
{amy.bohan;mark.keane}@ucd.ie

Abstract

This paper details the application of geometric proportional analogies in the sub-classification of polygons within a topographic (land cover) map. The first part of this paper concerns geometric proportional analogies that include attributes (e.g. fill-pattern and fill-colour). We describe an extension to the standard theory of analogy that incorporates attributes into the analogical mapping process. We identify two variants on this "attribute matching" extension, which is required to solve different types of geometric proportional analogy problems. In the second part of this paper we describe how we use the simpler of these algorithms to generate inferences in topographic maps. We detail the results of identifying a number of different structures on a sample topographic map.

1. Introduction

Sub-classification of polygon objects in maps can be used to improve the quality information stored on a topographic (land cover) map. For example *roads* can be sub-categorised into *cul-de-sacs, X-junctions* or *Y-junctions* while *buildings* can be sub-categorised as *houses* or *schools* etc. Currently, topographic maps (like OS MasterMap[1]) can be thought of as thousands of adjoining polygons, where only a minimum of information supplied about each polygon. Is this paper we show how a solution to a class of geometric analogy problems, can also be applied to improve the quality of information recorded on a topographic map.

---

[1] Crown Copyright, Ordnance Survey Research Centre, Southampton, UK.

A topographic polygon is an area bounded by a set of lines and each polygon is categorised as one of thirteen main themes including *road-or-track, rail, river, roadside, general surface, building* etc. Each theme typically becomes associated with a broad range of object types and the vagueness of these thirteen themes hinders many potential applications. For example, a polygon classified as a *road* may be a *road-segment*, a *crossroads (X-junction)*, a *cul-de-sac* or a *T-junction*. In order for topographic maps to be truly useful, as much information as possible should be assigned to each class of polygon. This is a particular problem for deriving automated solutions, such as route planning.

Another application area centres on building value estimation, as used by the insurance and investment industries. The theme "building" encompasses many different types of *building*, from *garden sheds*, to *semi-detached houses* to *hospitals*. It is commonly accepted that houses located on cul-de-sacs will appreciate more quickly in value houses located on main roads. However, the dearth of information recorded on topographic maps means that this folk wisdom can neither be tested, nor used to assist in the process of building value estimation.

Currently, any additional information supplied about map objects for computational processing, must be derived by hand. This is a slow, labour intensive and costly process. Automatic sub-classification of, say roads, can help to reduce this cost. It is also interesting to note that once the roads have been sub-categorised, they can then help to identify other objects. It is intended that the sub-categorisation of roads will form a foundation that can be built upon in order to further categorise other map objects, such as buildings. Even without further sub-categorisation of map objects, sub-categorising only roads has proven to be very useful. For example, the automatic identification of *houses* in a map that are located in a *cul-de-sac* could assist house buyers that are searching for such a property. Generating such information may also have implications for insurance and other industries, as these houses are often considered more valuable that equivalent houses not on a cul-de-sac. Also automatic identification of *Y-junctions* (or *T-junctions*) and *X-junctions* can easily be supported. Knowing how many junctions exist on a particular road may assist in deciding where to put a set of traffic lights for town planners.

We describe a method of identifying subcategories of polygons using their *context*. The context of a polygon refers to the other polygons (neighbours) that share a boundary line or boundary point with that central polygon. This context can prove invaluable in sub-categorising polygons. This is achieved by *analogical matching* [1, 2, 3, 4] to a previously defined polygon context. For example, a road network is composed of many individual *road* polygons, which are adjacent to one another, forming a network. Some of these polygons may in fact be junctions. If a *road* polygon is surrounded on three sides by *roadside* polygons and is adjacent to only one other *road* polygon, we may infer that this central polygon is actually a *cul-de-sac*.

This paper details the application of analogies in sub-classifying *roads* as *cul-de-sacs, Y/T-junctions* and *X-junctions*. To test our application we use a topographic map (from OS MasterMap), covering some of the region of Port Talbot. Before describing the application, we give an overview of geometric proportional analogies, which are the analogical comparisons used in the classification process. Section two therefore details the theoretical aspect of analogy and section three describes how this theory can be put into practice when sub-categorising roads.

2. Analogical Comparisons

In this section we examine geometric proportional analogies (GPAs) and discuss how they may be solved algorithmically. GPAs include those analogy problems commonly found in IQ tests. We then present a different type of GPA problem that includes attributes within the analogy process. We identify two distinct algorithms that are required to solve two different classes of GPA problems. In the following section we then develop one of these algorithms and illustrate its application to processing topographic maps. However, we begin by looking at plain GPAs.

2.1 Geometric Proportional Analogy (GPA)

Analogical comparisons are a primary means that people use to generate inferences. [1]. Analogies are comparisons between two systems of information, referred to as the *source* and *target* domains. The source provides the "inspiration" for solving the target problem. In this paper we focus on geometric proportional analogies (GPA's). GPAs are a type of analogy formed between two collections of geometric figures. They are of the form A:B::C:D, which we read as A is-to B as C is-to D. The *source* domain (A:B) identifies some transformation, which must then be applied to C, yielding D (See Figure 1). This analogy centres on partitioning the central polygon of part A to produce part B. This partitioning transformation must then be applied to C and this allows us to generate D.

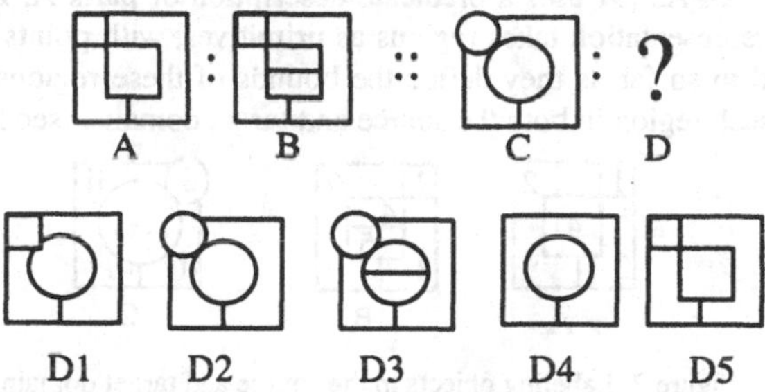

Figure 1: A Simple Geometric Proportional Analogy

There are two key points to note about GPAs. First, the change in the source domain (*i.e.* between A and B) is called the *transformation*. Second, parts A and C are used to identify the inter-domain *mapping* [1] i.e. small square (A) maps to small circle (C) and central square (A) maps to central circle (C). The combination of the transformation and mapping will yield the solution D.

2.2 Theoretical Background

ANALOGY [5] was the first computational model to solve GPA problems. It focused on geometric analogies involving plain figures, taking graphic images as input and making use of the geometry of the presented figures. Additionally, Evans' model selected the best D from a given list of alternative solutions.

More recent models of GPAs have made use of Gentner's structure mapping theory [1]. This states that all analogies may be solved by representing the source and target domains using predicates. Then the crucial inter-domain mapping between the source and target domains can be discovered by identifying the largest isomorphic mapping between the predicate structure of the two domain descriptions. Structure mapping theory has been successfully used in many models of conceptual analogies [6, 7, 8] as well as GPAs [6, 9, 10].

Previous models of GPA's determine the solution by selecting the best of a number of presented answers such as Tomai & Evans [5, 6]. The key distinction of our model is that it actually generates a description of the desired solution. This generation step will prove a key point when the geometric analogy algorithm is migrated to solving problems within topographic maps. This solution generation step will be elaborated later in the paper. Also in solving these GPA's we concentrate on the topology of parts A, B and C rather than the geometry of the figures they contain. That is, we ignore the shape of the individual polygons and concentrate on their topological arrangement. The following section details our model for solving GPAs.

2.3 Analogical Mapping

Our solution to GPAs [9] uses a predicate description of parts A, B and C of the analogy. Our representation takes regions as primitives, with points and lines only being admitted in so far as they define the bounds of these regions. We uniquely identify each such region in both the source and target domains (see Figure 2).

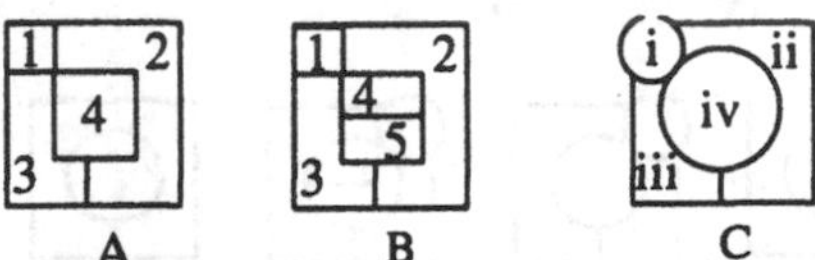

Figure 2: Labeling objects in the source and target domains

Having identified and labeled the distinct objects in the domain, we characterize the structure within each part (A, B, C) using two binary relations: *line-adjacent(x,y)* and *point-adjacent(y,z)*.

Line adjacent polygons are polygons that share at least one edge with the current polygon. Point adjacent polygons are polygons that are not line adjacent to the current polygon but that touch it at one or more points.

Figure 3: Line Adjacent Neighbours

Figure 4: Point Adjacent Neighbours

Part A of Figure 1 is therefore represented by the following collection of predicates, based on the labeling shown in Figure 2.

A	
line-adjacent(1,2)	*line-adjacent(2,3)*
line-adjacent(3,4)	*line-adjacent(4,2)*
point-adjacent(1,4)	

B	
line-adjacent(1,2)	*line-adjacent(2,3)*
line-adjacent(3,4)	*line-adjacent(4,2)*
point-adjacent(1,4)	*line-adjacent(4,5)*
line-adjacent(3,5)	*line-adjacent(2,5)*

Figure 5: Representation of the source domain of Figure 1

Next, we perform the central structure mapping step [1] that identifies the inter-domain *mapping* between the descriptions of part A and part C. (As the counterpart of B has yet to be generated, we ignore parts B and D at this stage). The inter-domain mapping consists of pairs of objects and relations, and these paired items represent counterparts of one another. So, object *1* in A is the counterpart of object *i* in C. This structure mappings process concentrates on the topological relations between objects, allowing different shaped polygons be placed in correspondence between parts A and C. So, the *square 1* of part A is mapped to *circle i* of part C (see Figure 2).

2.3.1 The Source Domain Transformation

The most important aspect of the source domain is the *transformation* it defines between parts A and B. This transformation is represented implicitly by the difference between the descriptions of these two parts. (Unlike [10] we do not use a separate vocabulary to represent the source domain transformation). The transformation in Figure 1 involves the insertion of an extra polygon by splitting an existing polygon. Therefore the solution to this problem is the application of this "insertion" transformation to the mapped equivalent in C – yielding D in Figure 1(ii).

Other GPA problems contain transformations in the source domain that insert or delete polygons from the source (and thus the target), or perform other modifications to it. GPA's may also perform translations and rotations on the objects or may replace an object by a different shape. However, our application domain of topographic maps makes best use of analogies that are translation, rotation, scale and shape invariant. That is, we wish to reason about topographic structures in different places and with objects of different shapes. Therefore, in this paper we focus on GPA's that are most similar to those we use in processing topographic maps.

We employ the standard algorithm for generating analogical inferences, which performs pattern completion on the information supplied in parts A, B and C to generate D. This is also known as the "Copy With Substitution and Generation" (CWSG) algorithm [11]. So, to generate the description of D we copy the structure of part B – but we substitute the object names of B with their mapped equivalents. Item 5 has no counterpart in the mapping, and so an appropriate token is generated for this in the description of D (such as *v*).

The source defines no transformation to the predicate description and the source (A) and target (C) predicate information is identical. We can copy the predicates in part C to generate the predicate description for the required solution D, but the object identifiers must be replaced by their mapped equivalents from C.

However, the application domain of topographic maps is not composed of undifferentiated polygons, but rather is composed of polygons each with a specific category. Incorporating this additional category information can be achieved by treating each category as an attribute of the relevant object. With this objective in mind, we explore geometric analogies that contain additional information.

2.4 Attributes in Geometric Proportional Analogies

We now describe a different type of GPA problem, which has not been addressed by previous models. These are GPA's that involve attribute transformations and attribute matching (see Figure 6). The attributes contained in these problems are vital to their solution and thus the attribute information cannot be overlooked. Keane *et al* [8] explored analogies involving attributes, but this work did not focus on proportional geometric analogies nor did it address attribute transformations. None of the existing models of geometric analogies looks to solve GPA problems such as that depicted in Figure 6.

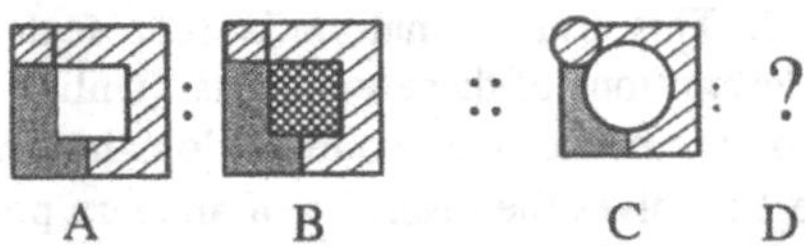

Figure 6: A Proportional Geometric Analogy involving Attributes

For example in Part A of Figure 6, we can see that one object is plain, two have a texture of diagonal lines and another object is grey. As qualities like *colour* and *texture* are associated with individual objects, this information is represented by single place predicates – or attributes. So, we add the attribute information about each polygon to the predicate descriptions (from above).

striped(1), striped (2), grey(3), plain(4).

Of course, we still identify the inter-domain mapping between the predicates of the source and target domains – or between part A and part C of Figure 6. This mapping process ignores the attribute information, and the attribute information is only utilised after the mapping has been identified. The presence of attribute information does necessitate an extra degree step in the solution process.

2.4.1 Attribute Transformations & Attribute Matching

The source domain (A:B) of Figure 6 includes a transformation to its attribute information, specifically to the *fill-pattern* attributes. As with the predicate information, the attribute transformation is represented implicitly by the difference in attributes in parts A and B. The attribute transformations (implicitly) defined by the source domain of this problem is:

A: *striped(1), striped(2), grey(3), plain(4)*

B: *striped(1), striped(2), grey(3), checkered(4)*

The attribute information from part C is added to its earlier predicate description. This information will prove crucial to the next attribute matching step, required to generate the correct D. The attributes added to predicate description of part C are:

C: *striped(i), striped(ii), grey(iii), plain(iv)*

2.4.2 Global Attribute Matches

We define *Attribute Matching* as the process of determining the attribute changes that occur across the transformation and mapping process. *Attribute matches* occur between the attributes of objects that map with one another. Therefore, attribute matching must occur after the structure mapping process has taken place. So the attributes of object 1 in the source, will be matched with the attributes of object i in the target, and so on for the other objects.

Attribute matching can manifest itself in two main ways: *Global attribute matches* and *Local attribute matches*. This distinction arises because there are multiple ways of identifying the mapping between these attribute transformations. We begin with the simpler form of attribute matching - global attribute matching. We define a *global attribute match* as a match between attributes where there is a 1-to-1 correspondence between all attributes in the source and target domains.

Now we identify the 1-to-1 correspondence between the attributes of parts A and C. So, *striped(1)* matches with *striped(i)* etc. Table 1 details the attribute matching required for the problem in Figure 6. In this problem, the attributes that are mapped together are also identical. These are among the easier class of problem to involve attributes. Crucially, this is also the type of attribute matching that we shall make use of in our application for processing topographic maps.

Table 1 Global Attribute Matching

Source		Target	
A	B	C	D
striped(1) ->	*striped(1)*	*striped(i)* ->	
striped(2) ->	*striped(2)*	*striped(ii)* ->	
grey(3) ->	*grey(3)*	*grey(iii)* ->	
plain(4) ->	*checkered(4)*	*plain(iv)* ->	

Figure 6 may be solved by use of the global attribute matching, generating the solution depicted in Figure 7.

Figure 7: Solution to the Geometric Proportional Analogy in Figure 6

There is also a local *attribute matching algorithm* that is required to solve more complex GPA problems. This algorithm is required in cases where there are multiple matchings for an attribute across different objects. However, we have found that most problems in topographic maps can also be solved using global attribute matches. However, the possibility of more complex local attribute matches occurring can not be ruled out. For further information on local attribute matching see [9].

3. Geometric Proportional Analogies in Topographic Maps

We now apply our geometric proportional analogies to the task of processing topographic maps. A topographic map can be thought of as a large collection of (mostly) non-overlapping polygons describing homogenous collections of land cover across an area. OS UK categorise polygons into one of approximately 13 themes (categories), including; *road-or-track, rail, river, roadside, building* and *general surface*. However, many of these categories are very broad. The remainder of this paper centres on (automatically) improving the quality of the data recorded on OS UK's MasterMap map of Great Britain.

Figure 8 depicts a source domain representing a T-shaped collection of polygons, which are all from the same category. The attributes of the central polygon are modified by the source domain transformation of the GPA. The target domain (C) represents a collection of polygons located within a topographic map. Three of these polygons are from the *road* category (theme).

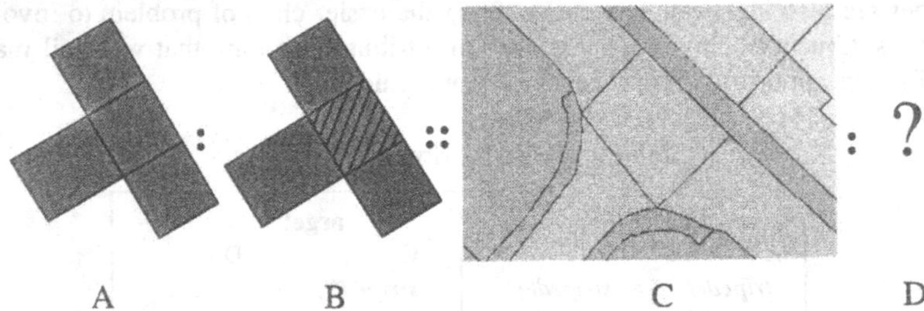

Figure 8: A Geometric Proportional Analogy within a Topographic Map

3.1 How do we find the cul-de-sacs?

A *cul-de-sac*, or dead end, is a road that is blocked off and can only be accessed through one entrance. They are often found in housing estates, but they can be found anywhere, in industrial estates, hospitals, in the countryside and the city centre.

It is useful to know where cul-de-sacs are for several reasons. It is a commonly held belief that houses situated in a *cul-de-sac* tend to be more expensive than houses that are situated on the main *road*. This is largely due to the fact that *cul-de-sacs* are seen as being quieter, with less traffic and are safer for pedestrians and children. Cul-de-sacs may be useful in route planning

A cul-de-sac can be thought of as a *road* segment (polygon) that is connected to only one other *road* segment. In this way the task can be reduced to finding all of the *road-or-track* polygons in a map that are line adjacent to only one other *road-or-track* polygon and identifying each as a *cul-de-sac*. The shape or size of the polygons does not need to be taken into account. If a road segment is *line-adjacent* to two or more different road segments, it is not considered a cul-de-sac.

In order to find a *cul-de-sac*, first we generate a list of *line-adjacent* polygons for each individual polygon in the map. In order to be certain that we have found a cul-de-sac, the list of polygons that are *line-adjacent* to the road-or-track polygon in question must be checked and the numbers of road-or-track polygons that appear in its *line-adjacent* list are counted. If this total is equal to one, then we have found a cul-de-sac. This task does not require us to consider *point-adjacent* polygons.

Sometimes, in looking for cul-de-sacs, errors occur due to rivers or railways crossing over a road. This is known as the occlusion problem. These occlusions can be removed before categorising the cul-de-sacs by finding where two roads are separated by only a river or railway polygon and replacing this occluding polygon with another road polygon [12].

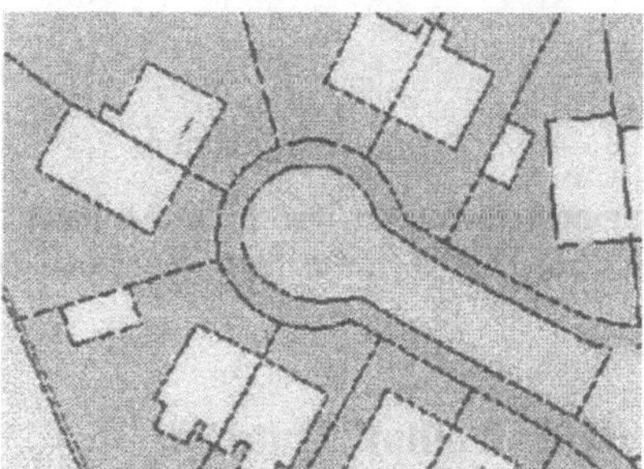

Figure 9: A cul-de-sac within a housing estate

It is also interesting to note that because duplicate line and point adjacencies are removed by the CSM algorithm, we do not have any problem with categorising cul-de-sacs that are adjoined to the same road twice (see Figure 10).

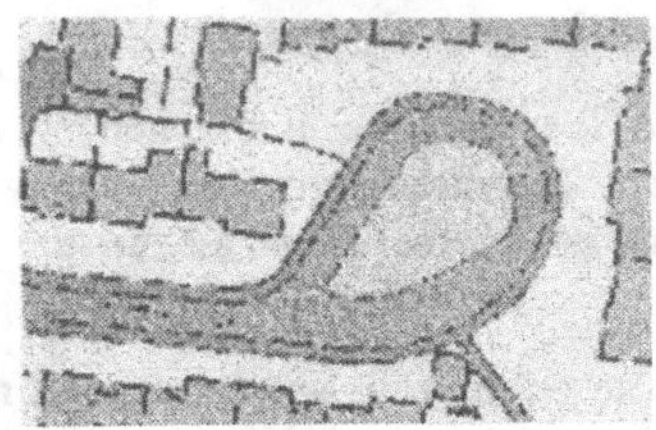

Figure 10: A cul-de-sac line-adjacent to the same road twice

3.1.1 *Finding Y-junctions and X-junctions*

We can also find Y-junctions and X-junctions, in a similar manner. A Y-junction, or T-junction, is a road segment where there is a choice of two different routes that can be taken. It can be thought of as a road segment that is line adjacent to three other road segments. In order to find all of the Y-junctions in a map, we use the same algorithm that we used to find the *cul-de-sacs* and we check if the total number of road-or-track polygons that are *line-adjacent* to a road-or-track polygon being considered is equal to three. If this is the case we have found a Y-junction.

An X-junction is a road segment where there is a choice of three different routes that can be taken. We define it as a road segment that is line-adjacent to four other road segments. We find X-junctions in the same manner as we find Y-junctions, except that we look for the polygons that are line-adjacent to a total of four other road-or-track polygons.

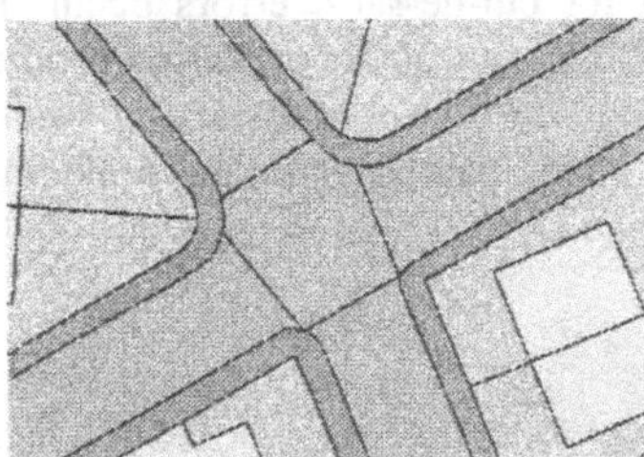

Figure 11: X-junction

If a road-or-track segment is found that is line-adjacent to two road-or-track polygons, or if it is line-adjacent to more than four road-or-track polygons, it is discarded.

3.2 Tests on the "Port Talbot" Dataset

The results below are based on the OS MasterMap data for Port Talbot, which is mainly a residential area containing over 5000 non-overlapping independent polygons. For our purposes we have looked only at the topography layer, which contains large-scale data of the town's real world surface features, to find cul-de-sacs, Y-junctions and X-junctions. This is a convenient data form to use as it contains a lot of detail about features in the area and their adjacencies. Examining the data is also quite simple and road segments can be found with relative ease.

We have decided to omit polygons that are on the edge of the map from our testing, as these polygons would produce unreliable results. We have also omitted possible occlusions, which can be removed before sub-categorising cul-de-sacs.

In each case, all of the cul-de-sacs, Y-junctions and X-junctions in the map were verified independently and systematically by hand, using two human map readers. First, each *cul-de-sac, Y-junction* and *X-junction* in the map was found manually, and separately, by both map readers. It was confirmed that they had both found the same number of objects in each category. Secondly, we used the algorithm detailed in section 3.1 to find each instance of a cul-de-sac, Y-junction and X-junction in the map. Finally, we compared the map readers results against the results derived from using our algorithm. This was carried out to assess the accuracy of our algorithm at identifying all members of each category. We also wanted to ensure that our definition of each category did not deviate from what the map readers perceived to be a cul-de-sac, Y-junction or X-junction.

In order to analyse our results we will look at them in terms of *precision, recall* and *F-measure* [13]. In this case, the *precision* is the ratio of the number of correctly identified road segments to the total number of road segments returned by our algorithm.

$$precision = \frac{number\ of\ correct\ answers\ given}{total\ number\ of\ answers\ given}$$

Recall is the ratio of the total number of correct answers returned from a dataset, over the total number of correct answers contained in the dataset.

$$recall = \frac{number\ of\ correct\ answers\ given}{total\ number\ of\ possible\ correct\ answers}$$

The *F-measure* combines the values of both precision and recall. The beta (β) is a parameter used to assign the relative importance of precision to recall. In our example, we have allowed beta to assume a value of 1, meaning that precision and recall are given equal importance.

$$F - measure = \frac{(\beta^2 + 1) precision * recall}{\beta^2 precision + recall}$$

Table 2 Accuracy of the Sub-classification tasks

	Precision	Recall	F-measure
Cul-De-Sac	100%	100%	1
Y-junction	93.5%	100%	0.966
X-junction	91%	100%	0.953

3.2.1 Cul-de-sac Results

Our results indicate that, by our definition, there are 133 cul-de-sacs and junctions in Port Talbot. Further inspection by hand concluded that all of the polygons returned do, in fact, correspond to cul-de-sacs and junctions.

Looking at these results in terms of precision, the total number of correctly identified cul-de-sacs was equal to the total number of answers returned. This gives us a precision of 100%, which means that every cul-de-sac that was returned was correctly identified as a cul-de-sac. There was no case in which a polygon was incorrectly identified as a cul-de-sac.

With regard to recall, the number of correct answers returned for our definition of a cul-de-sac was equal to the total number of correctly identified cul-de-sacs. This gives us a recall of 100%, which means that every cul-de-sac in Port Talbot was identified. The F-measure for cul-de-sacs is equal to one. This is to be expected, as both precision and recall are also equal to 100%.

3.2.2 Y-junctions Results

Y-junctions are defined as a road segment that is line adjacent to three other road segments. Our algorithm returned more results for y-junctions than were found by hand. This discrepancy in our results gives us a precision of 93.5%. The incorrect polygons are slip-roads onto a motorway. In the future we hope to be able to identify the motorway and exclude it from our testing in order to improve results. The results returned by our algorithm include every Y-junction that exists in the Port Talbot dataset.

The total number of correct answers given by our algorithm was equal to the total number of possible correct answers, and so the recall is 100%. We can be sure that no Y-junction exists in the map that does not appear in our list of results. Given the precision and recall, the F-measure for Y-junctions is 0.966.

3.2.3 X-junctions Results

The definition of an X-junction is a road segment that is line adjacent to four other road segments. Although all of the eleven road segments that are returned as part of our results are adjacent to four other road segments, one of the results could not be classed as an X-junction by our map readers as it is a motorway entrance.

Looking at the number of correct answers found manually against the total number of answers returned by our algorithm gives us a precision of 91%. 100% of the X-junctions that actually exist in the Port Talbot dataset were found, and so we have 100% recall. The F-measure for X-junctions, given the precision and recall, is 0.953.

3.2.4 Future Work

It is important to note that while our precision may have dropped below 100%, our recall remained at 100%. Some answers that were returned were false positives, but every cul-de-sac and junction that exists in the map has been successfully identified. This is a very encouraging outcome. Although our precision is already consistently above 90%, we are hopeful that future work in this area will remove some of the obstacles that are faced with removing false positives and improve the precision even further.

4. Conclusion

In the beginning of this paper we set out to show that road segments in topographic maps could be successfully sub-categorised from the current *road-or-track* category into the sub-categories of *cul-de-sac, Y-junction and X-junction.* This can be found by looking at the geometric analogies, along with attributes, in topographic maps. The results have shown that that this method works extremely well for sub-categorising cul-de-sacs as well as different types of junctions, such as Y-junctions and X-junctions. By ignoring the shape of the polygons and concentrating on the local topology between polygons, i.e. the neighbouring polygons in the map, we have reduced this complex problem into something that is simpler to represent.

We examined proportional geometric analogies that include attribute information (fill-colour, fill-pattern etc) in the analogy process. We then described the attribute matching extension to the standard structure mapping algorithm employed by virtually all models of the analogy process. We specified two variants on this structure matching extension that can be use to solve different types of these geometric analogy problems. We then described how one of these algorithms was adapted to identifying localised collections of polygons within topographic maps.

Our contextual structure matching (CSM) algorithm appears to be a successful method for classifying different types of road segments, namely *cul-de-sacs*, *Y-junctions* and *X-junctions*. In fact, by using this method, cul-de-sacs, Y-junctions and X-junctions were sub-categorised with over 90% accuracy. In the case of cul-de-sacs the results could not be any better than 100%, although this figure may drop when different topographic maps are used. Preliminary results (on other maps) suggest that, for cul-de-sacs, the accuracy should not drop below 90%. In the case of Y-junctions and X-junctions, there was only one object on the map that caused incorrect data to be returned. However, using further sub-categorisation experiments, we may be able to fix this problem by identifying the motorway and excluding it from all other Y-junction and X-junction calculations. It is hoped that the more sub-categorisations of roads that we can find, the more accurate the results will become.

References

1. Gentner, D. "Structure-Mapping: A Theoretical Framework for Analogy", Cognitive Science, 7, 155-170, 1983.
2. Mulhare, L. O'Donoghue, D. Winstanley A. C. "Analogical Structure Matching on Cartographic Data", 12th Artificial Intelligence and Cognitive Science AICS-2001, NUI Maynooth, Ireland, pp 43-53, Sept. 5-7, 2001, ISBN 0-901519-48-0,.
3. O'Donoghue, D. Winstanley, A.C. "Finding Analogous Structures in Cartographic Data", 4th AGILE Conference on G.I.S. in Europe, Czech Republic, April, 2001,.

4. Winstanley, A.C. O'Donoghue, D. and Keyes L. "Topographical Object Recognition through Structural Mapping", 1st International Conference on Geographic Information Science - GIScience 2000, Savannah, Georgia, USA, October 28-31, 2000.
5. Evans, T.G "A Program for the Solution of a Class of Geometric Analogy Intelligence-Test Questions", in Semantic Information Processing, (Ed.) M. Minsky, MIT Press, 1967.
6. Tomai, E. Forbus Kenneth D. Usher, J. "Qualitative Spatial Reasoning for Geometric Analogies", 18th International Workshop on Qualitative Reasoning, August 2-4, 2004, Northwestern University, Evanston, Illinois, USA (during 26th Annual Meeting of the Cognitive Science Society).
7. Falkenhainer, B. Forbus, K.D. Gentner, D. "The Structure Mapping Engine: Algorithm and Examples", Artificial Intelligence, 41, 1-63, 1989.
8. Keane, M. T. Ledgeway T. and Duff, S. "Constraints on Analogical Mapping: A Comparison of Three Models", Cognitive Science 18, 387-438 (1994)
9. Bohan, A. O'Donoghue D. "A Model for Geometric Analogies using Attribute Matching", AICS-2000 11th Artificial Intelligence and Cognitive Science Conference, Aug. 23-25, NUI Galway, Ireland, 2000.
10. Davies, J. Goel, A. K. "Visual analogy in problem solving", Proceedings of the International Joint Conference on Artificial Intelligence 2001, Morgan Kaufmann publishers, pp 377-382, 2001.
11. Holyoak K. J. Novick L. Melz E. "Component Processes in Analogical Transfer: Mapping, Pattern Completion and Adaptation", in Analogy, Metaphor and Reminding, Eds. Barnden and Holyoak, Ablex, Norwood, NJ: 1994.
12. O'Donoghue, D. Loughlin, A. "Using Context to Repair Partial Occlusions in Topographic Data", Proceedings of GISRUK - Geographical Information Science Research Conference, Norwich, UK, pp 15-18, 28-30 April, 2004.
13. Jurafsky D. & Martin J, "Speech and Language Processing", Prentice Hall, 2000.

Experience with Ripple-Down Rules*

P.Compton, L.Peters†, G.Edwards†, T.G.Lavers†
University of New South Wales, Sydney, Australia
†Pacific Knowledge Systems Pty. Ltd, Sydney, Australia
contact: compton@cse.unsw.edu.au

Abstract

Ripple-Down Rules (RDR) is an approach to building knowledge-based systems (KBS) incrementally, while the KBS is in routine use. Domain experts build rules as a minor extension to their normal duties, and are able to keep refining rules as KBS requirements evolve. Commercial RDR systems are now used routinely in some Chemical Pathology laboratories to provide interpretative comments to assist clinicians make the best use of laboratory reports. This paper presents usage data from one laboratory where, over a 29 month period, over 16,000 rules were added and 6,000,000 cases interpreted. The clearest evidence that this facility is highly valuable to the laboratory is the on-going addition of new knowledge bases and refinement of existing knowledge bases by the chemical pathologists.

1. Introduction

The aim of this paper is to provide data on the use of the Ripple-Down Rule (RDR) knowledge acquisition technique. RDR is a general knowledge acquisition technique, but the particular application area considered here is adding clinical comments or interpretations to laboratory reports to assist the referring clinicians. That is, the clinician who orders some chemical pathology blood tests, receives not only the laboratory results but advice from the pathologist on interpretation of the results, further testing that may be required and so on. Many pathology reports have some sort of simple canned comment; the aim of using a KBS is to provide much more detailed comments providing expert pathologist advice on the clinical management of the specific patient.

The advantage of this area for an expert system or other AI technology is that there is no demand or expectation placed on the clinician receiving the report. The clinician does not have to interact with the system, or change their mode of operation in any way. Since a clinician chooses to order diagnostic tests for a patient presumably they will wish to view the report, including any interpretative comments. Of course, the quality of the comments will be critical in whether the

* This paper describes results generated by Labwizard, a software system produced by Pacific Knowledge Systems (PKS). The first author has a small shareholding in PKS, while the other authors are employees and hold shares and/or options in PKS; thus all may benefit from any increased reputation of Labwizard.

clinician pays attention to them, but the quality of the comments depends purely on the level of expertise of the system, not on issues of integration into the clinical workflow. Buchanan's 1986 report of expert systems in routine use noted that three of the first four medical systems in routine use provided clinical interpretation of the results of diagnostic testing [1].

RDR were initially developed to deal with the maintenance problems of one of these first medical expert systems [2]. They were first tested in medicine in the PEIRS system [3]; however, in these studies there was a single domain expert who was intimately involved in the development and use of the system, so there has always been a question whether the technique would be as useful in other hands. There has been a range of other evaluation for different problems types, but this has all been in the research context. The following paper describes results based on commercial use of the Labwizard version of RDR developed by Pacific Knowledge Systems (PKS) (www.pks.com.au). Results are presented from one particular laboratory customer of PKS and the data was collected by automatic logging of all activity on the system. The chemical pathologists responsible for developing the KBs have had no involvement in this analysis and we have therefore masked the identity of the laboratory and the various areas of chemical pathology covered.

2. Methods

RDR was developed to deal with the contextual nature of expert knowledge [4, 5]. In brief, when a domain expert is asked to explain how they reached a specific conclusion, they provide a justification that their conclusion is correct. Implicitly or explicitly they provide a justification that shows that their conclusion is to be preferred to other conclusions that might be considered in the context.

The two key features of RDR to facilitate adding knowledge in context are:

- Firstly, when a conclusion provided by a KBS is incorrect, a refinement rule is linked to the incorrect rule so that the refinement rule is only ever evaluated in the same context, that is, when the parent rule also has fired. The conclusion of the refinement rule is used rather than the conclusion of the parent rule if both fire.
- Secondly, the expert only ever adds a rule to deal with a particular case, so that every rule has an associated case called a cornerstone case. If the expert creates a rule that will fire not only on the case in hand, but on other cornerstone cases, they are asked to add conditions to the rule to distinguish the case from the other cornerstone cases or to accept that the refinement rule should apply to one of more cornerstone cases.

There are many different RDR structures, implementing these key features in different ways e.g [6, 7] and a range of other work linking RDR to machine learning e.g. [8].

An RDR system is built while the system is in use; it starts with an empty KBS and is built gradually over time as cases are processed. The expert monitors the output and gradually adds rules until the conclusions provided reach the standard required. As the system evolves the conclusion given for a case will be either correct, incorrect or missing. If it is incorrect or missing the expert adds rule which gives the correct conclusion for the case. This rule is automatically added to the KB as a refinement of the rule that gave the incorrect conclusion, and is only evaluated in this same context, or is added at the end of the previous rules and is only evaluated after the previous rules have been evaluated. This is the simplest of a range of RDR structures. With this structure only a single cornerstone case, the case associated with the parent rule, needs to be considered.

Labwizard uses a variant of the Multiple-Classification RDR structure (MCRDR) [9]. This structure is based on an n-ary tree allowing many rules to fire on a case and potentially giving many conclusions. With MCRDR many cornerstone cases also may fire on a new rule that is added. This is handled by showing any conflicting cases to the expert one by one, for the expert to refine the rule they are developing, or to allow its conclusion to be applied to the cornerstone cases. In practice only two or three cases out of possibly thousands need to be considered before a sufficiently precise rule is arrived at.

A critical feature of Labwizard is that all data available on a patient can be passed to the KBS including up to three years of past test results and clinical notes. This allows for highly patient specific comments to be made. Another critical feature is Labwizard's integration into the laboratory workflow [10]. The laboratory information system (LIS) sends reports ready for output to the Labwizard server along with all other information and past results available on each patient. The server can handle multiple KB and comments are appended to the report. The report is then validated by a pathologist to see if it should go out to the referring clinician or whether the interpretative comment is incorrect and a new rule should be added.

It is too tedious to keep checking reports where the pathologist knows from experience the system is fully reliable. To deal with this, auto-validation is provided which allows some reports to go straight to the referring clinician. Auto-validation is based on particular combinations of comments that the expert believes can be sent out unchecked, but the expert can also set the system so some percentage of these reports are sent for manual validation as a way of on-going monitoring. The human validator either confirms the comment or changes it and the report is then sent out. Any changed comments are queued for knowledge acquisition. The expert responsible for building rules for a KB reviews the cases where comments have been changed and may or may not decide to add a rule. Labwizard supports a very distributed environment: reports may come from geographically distinct laboratories, may be sent elsewhere for validation, and rules may be built at a yet another location. Although all rules may be added to the one KB, laboratories tend to develop a number of KB for different sub-domains managed by different experts. The Labwizard server supports multiple concurrent KBs.

3. Results

The data all come from one particular commercial chemical pathology provider. The most significant results are shown in Fig 1. Over the 29 month period since Labwizard was introduced more and more KBs were put into use and more and more patient reports were processed by the system. The KBs cover different sub-domains of chemical pathology. A particular KB is activated if the data contains relevant laboratory results, but all data available on the patient is passed to the KB. The same patient data may be passed to various KBs, e.g thyroids and lipids.

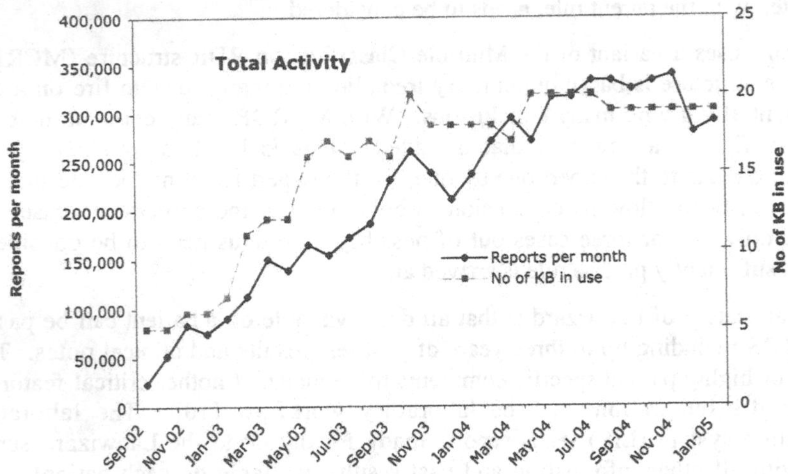

Figure 1. The total number of patient reports processed and issued per month and the number of knowledge bases in use.

The PKS payment model is based on the volume of reports processed. Broadly, the more reports that are processed, the more the laboratory pays PKS. This model was used to facilitate the introduction of a new technology where laboratories were unsure of the value of the technology. Fig 1. shows the ongoing introduction of new KBs despite the increased costs that this produces. This provides very strong evidence that this particular pathology provider considered automated interpretations improved the quality of their clinical reports and their ability to provide a better quality service to referring clinicians. It is beyond the scope of the paper to consider the evidence that referring clinicians find the interpretative comments helpful, but it is clear the laboratory considers that it is achieving increased customer satisfaction.

Figure 2 shows that the rate at which comments on reports are edited before the report is sent out. Comments are edited at the validation stage and the pathologist doing the validation is free to edit the comments on the report in any way they wish. They edit comments in three ways:

- The report does not have any comment, so a clinically useful comment is added.
- The report has a comment that is incorrect and which the pathologist changes before the report goes out.
- The pathologist deletes the comment and may refer the report back to the laboratory.

The last case covers the use of Labwizard for internal laboratory quality assurance. Laboratories have realized that it can be very useful to write rules to pick up anomalous sets of results which should be referred back to the laboratory for further testing or other checking. The logs we have used for the data in this paper count all these changes to reports, but do not distinguish between them. Only the first two indicate an error or inadequacy in the KB and may result in a new rule being added; however, a new rule is not necessarily added when the comment on a report is changed. The validating pathologist may wish to add some further highly patient-specific information, perhaps because of a conversation he or she has had with the referring clinician. This case is then kept for knowledge acquisition, but the expert who adds rules (perhaps the same pathologist) may consider it is inappropriate to add a rule to provide such a patient-specific comment.

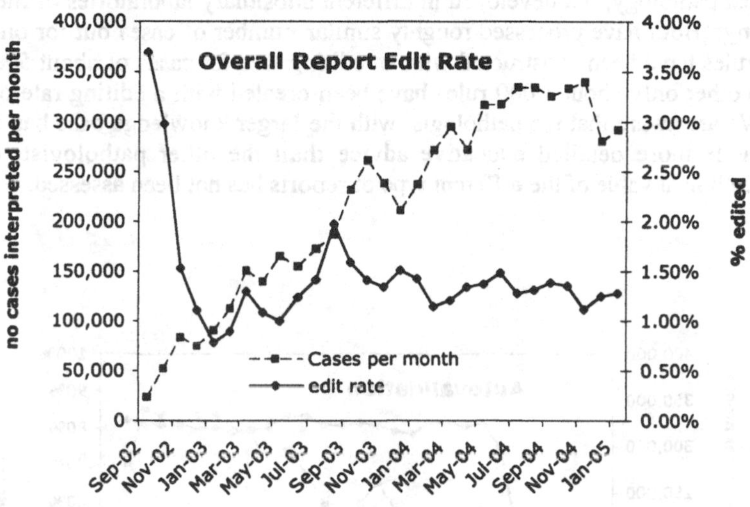

Figure. 2. The number of reports where interpretative comments have been added, changed or deleted.

Figure 2 shows that the fraction of reports edited rapidly drops to less than 1.5% of reports processed. This figure combines the results from all KB in use, regardless of how recently they have been introduced. If we assume 20 working days per month (although there is work done on weekends), about 220 reports per day have comments edited. Averaged across 20 knowledge bases, this is about 11 reports per day. Figure 6 shows the same data for individual KB. It may seem surprising that the initial rate at which reports are edited is low. This may be because the experts initially add comments only for the more critical cases and allow the rest to go out without a comment. However, another important factor is the logs we have used provide only monthly totals and this masks an initially higher editing rate. Figure 6 shows that relatively large numbers of rules tend to be added initially, and past experience with such systems shows a fairly high level of accuracy is rapidly reached. Since the fraction of reports edited drops to less than 1.5% of reports issued, and this includes quality assurance comments, the overall error rate end up less than 1.5%. Another way of looking at accuracy is the number of rules added. The number of rules added is 0.26% of the total number of cases processed or less in the later stages of development. In conclusion is seems reasonable to surmise that this group of KBs has an overall error rate of less than 1.5%. This compares very favourably with other KBS technology, but with the added advantage that RDR allows for further correction of errors at any stage.

Since a KBS is meant to capture the expertise of the relevant domain expert, we consider an accurate / appropriate / correct comment for a report is one that the domain expert pathologist is happy with. It is the pathologist who provides advice to the referring clinician; is he or she happy that the advice provided through Labwizard is appropriate? Clearly the notion of appropriate advice varies. Included in the results below are two KBs (E & E') for the same sub-domain of chemical pathology, but developed in different subsidiary laboratories of the parent company. Both have processed roughly similar number of cases but for one about 9,000 rules have been constructed with an editing rate for cases of about 5%, while for the other only about 1,000 rules have been created with a editing rate of about 1%. We are aware that the pathologist with the larger knowledge base has decided to provide more detailed educative advice than the other pathologist, but the relative clinical value of the different type of reports has not been assessed.

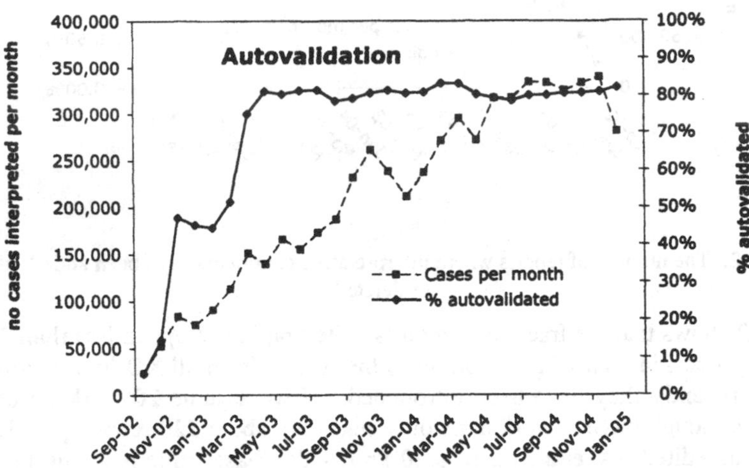

Figure 3. The percentage of interpreted reports that are sent out without being manually checked.

Labwizard's auto-validation facility enables a laboratory to decide which particular interpretations and combinations of interpretations are so reliable that the can be sent out without being validated by a chemical pathologist. The pathologist can choose to send out all interpretations of a particular type, or can choose that a random selection of these should be checked, say 5% or 10%. Reports that are auto-validated tend to be close to 100% auto-validated. Some types of reports are never auto-validated such as comments that refer a report back to the laboratory scientists for quality assurance purposes. Figure 3 shows the overall auto-validation levels for the laboratory. Within 5 months of the introduction of Labwizard, regardless of new KBs being introduced, over 80% of reports were auto-validated. Considering that 20 sub-domains are involved, about 100 reports per sub-domain per day need to be checked.

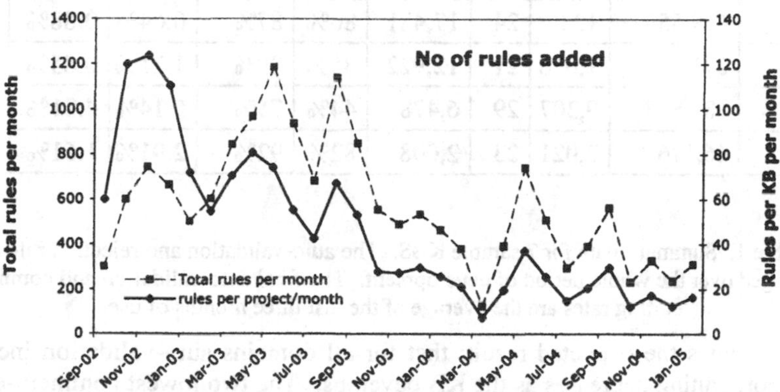

Figure 4. The rate at which rules are added both across the whole laboratory and per KB.

Checking interpreted reports may result in new rules being added when cases are found for which the KB's interpretation is missing or incorrect. Figure 4 shows the rate at which rules are added. It shows the total rules per month as well as the average number of rules per KB per month (note: the average is taken of the individual rule/month data). When all the KB were new over 100 rules were added per KB per month – about 5 per day. The time taken to add a rule is discussed further below, but overall it took 353 hours, about 10 man weeks, to add the rules; i.e an average time of 77 seconds per rule over 16,000 rules. At the peak development time the laboratory was investing about 20 hours per month, about an hour per day, in rule development. Towards the end of the 29 month period this was about 6 hours per month, less than 20 minutes per day.

3.1 Individual KB results

Data on some of the individual KBs are presented to demonstrate the variety that can occur. The domains for these KBs are specified as A,B,C etc as it is beyond the scope of this paper to consider how the differences in the KBs relate to particular sub-domains of chemical pathology; however, we note that E and E' are both for the same sub-domain of chemical pathology but were developed by different experts for different local laboratories within the overall company.

	Total cases interpreted	Total rules added	Months in use	Cases per month	Auto-validation rate	Final auto-validation rate	Comment-editing rate	Final comment-editing rate
A	1,490,767	1,061	29	51,406	92%	97%	0.23%	0.13%
B	1,333,598	1,091	18	74,089	72%	73%	2.20%	1.86%
C	1,205,566	339	28	43,056	86%	97%	0.22%	0.12%
D	419,555	123	24	17,481	86%	87%	0.64%	0.88%
E	271,371	1,036	21	12,922	85%	89%	1.21%	0.85%
E'	187,848	9,307	29	6,478	44%	75%	5.14%	4.81%
F	46,176	2,021	23	2,008	82%	92%	2.91%	1.61%

Table 1. Summary data for 7 sample KBS. The auto-validation and rejection rate are averaged over the whole period of development. The final auto-validation and comment-editing rates are the average of the last three months of use.

Table 1 shows the expected result: that for all domains auto-validation increases and report editing decreases as the KB develops. The two lowest comment-editing rates also have the highest auto-validation rates. Although both have processed over 1 million reports one has 1061 rules, while the other has 339 rules. We assume the very low comment-editing rates and high auto-validation rates are because these KBs are not used significantly for internal quality assurance, which necessarily increases the apparent comment-editing rate. E' is particularly interesting in that the number of rules constructed approximates the number of cases edited, suggesting the very high rejection rate is because this particular expert is seeking to develop very specific comments. Despite the relatively high and continuing comment-editing rate, the expert has been willing to markedly increase the auto-validation rate over the development.

Figure 5 shows the average time taken to add a rule at different stages of development. Data for the graphs was obtained by taking average rule creation time from the logs at approximately 100, 250, 500, 1000 rules etc. We are only able to provide average data as the logs used provided total time adding rules and the number of rules added since the last log download. The time adding a rule is the total amount of time the expert is logged on to the knowledge acquisition module constructing a rule for a case. It includes time for interruptions such as answering the phone, getting coffee etc. However, assuming that the rate at which these interruptions occur does not increase with KB size, the average time taken should provide a reasonable indicator of the relationship between knowledge acquisition and KB size.

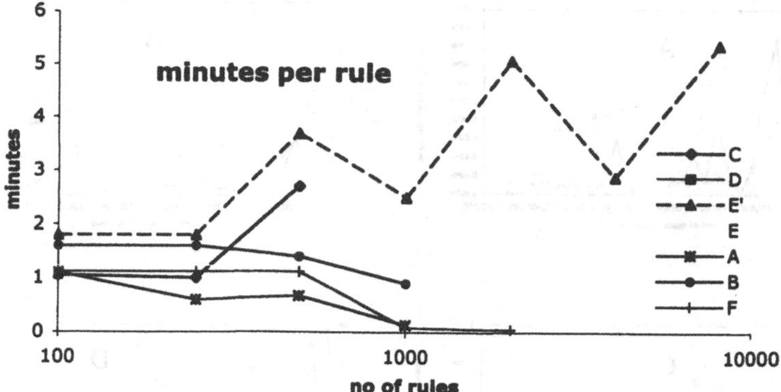

Figure 5. shows the average time taken to add a rule at different KB sizes for some sample KBs

The time taken to add a rule for some KBs decreases as the KB grows, and for two of the KBs is very small. It should be noted that we are measuring only knowledge engineering time, not the time taken in medical decision-making. The pathologist who validates the report considers whether the comment is appropriate and constructs a new comment or finds an appropriate comment to reuse. The expert who adds a rule only has the task of deciding what features distinguish a case for which this interpretation is appropriate from other cornerstone cases. This is the only knowledge engineering task in RDR and is what has been measured in these studies. This is a very rapid point and click task particularly if the same pathologist who validated the report is the expert adding the rule.

E' provides the most interesting data because of its much larger size and the average time to add a rule to E' increases roughly proportional to the log of KB size. There are four possible reasons why the knowledge acquisition time increases as KB size increases:

- The cases being dealt with are increasingly unusual and may take more time to think about.
- The number of cornerstone cases that the expert has to consider, increases.
- The number of cornerstone cases that have to be processed by the system during knowledge acquisition, increases.
- Because the rule building for E' takes place at a remote site from the server, with a relatively poor link, downloading increasing numbers of cornerstone cases may slow the process.

Despite this combination of factors, these results are consistent with informal observations of experts where they generally take a minute or two to add a rule. The major claim of RDR that it is very simple and rapid to add a rule, largely independent of KB size, is supported by this data.

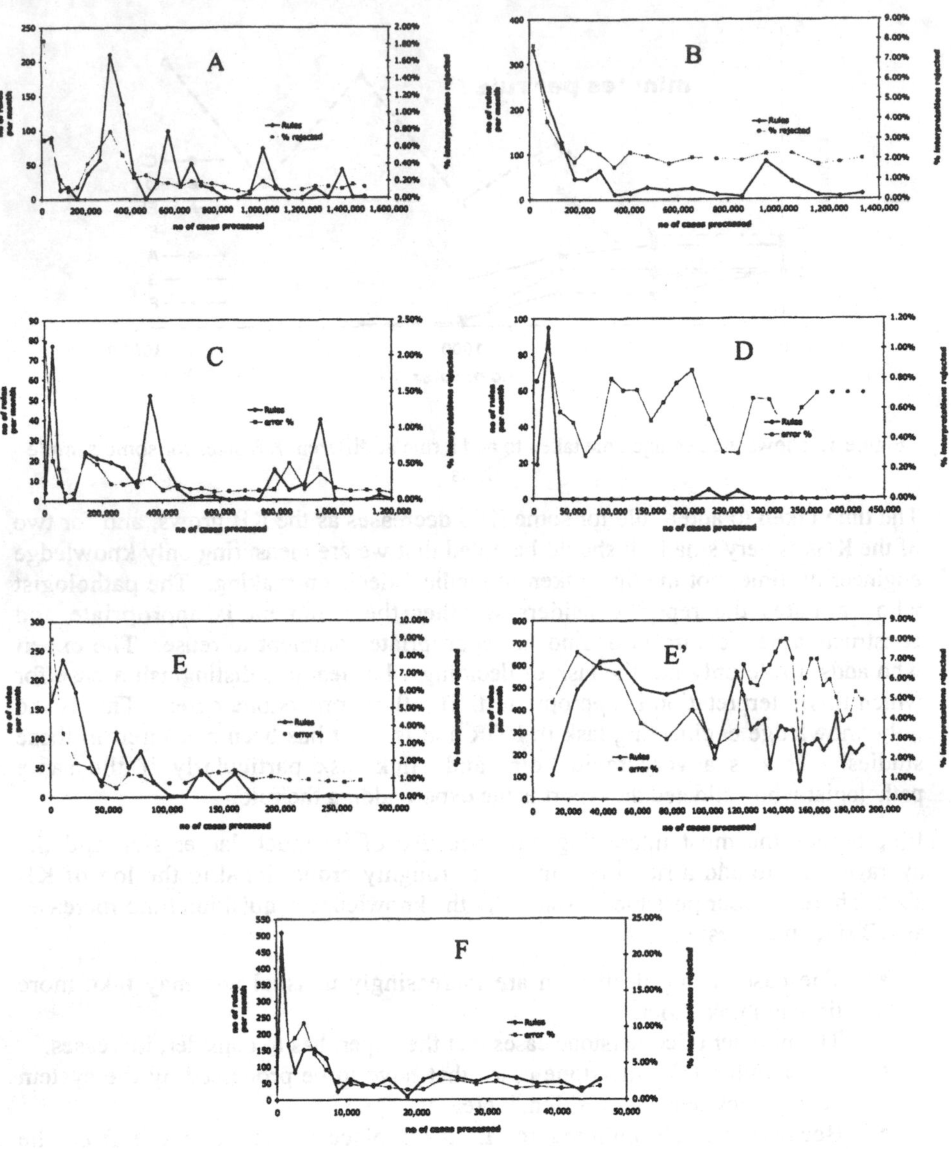

Figure. 6. A selection of knowledge bases, showing the number of rules added per month and the percentage of reports rejected, i.e. where the comments are edited before reports go out, against the number of cases processed.

4. Conclusions

Relatively few medical systems reach routine clinical use, and of those that do, the reasons are often unclear: is it because of the clinical value of the system or because of the particular values and interests of the organization or individuals involved? In the data that is presented here, the pathology provider using Labwizard is a commercial company whose aim is to generate financial returns for shareholders by providing high quality diagnostic laboratory services. Despite an explicit link between the volume of Labwizard usage and costs, the pathology company has chosen to increase its use of Labwizard by adding new knowledge bases throughout a 29 month period. The conclusion from this is that the pathology provider believes that the very specific clinical advice provided through Labwizard is of considerable value in satisfying its clinician customers and thereby increasing market share.

A central claim for RDR has been that new rules can be added throughout the life of the system, very simply and easily. The data presented show that rules are added throughout the life of the KB, and that the time taken to add a rule is only a few minutes regardless of the size of the KB. The maintenance of a KB is carried out by the relevant chemical pathologist and is at their discretion. The ongoing addition of rules suggests that pathologists see a value and little cost in adding further refinements as required. It has also been argued that the incremental approach of RDR also enables the KB to evolve as requirements in the domain evolve.

Although the time to build an individual rule is small, the question remains of whether the RDR structure is efficient or whether perhaps the expert is required to add repeat knowledge, with the same knowledge added in different contexts. We do not have a definitive answer to this except to note that simulation studies show RDR produce KB similar in size to those developed by machine learning [11]; that attempts to compress early Labwizard KBs resulted in only about 10% compression [12], and above all that there is very little complaint from the pathologists concerned about the knowledge acquisition process. We have studies under way comparing the efficiency of a number of KBS structures. The conclusion of all this is that although RDR structures may introduce some repetition, the cost of this is small compared to the ongoing ease of adding rules. By any measure, an overall total of 353 hours to build the KBs described here is a very small investment.

A question that arises from this study is: what is the appropriate level of specificity in interpretative comments? Comments that are too general, or cover too many different cases, rather than the specific situation of the patient will tend to be ignored by the clinician receiving the report. For a comment to provide useful management advice, it must take into account the patient test history, medication, clinical notes and demographics, not just the clinical guidelines for the current tests. That is, it should answer the specific question the clinician is asking with regard to this patient. Secondly the comment needs to be directed to the clinician who requested the diagnostic tests. What sort of information will be helpful to him or her; what are they likely not to know or to miss? Obviously it is superfluous to tell a specialist about their area of specialty so the simple comment "specialist management noted" may be preferred in some cases. The graphs in figure 6 show a very rapid decrease in the comment-editing rate in the early stages of development. Probably a good strategy for the expert is to produce rules for fairly general and common comments early on, or to concentrate on a few clearly defined objectives such as "normals". In this way auto-validation can be set high early in the project's development, reducing the manual validation load on the expert. Over time the expert adds more and more refined and patient specific comments as seems appropriate.

There has been a strong move in medicine towards standardization. In contrast Labwizard is used by laboratories to compete for market share by having higher quality, more helpful, interpretative comments than other laboratories – comments that are aimed specifically at the clinicians likely to use the laboratory and the type of patients they have. The data from E and E' shown here, suggest that there might be quite significant differences between how expert pathologists prefer to advise other clinicians, even in the same sub-domain. Although pathologists can be trained in a few hours to use build rules, it can some time building rules before they appreciate the best level of granularity for rules and comments. Some pathologists will tend initially to use Labwizard as another way to produce very coarse generic comments, while others will develop rules that are so specific they are unlikely to be used again. It is unclear whether the large size of E' compared to E is because of the more educative nature of the comments or because the rules are unnecessarily specific. It will be fascinating to compare KB for the same sub-domains by different experts, with perhaps different purposes, and some initial steps have already been taken in developing techniques to do this [13].

The application described here has been in medicine, but this gradual approach to building a system over time can be applied to any area where it is natural and appropriate to monitor the performance of the system. Help desks are an obvious example. Other examples included financial systems such as loan systems or monitoring for fraud. In fact most industrial and commercial applications of KBS deal with a stream of cases. A system can be built and then tested on the stream of cases, or with the RDR approach the stream of cases can be used to build the system. The rate at which changes need to be made in the RDR system at a particular stage of development corresponds to the error rate on unseen test cases in a more conventional evaluation. The difference is that with the RDR system the errors in the test cases can also be fixed and the system further improved.

Acknowledgements

RDR research has had long-term support from the Australian Research Council and PKS development was assisted by a grant from AusIndustry. The authors thank the referees for their helpful comments.

References

1. Buchanan, B. Expert systems: working systems and the research literature. Expert Systems 1986; 3: 32-51
2. Compton, P., Horn, R., Quinlan, R., and Lazarus, L., Maintaining an expert system. In: Quinlan, J.R. (ed) Applications of Expert Systems, Addison-Wesley, 1989, pp 366-385
3. Edwards, G., Compton, P., Malor, R., Srinivasan, A., and Lazarus, L. PEIRS: a pathologist maintained expert system for the interpretation of chemical pathology reports. Pathology 1993; 25: 27-34
4. Compton, P. and Jansen, R. A philosophical basis for knowledge acquisition. Knowledge Acquisition 1990; 2: 241-257
5. Richards, D. and Compton, P. Taking up the situated cognition challenge with ripple down rules. International Journal of Human Computer Studies 1998; 49: 895-926
6. Beydoun, G. and Hoffmann, A. Theoretical basis for hierarchical incremental knowledge acquisition. International Journal of Human Computer Studies 2001; 54(3): 407-452
7. Cao, T.M. and Compton, P. A simulation framework for knowledge acquisition evaluation. In: V. Estivill-Castro (ed) Twenty-Eighth Australasian Computer Science Conference (ACSC2005), Newcastle, 2005, pp 353-360
8. Yoshida, T., Motoda, H., and Washio, T. Adaptive ripple down rules method based on minimum description length principle. In: Proceedings of the 2002 IEEE International Conference on Data Mining (ICDM 2002), IEEE Computer Society, 2002, pp 530-537
9. Kang, B., Compton, P., and Preston, P. Multiple classification ripple down rules. In: Mizoguchi, R. (ed) Proceedings of the Third Japanese Knowledge Acquisition for Knowledge-Based Systems Workshop (JKAW'94), Japanese Society for Artificial Intelligence, 1994, pp 197-212
10. Compton, P., Edwards, G., Lazarus, L., Peters, L., and Harries, M., Knowledge based system, U.S Patent 6,553,361, 2003.
11. Compton, P., Preston, P., Kang, B., and Yip, T. Local patching produces compact knowledge bases. In: Steels, L. Schreiber, G. and Van de Velde (eds)W. A Future for Knowledge Acquisition: Proceedings of EKAW'94, Springer Verlag, 1994, pp 104-117
12. Suryanto, H., Richards, D., and Compton, P. The automatic compression of multiple classification ripple down rule knowledge base systems: preliminary experiments. In: Jain, L. (ed) Proceedings of the Third International Conference on Knowledge-Based Intelligent Information Engineering Systems. (IEEE Cat. No. 99TH8410), 1999, pp 203-206
13. Suryanto, H. and Compton, P. Discovery of ontologies from knowledge bases. In: Gil, Y. Musen, M. and Shavlik, J. (eds) Proceedings of the First International Conference on Knowledge Capture, ACM, New York, 2001, pp 171-178

Applying Bayesian Networks for Meteorological Data Mining

Estevam R. Hruschka Jr, DC-UFSCar/ Federal University of Sao Carlos, Brazil

Eduardo R. Hruschka, Catholic University of Santos (UniSantos), Brazil

Nelson F. F. Ebecken, COPPE/ Federal University of Rio de Janeiro

Abstract

Bayesian Networks (BNs) have been recently employed to solve meteorology problems. In this paper, the application of BNs for mining a real-world weather dataset is described. The employed dataset discriminates between "wet fog" instances and "other weather conditions" instances, and it contains many missing data. Therefore, BNs were employed not only for classifying instances, but also for filling missing data. In addition, the Markov Blanket concept was employed to select relevant attributes. The efficacy of BNs to perform the aforementioned tasks was assessed by means of several experiments. In summary, more convincing results were obtained by taking advantage of the fact that BNs can directly (i.e. without data preparation) classify instances containing missing values. In addition, the attributes selected by means of the Markov Blanket provide a simpler, faster, and equally accurate classifier.

1 Introduction

The availability of climate observational records and the increasing computational processing power have motivated the application of several statistical and data mining techniques (e.g. linear regression, principal component analysis, canonical correlation analysis, neural networks, clustering methods, etc.) in meteorology [1-3]. Following this trend, recently Bayesian Networks (BNs) have been successfully employed in meteorology [2], mainly because they offer a sound and practical methodology for discovering probabilistic knowledge in databases as well as for building intuitive and tractable probabilistic models, which can be used to solve a wide variety of problems. In addition, Bayesian Networks (BNs) can directly (i.e. without data preparation) process instances containing missing values [4]. Finally, BNs can also be employed for data preparation, particularly for filling missing data [2, 5] and for attribute selection [6,7].

Under this perspective, this paper describes a case study of the application of BNs for mining weather data, which are generally voluminous and can be mined for occurrence of particular patterns that distinguish specific weather phenomena [1].

More specifically, we employ a weather dataset collected at the International Airport of Rio de Janeiro and that discriminates "wet fog" instances from "other weather conditions" instances. The processes of fog formation and dissipation are controlled by a complex combination of meteorological processes operating on many different scales. No single process dominates.

Fog continues to be an important forecast challenge for aviation. Airlines specializing in express package delivery are especially vulnerable to the impacts of fog due to the high number of arrivals scheduled close to sunrise, when fog frequency peaks. While nearly all forecasters are familiar with the fundamental forecasting concepts, skill scores for predicting fog continue to lag those of most other terminal forecast variables.

Accurate short-term forecast of fog and low clouds is of the utmost importance to air traffic operation. The understanding of the conditions in which wet fog occurs is relevant for airport operation and it can be considered as the main goal of a data mining task in this dataset. However, real-world data are usually of low quality, mainly when they were not collected specially for data mining purposes. Also, they may contain measurement errors, missing values, redundant attributes, and so on. In this context, data preparation techniques may lessen the influence of low quality data, consequently increasing the probabilities of successful applications of data mining algorithms, which usually assume that datasets to be processed are error free. In this work we evaluate BNs both as classifiers and as data preparation tools (to impute missing values and to select relevant attributes).

The remainder of the paper is organized as follows. Section 2 briefly describes the algorithm employed to learn BNs from datasets. Section 3 addresses the employed methods for data preparation, whereas Section 4 reports our experimental results. Finally, in Section 5 we summarize our contributions and point out some future work.

2 Bayesian Networks

Bayesian Networks (BNs) are graphical representations of multivariate joint probability distributions. They are represented by directed acyclic graphs in which the nodes represent the variables and the arcs represent probabilistic dependencies among connected variables. The strength of each dependency is given by the conditional probability P(Xi|∏Xi) (Xi being the *i*-th variable, and ∏Xi the set of parents of Xi in the graph). The variables that are not connected by an arc can be considered as having no direct influence among them. The use of conditional independence is the key to the ability of Bayesian Networks (BNs) to provide a general-purpose compact representation for complex probability distributions [8,9].

A classic example of a Bayesian Network (BN) is the metastatic cancer problem [10] shown in figure 1. The nodes represent the variables (Cancer, Brain Tumor, Increased Total Serum Calcium, COMA and Severe Headaches) and the links show the probabilistic dependencies among them.

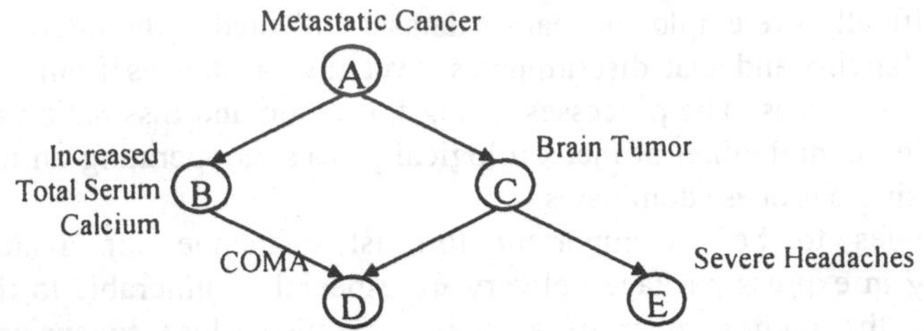

Figure 1. Bayesian network representing the Metastatic Cancer problem (taken from [10])

When a human expert is available, BNs can be built directly from domain knowledge (without data), and subsequently, the achieved BNs can be used for probabilistic inference. On the other hand, when a human expert is not accessible, BNs can be learned from data.

Learning BNs from data became an effervescent research topic in the last decade [11], and there are two main classes of methods to perform this task: methods based on heuristic search and methods based on the conditional independence (CI). References to both classes of algorithms can be found in [12].

In a process of learning BNs from data, the BN variables represent the dataset attributes (or features). When using algorithms based on heuristic search, the initial order of the dataset attributes is considered an important issue. Some of these algorithms depend on this ordering to determine the arcs direction such that an earlier attribute (in an ordered list) is a possible parent only of the later ones. On the other hand, the conditional independence (CI) methods try to find the arcs direction without the need of ordering the attributes. However, even for the CI methods, when a suitable ordering is known the algorithms can be improved [13].

The BN learning algorithm applied in our experiments is based on the K2 algorithm [14], which constructs a BN from data and uses a heuristic search for doing so. It assumes that: (i) the attributes are discrete; (ii) all the possible instances (cases) are present in the dataset; (iii) the dataset has only independent cases; and (iv) all attributes must be preordered. Considering these assumptions, the algorithm searches for a BN structure that represents the dataset.

The attributes pre-order assumption is an important aspect of K2. It uses an ordered list (containing all the attributes including the class), which asserts that only the attributes positioned before a given attribute A may be parent of A in the graph structure. Hence, the first attribute in the list has no parent (it is a root node in the BN). To keep the class attribute as a root node, in this work it is always put as the first one in the ordered list. Thus, the class attribute is a candidate parent of all other attributes.

The network construction uses a greedy method to search for the best structure. It begins as if every node had no parent. Then, beginning with the second attribute (the first one is the class) from the ordered list, the possible parents are tested and the ones that maximize the whole probability structure are added to the network. This process is repeated for every attribute, thus the best structure can be achieved.

With the best structure previously defined, the network conditional probabilities must be determined. It is done using a Bayesian estimation of the (predefined) network structure probability.

In our work, the implementation of K2 has two additional assumptions. The first is that the a priori knowledge about the class attribute is given as a uniform distribution and not according to the number of instances of each class in the dataset. It is done trying to minimize the effects of unbalanced datasets, therefore the a priori belief in each possible state of the class attribute has the same value. The second new assumption is that all the zero-values in the conditional probability distribution table are substituted by 0.00001. Accordingly, the instances that are not present in the dataset are not considered as impossible cases, because their probabilities are different from zero. It does not influence the knowledge represented by the network, and eliminates the non-permitted cases in the classification/prediction task. Other methods to deal with the a priori knowledge and the zero-values in conditional probability distribution can be found in [15,16].

The use of K2 for learning BNs from data is often motivated by its ability to find the network structure efficiently [2,17] given that a reasonable variable ordering is provided. As stated in [18], the Chi-square (χ^2) statistical test allows finding conditional independence relationships among attributes. Such relationships can be used as constraints to construct a BN. Thus, trying to get the most out of the K2 algorithm results, besides the two new assumptions, in this work we use an attribute ordering optimization method based on the chi-square (χ^2) statistic test. It consists in generating the pre-ordered attribute list using the χ^2 measure among the class and all the other attributes. Thus, the χ^2 statistic test is used to rank the attributes before the K2 application. Therefore, such a BN learning method is called K2χ^2, in which the attributes are decreasingly ordered according to the χ^2 scores. The first attribute in the ordered list has the highest χ^2 score, i.e. it is the most dependent upon the class attribute. All the BN learning tasks described in this paper use K2χ^2 algorithm [7].

BNs can be built on any combination of quantitative (continuous) and qualitative (discrete) variables. When a dataset contains quantitative information, two approaches are possible for BN learning: discretization of the quantitative attributes, or probability density estimation of them.

The main difficulty of using probability density estimation is to define the correct form of the original probability density of each quantitative attribute in the dataset. It was shown in [19] that the ACCRs (Average Correct Classification Rates) of a Bayesian classifier tend to fall down when the assumed density is not a proper estimate of the true one.

This work is restricted to networks containing only discrete variables with finite domains. It is done to follow the first assumption given by the K2 definition. Thus, whenever a continuous attribute is found, a discretization approach is applied.

In spite of avoiding the difficulties described above, discretizing numerical attributes into a small number of ranges may not guarantee that the Bayesian classifier will perform with the best accuracy. As discretizing an attribute means to substitute the original (quantitative) data with new (qualitative) ones [19], the discretization process may produce information loss. Thus, it is important to use an adequate process to represent the quantitative data in a qualitative style. In this work, we apply the PKI-Discretization [20], whose implementation is available in the Weka System [21], that has shown to be useful for Bayesian classifiers.

Considering data mining tasks, one of the most powerful qualities of a Bayesian Network (BN) is its ability to deal with missing values [4]. However, it is important to mention that the BN ability to deal with missing values is not present in the learning process. In other words, traditional BN learning algorithms (K2, for example) are not designed to learn from data containing missing values. To do so, missing values must be imputed, or sampling methods such as EM [22] or Gibbs [23,24] must be applied.
In this work, we first use BNs to classify instances from the target dataset without any data preparation (i.e. attribute selection and/or missing values treatment). Subsequently, we use BNs to select the most relevant attributes and impute suitable values to substitute the missing ones. The next section describes how BNs can be employed for data preparation.

3 Data Preparation using Bayesian Networks

Data mining is a process focused on the automated discovery of new facts and relationships in data, and it consists of three basic steps: data preparation, information discovery, and analysis of the mining algorithm output [25]. The data preparation step involves techniques such as data cleaning, integration, transformation, reduction, discretization and generation of concepts hierarchies [26]. As previously mentioned, in this work BNs are employed for both information discovery (to classify instances – as described in Section 2) and data preparation (to select relevant attributes and to impute missing values).

3.1 Attribute Selection

Reunanen [27] observes that there can be many reasons for selecting only a subset of the attributes: (i) it is cheaper to measure only a subset of attributes; (ii) prediction accuracy might be improved through exclusion of irrelevant attributes; (iii) the predictor to be built is usually simpler and potentially faster when less input attributes are used; (iv) knowing the relevant attributes can give insight into the nature of the prediction problem at hand.
There are two fundamentally different approaches for attribute selection [28]: wrapper and filter. The first evaluates the subset of selected attributes using the data mining algorithm that will ultimately be employed for information discovery, i.e. the data mining method is wrapped into the selection procedure. The second approach involves performing attribute assessments based on general characteristics of the data, i.e. the attribute subset is filtered without considering the data mining algorithm to be used.
Wrapper methods are often criticized because they require massive amounts of computation [29]. In real-world applications, in which large datasets are mined, the use of wrapper methods is usually unfeasible. In these cases, it is interesting to employ filter methods, which are usually more efficient than wrappers. We refer the reader interested in traditional filter methods to [1,28,29] and references therein.
The concept of Markov Blanket can be used to simplify an induced BN in relation to the number of employed attributes. Let us assume a BN in which Λ_A is the set of

children of node A and Π_A is the set of parents of A. The subset of nodes containing Π_A, Λ_A and the parents of Λ_A is called Markov Blanket of A (see Figure 2). As shown in [8], the network nodes that have influence on the conditional distribution of A (given the state of all remaining nodes) are only those that form the Markov Blanket of A. Thus, after defining the BN structure that models a dataset, the Markov Blanket of the class variable can be used as an attribute subset selection criterion. This subset of attributes that form the Markov Blanket can be used by other classifiers. In this sense, the Markov Blanket concept can be employed as a heuristic filter approach for other classifiers [7]. In this work, we employ the Markov Blanket to select relevant attributes for classifying instances describing meteorological conditions. The main steps to select the subset of attributes is:

1) Learn a BN from data using $K2\chi^2$;
2) Define the Markov Blanket of the Class attribute;
3) Remove the attributes outside the Markov Blanket.

Further details about this method can be found in [7]. In summary, the task of data preparation performed in this work considers two successive steps: (i) attribute selection and (ii) missing values imputation, which is addressed in the next section.

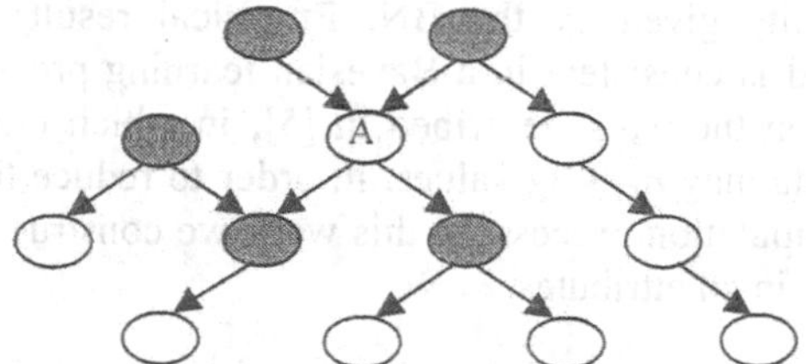

Figure 2. The shadowed nodes represent the Markov Blanket of A.

3.2 Missing Values Imputation

In real-life databases, some observations of one or more attributes are typically missing. These missing values are a critical problem for data mining methods, which are usually not able to cope with them in an automatic fashion, i.e., without data preparation. In general, there are many approaches to deal with the problem of missing values [26]: i) Ignore the instances containing missing values; ii) Fill the gaps manually; iii) Substitute the missing values by a constant; iv) Use the mean or the mode of the instances as a substitution value; and v) Get the most probable value to fill the missing ones. The first approach involves removing the instances and/or attributes with missing values. However, the waste of data may be considerable and incomplete datasets may lead to biased statistical analyses. The second approach is usually unfeasible in data mining tasks, because of the huge dimensionality of employed datasets. The third approach assumes that all missing values represent the same value, probably leading to considerable distortions. The substitution by the mean/mode value is a common practice and sometimes can even lead to reasonable results. However, it does not take into consideration the between-attribute relationships, which are useful to the process of missing values substitution.

Therefore, in general the best approach involves trying to fill the missing values with the most probable ones.
The substitution of missing values, also called missing values imputation [30], should not change important characteristics of the dataset. In this sense, it is necessary to define the important characteristics to be maintained. Data mining methods usually explore relationships between attributes and, thus, it is critical to preserve them, as far as possible, when replacing missing values.
The substitution process employed in our work starts with the selection (from the original sample) of all sample instances that do not have missing data. These instances form a clean sample, which is used as a clean training dataset to the BN construction. Afterwards, the K2χ^2 algorithm is applied to construct a BN, which is used to substitute the missing values. The substitution process can be summarized as follows:

1. Generate a clean training dataset from the original data;
2. Construct a BN from the clean training dataset;
3. Infer the best values to substitute the missing ones.

The values used to fill in the gaps in the datasets are the ones that have the highest posterior probability given by the BN. Empirical results have shown that this imputation method is consistent in a Bayesian learning process [5]. Our imputation method is based on the work described in [5], in which one BN is constructed to each attribute containing missing values. In order to reduce the computational effort involved in the imputation process, in this work we construct a single BN to impute the missing values in all attributes.

4 Experimental Results

The employed dataset was collected at the International Airport of Rio de Janeiro and it is formed by 87,075 instances, of which only 1,452 do not contain missing values. Each instance is described by 27 attributes (e.g. pressure, temperature, humidity, precipitation, etc.) and the associated class label (i.e. either wet fog or another weather condition).
The efficacy of BNs was evaluated in two kinds of datasets: original and prepared (i.e. after missing values imputation and/or attribute selection). Thus, before reporting our experimental results, let us define some terms and their corresponding acronyms. In general, a dataset D is formed by instances with and without missing values. We call C (complete) the subset of instances of D that do not have missing values, and M (missing) the subset of instances of D with at least one missing value. After imputing the missing values in M, a filled dataset F, which contains only instances with imputed values, can be obtained. We call D' the dataset that contains the original complete values and the filled ones, i.e. D'={C+F}. Table 1 summarizes the quantity of instances in each of these datasets. The BN efficacy to classify weather data was estimated by the Average Correct Classification Rate (ACCR), also known as success rate [21], considering ten-fold cross validation procedures. A summary of the achieved results is reported in Table 2. The attribute selection performed by means of the Markov Blanket changes the data distribution (last row of

Table 1), because in this case only the selected attributes are considered to separate complete instances from those with missing values. Further details about the data distribution in each employed dataset are provided in the experimental analyses performed in the sequel.

Table 1. Quantity of instances in the employed datasets.

Dataset	Other weather conditions	Wet fog	Total
D and D'	68,173	18,902	87,075
C	899	553	1,452
M and F (all attributes)	67,274	18,349	85,623
M and F (selected attributes)	56,640	15,323	71,963

Initially, the efficacy of BNs was assessed in the raw data, i.e. in the original dataset D. In this case, a BN was induced from C and used as a classifier in D, according to the procedure described in Section 2. Since meteorological data usually describe complex phenomena, the obtained results reported in Table 2 are promising. It is also interesting to observe that the attributes selected by means of the Markov Blanket (horizontal visibility, relative humidity and pressure variation), which correspond to 11% of the total number of attributes, provide a simpler, faster, and equally accurate classifier.

The total ACCR in the complete instances (C), considering all attributes, was similar to the one achieved in D. However, the employed dataset is unbalanced, i.e. the class "wet fog" has significantly less instances than the other one. Thus, in order to avoid biased analyses, the proportions of instances of each class must be somewhat considered to evaluate the experimental results. A simple way of performing fair analyses involves reporting the ACCRs for each class. In this sense, the ACCR in the wet fog instances of C (81.60%) is significantly better than the corresponding ACCR in D (68.68%). We believe that this difference is mainly due to the fact that the proportion of "wet fog" instances in C is higher than in D. Similarly, the ACCR in the "other weather conditions" instances is correspondingly affected. The attributes selected by means of the Markov Blanket in C and D have provided consistent results.

The total ACCRs obtained in D' were similar to those achieved in both C and D. Since the proportions of instances of each class in M are similar to those observed in D, similar ACCRs in D and D' could be expected. However, the complete dataset (C), which contains only 1.67% of D, was used to impute the missing values in the remaining instances, which represent 98.33% of D'. Depending on the proportion of missing values, substitution methods may have problems to infer suitable values to be imputed. From a general standpoint, there is a relationship between the quality of imputations and the availability of instances in C. The more instances in C, the better the imputations tend to be, because there is more information available. Thus, high proportions of missing values tend to degrade the results of imputation methods. In this sense, we believe that considerable distortions were inserted by the imputation process and this aspect will be studied in a future work.

All the described experiments were run on an ordinary desktop PC with a 3.0GHz Pentium IV processor and 1GB of memory. We measured the computational performance in our experiments and, to get a rather detailed picture of how the total time requirement is composed, separate measurements were carried out. Table 3 summarizes the CPU time.

Table 2. Average Correct Classification Rates (ACCRs).

Dataset	Other weather conditions	Wet Fog	Total
D	85.26 %	68.68 %	81.66 %
D (Markov Blanket)	84.92 %	68.67 %	81.39 %
C	81.03 %	81.60 %	81.19 %
C (Markov Blanket)	81.75 %	81.15 %	81.52 %
D'	97.88 %	16.51 %	80.23 %
D' (Markov Blanket)	94.91 %	42.63 %	83.55 %

Table 3. CPU time.

Implemented Simulations	Times in seconds
Learn BN using D'	49.13
Learn BN using D' (Markov Blanket)	0.48
Learn BN using C	2.75
Learn BN using C (Markov Blanket)	0.03
Substitution of missing values using M	550.10
Substitution of missing values using M (Markov Blanket)	19.45

The two last lines in table 3 show that the substitution process takes more time than the learning task. It is important to notice that the time for substituting missing values reported in table 3 does not include the generation of the clean BN. It only considers the time to infer (using the clean BN and the propagation algorithm described in [31]) a suitable value to fulfil each gap in the M dataset, plus the time to generate the F dataset. Another interesting aspect revealed by table 3 is that, the use of Markov Blanket feature selection method brought a significant computational time reduction to both learning and imputation tasks.
In summary, more convincing results were obtained in D, taking advantage of the fact that BNs can directly (i.e. without data preparation) process datasets containing missing values. The attributes selected by means of the Markov Blanket have also provided interesting results.

5 Conclusions and Future Work

This paper described a case study of the application of Bayesian Networks (BNs) for mining meteorological data, which were collected at the International Airport of Rio de Janeiro and that discriminates "wet fog" instances from "other weather conditions" instances. BNs were employed not only to classify instances, but also to impute missing values and select the most relevant attributes. The Markov Blanket was employed to select relevant attributes. In this context, the efficacy of BNs was assessed by means of several experiments. The attributes selected by the Markov Blanket have provided promising results. Due to the high proportion of missing values, more convincing results were obtained by taking advantage of the fact that BNs can directly (i.e. without data preparation) process datasets containing missing values. Indeed, high proportions of missing values tend to degrade the results of imputation methods. Thus, we believe that considerable distortions were inserted by the imputation process and this aspect will be investigated in a future work. Finally, the obtained results will be presented to domain experts in order to precisely assess their usefulness for the airport operation.

Acknowledgments

The authors thank CNPq, FAPESP and FAPERJ for their financial support.

References

1. Basak, J., Sudarshan, A., Trivedi, D., Santhanam, M.S., Weather Data Mining Using Independent Component Analysis, Journal of Machine Learning Research, n.5, pp. 239-253, 2004.
2. Cano, R., Sordo, C., Gutiérrez, J.M., Applications of Bayesian Networks in Meteorology, Advances in Bayesian Networks, Gámez, J.A. et al. eds., pp. 309-327, Springer, 2004.
3. Cofiño, A.S., Gutiérrez, J.M., Jakubiak, B., Melonek, M., Implementation of data mining techniques for meteorological applications. In: Realizing Teracomputing, Zwieflhofer, W. & N. Kreitz eds., pp. 256-271, World Scientific Publishing, 2003.
4. Heckerman, D. "Bayesian networks for data mining," Data Mining and Knowledge Discovery, vol. 1, pp. 79-119, 1997.
5. Hruschka JR., E. R., Hruschka, E. R., Ebecken, N. F. F. A Data Preparation Bayesian Approach for a Clustering Genetic Algorithm. In: Frontiers in Artificial Intelligence and Applications, Soft Computing Systems: Design, Management and Applications, IOS Press, v.87, pp. 453-461, 2002.
6. Blum, A.L., Langley, P., Selection of Relevant Features and Examples in Machine Learning, Artificial Intelligence, pp. 245-271, 1997.
7. Hruschka JR., E. R., Hruschka, E. R., Ebecken, N. F. F. Feature Selection by Bayesian Networks In: The Seventeenth Canadian Conference on Artificial Intelligence, 2004, London, Ontario. Lecture Notes in Artificial Intelligence. Berlin: Springer-Verlag, v. 3060, pp. 370–379, 2004.
8. Pearl, J., Probabilistic Reasoning in Intelligent Systems: Networks of Plausible Inference, Morgan Kaufmann, San Mateo, CA, 1988.
9. Friedman, N. and Koller, D., Being Bayesian about network structure. A Bayesian approach to structure discovery in Bayesian networks, Machine Leraning 50 (1-2): 95-125, 2003.
10. Cooper, Gregory F. NESTOR: A computer-based medical diagnostic aid that integrates causal and probabilistic knowledge, PhD. thesis, Rep. No. STAN-CS-84-48 (also HPP-84-48), Dept. of Computer Science, Stanford Univ., CA, 1984.
11. Chickering, D. M., Optimal Structure Identification with Greedy Search, Journal of Machine Learning Research, (3):507-554, 2002.

12. Spirtes, P., Glymour, C. and Scheines, R., Causation, Prediction, and Search, (Adaptive Computation and Machine Learning), 2nd edition, Bradford Books, 2001.
13. Cheng, J., Greiner, R., Kelly, J., Bell, D., Liu, W.R., Learning Bayesian networks from data: An information-theory based approach. Artificial Intelligence, 137 (1-2): 43-90, 2002.
14. Cooper G. & Herskovitz, E.. A Bayesian Method for the Induction of Probabilistic Networks from Data. Machine Learning, 9, 309-347, 1992.
15. Langley, P. & Sage, S., Induction of Selective Bayesian Classifiers. Proceedings of the Tenth Conference on Uncertainty in Artificial Intelligence, Seattle, 1994.
16. Anderson, J. R. & Matessa, M., Explorations of an Incremental Bayesian Algorithm for categorization. Machine Learning, 9, 275-308, 1992.
17. Hsu, W. H., Genetic Wrappers for feature selection in decision tree induction and variable ordering in Bayesian network structure learning, Information Science, 163, pp. 103-122, 2004.
18. Cheng, J. and Greiner, R., Comparing Bayesian Network Classifiers, Proc. of the Fifteenth Conference on Uncertainty in Artificial Intelligence (UAI '99), Sweden, pp. 101-108, 1999.
19. Ying, Y. and Webb, G., On Why Discretization Works for Naive-Bayes Classifiers. In Proceedings of the 16th Australian Conference on AI (AI 03), Lecture Notes AI 2903, 440-452. Berlin: Springer, 2003.
20. Ying, Y., Discretization for Naive-Bayes Learning. PhD. Thesis, Monash University, 2003b. http://www.cs.uvm.edu/~yyang/Yingthesis.pdf
21. Witten, I. H., Frank, E., Data Mining – Practical Machine Learning Tools and Techniques with Java Implementations, Morgan Kaufmann Publishers, USA, 2000.
22. Dempster, A. P., Laird, N. M., Rubin, D. B., Maximum Likelihood from Incomplete Data via the EM algorithm, Journal of the Royal Statistical Society B, 39, 1-39, 1977.
23. Gelfand, A.,E. and Smith, A. F. M., Sampling-based approaches to calculating marginal densities. J. American Statistical Association, 85:398--409, 1990.
24. Casella, G. and George, E. I., "Explaining the Gibbs sampler," Amer. Statist., vol. 46, pp. 167-174, 1992.
25. Bigus, J. P., Data Mining with Neural Networks , First edition, USA, McGraw-Hill,1996.
26. Han, J. and Kamber, M., Data Mining, Concepts and Techniques. Morgan Kaufmann, 2001.
27. Reunanen, J., Overfitting in Making Comparissons Between Variable Selection Methods, Journal of Machine Learning Research 3, pp. 1371-1382, 2003.
28. Liu, H. and Motoda, H., Feature Selection for Knowledge Discovery and Data Mining. Kluwer Academic, 1998.
29. Guyon, I., Elisseeff, A., An Introduction to Variable and Feature Selection, Journal of Machine Learning Research 3, pp. 1157-1182, 2003.
30. Little, R., & Rubin, D. B., Statistical Analysis with Missing Data. Wiley, New York, 1987.

31. Lauritzen, S. L., & Spiegelhalter, D. J., Local computations with probabilities on graphical structures and their application to expert systems. J. Royal Statistical Society B, 50, 157–224, 1988.

SESSION 4:

INDUSTRIAL APPLICATIONS

WISE Expert: An Expert System for Monitoring Ship Cargo Handling

T. R. Addis
University of Portsmouth
Tom.Addis@port.ac.uk
www.tech.port.ac.uk/staff/addist/intel.htm
J. J. Townsend Addis
Clarity Support Ltd
Jan.Addis@clarity-support.com
www.clarity-support.com
R. Gillett
L3 MPRI Ship Analytics
pchemx@interalpha.co.uk
http://www.shipanalytics.com/MS/wise_index.asp

Abstract

WISE Expert is a general-purpose system that can be used for monitoring or controlling, in real time, complex systems that have recurring sub-structures. The system has been developed using a unique schematic development tool that ensures coherency of structure during design and construction. The design of the Expert System takes advantage of a distinction between the monitored system structure and expert knowledge so that the structure description can be used to generate specific rules for the system automatically. The system has been tested as an overseer during the running of trainee mariner exercises with a liquid cargo simulator and is now operational at over 35 customer sites throughout the world.

1 Introduction

WISE Expert is an expert system that was initially designed specifically to monitor a simulation of liquid cargo vessels.

As part of the process of training ships officers simulators are used to provide some of the training in a real world environment. With respect to the handling of bulk liquid cargoes such as chemicals, liquefied gases and oil a Liquid Cargo Handling Simulator (Lchs) is used. Such a simulator provides a representation of all the cargo storage tanks and associated pipeline systems, valves, control systems and equipment that are required to load/unload the cargo and maintain it in an appropriate condition during the voyage. The models simulate all the thermo and fluid dynamics of the various mixtures of liquids and gases within the systems and hence together allow students to undertake all the tasks associated with preparing the vessel and handling the appropriate cargoes. Traditionally simulators of this type were shore based, located in specific training institutions. This was because of the need for both the hardware and skilled instructors (or overseers). They were required to provide the training and monitor the student's activities during the simulation exercise to ensure that the student did not learn bad techniques, pursue bad practices or enter into dangerous situations during cargo management exercises. With the introduction of PC technology, the hardware became less of an issue but the need for a skilled instructor remained. In 1997 it was becoming apparent that with the reduction in crew numbers the shipping companies were experiencing increasing logistical difficulties in being able to release sufficient personnel to attend shore based courses. Consequently, to ensure the training in this field could be delivered at the required level it was decided to investigate a way in which the need for the skilled instructor could be replaced by a computer based system. This allows the simulator to be used safely by a student for self-study without an instructor being available, such as in an onboard environment [1].

The Lchs cannot only be used to simulate different vessel types but also different variations of the same type, such as oil tankers of varying capacities. In the latter case the basic structure of the vessel and the principles of operation remain the same but the actual configuration of pumps, tanks and other structural elements will change. Consequently, it was important in designing WISE Expert to ensure that the knowledge base produced for one vessel could be easily adapted for use on another vessel of the same type but of a different configuration. This would then allow new models to be produced quickly and easily.

It was proposed in 1998 that an expert system could be created that would take the place of the marine tutor in monitoring students' actions and warning students of potential or real hazards during exercises.

If such a system could be created then this would lead to a range of other uses such as improved classroom response and the monitoring of real ships at sea. Improved classroom response could be achieved if student monitoring could also be networked. Then major warnings could be fed back to a central overseeing station. This would then release the tutor to concentrate on difficult problems and thus improve the student-learning environment. The monitoring of real ships at sea, if logged, would also provide feedback into the expert system from actual events. This would produce a continually improved product, providing a richer resource for training and extending the capability of a shipboard monitor.

Investigations of a sample of expert system products showed no commercial off-the-shelf systems that can cope with this requirement [2]. The problems with these standard expert systems were:

- Expensive – commercial licensing
- Self contained – links to the simulator would be difficult
- Networking – not available.
- Knowledge only in rule form – ship structures for example would have to be defined as rules (see section 2)
- No assurance that there is coherence of the knowledge base

- ➢ Presumptions of use – we are not requiring a 'solution' to be discovered. We have no goal other than monitoring for problems (although control goals are also a potential option).
- ➢ Limited extendibility – decisions based on calculations are restricted
- ➢ Slow – all rules work through a general inference engine
- ➢ Depth first assumption – only crude heuristic control over rule access order is possible.
- ➢ There seemed no way to take advantage of the repetitiveness of ship storage systems for automatic rule generation thus saving the expert effort.

It was decided to create a special expert system from first principles that would address the unique problem of overseeing the simulator. It had to have the following properties:

- ✓ Inexpensive – no license fee and minimum development time
- ✓ Easy links to other programs and threads
- ✓ Networked communication between different simulations
- ✓ Communication hub for an overseeing instructor
- ✓ Pattern sensitive monitoring rather than goal seeking.
- ✓ Extendable – so that any kind of procedure can be done within a decision rule
- ✓ Flexible – be able to change easily for different ships, addition of new rules to be applicable to all ships. For example, the automatic generation of rules from structural information
- ✓ Continuous development of the rule base to be rendered in house
- ✓ Knowledge base to be limited to only explicitly specified dependencies
- ✓ Fast – a complete scan of all possibilities should take no more than 10 seconds
- ✓ Control over rule access to be under precise control

Further, given the right development tool it is not too difficult to create a bespoke expert system [2]. We can then have complete control over our design by avoiding the constraints of someone else's paradigm. The first operational system was designed and constructed in about four man-months.

2 Rules for all Occasions – The Standard Approach

One of the obvious characteristics of a liquid cargo ship is that it consists of a collection of tanks. Each tank represents a single system that has valves and gauges indicating its state. There will be rules associated with each tank such as:

Rule#	Monitoring Rules	Message/Meaning/Action
1	**If** Cargo tank pressure < 0 **&** Cargo tank P/R valve open	Cargo tank **Object (Rule#1)** in vacuum. Relief valve open
2	**If** Cargo tank pressure >= 1400 **&** Cargo tank P/R valve open	Very high pressure in cargo tank **Object (Rule#2)**

If this were to be done by a typical expert system then associated with these rules would be another set of rules that define the structure of the ship. Here rules include facts and clauses [2]. The need for structure rules in the expert system is that the conditions to be monitored depend upon a different but overlapping set of structure relationships than used by the simulator. These expert structure rules would include the 3000 different variables that define the state of a simulation (or even a real ship with respect to the cargo). Other rules would be there to identify the different objects (e.g. tanks). There would also be rules that simply act as intermediate links between other rules to allow inference to occur. For a typical liquid cargo vessel we estimate that there would be about 10,000 or more rules of this kind. The process of automating the overseeing would be to take each Monitoring Rule and expand it using the Structure Rules.

Rule#	Structure Rules	Variable/Object/Relation
S1	**If** Cargo tank pressure	**Variable** VPP(1)
S2	**If** Cargo tank pressure	**Variable** VPP(2)
O1	**If** VPP(1)	**Object** (Number 1, Port)
O2	**If** VPP(2)	**Object** (Number 1, Starboard)
S17	**If** Cargo tank P/R valve	**Variable** FLOPAR(?,303)
S18	**If** Cargo tank P/R valve	**Variable** FLOPAR(?,304)
O17	**If** FLOPAR(?,303)	**Object** (Number 1, Port)
O18	**If** FLOPAR(?,304)	**Object** (Number 1, Starboard)

For example in Monitoring Rule#1 above we would need to take all the alternatives that the structure rules express. In a typical case this would be replaced by 16 or so possibilities and would require at least three stages of inference for each of them not including all the potential paths that fail.

Rule#	Constructed Rules	Constructed Message/Meaning/Action
C1	**If** VPP(1) < 0 **&** FLOPAR(?,303) = Open	Cargo tank (Number 1 & Port) in vacuum. Relief valve open
C2	**If** VPP(2) < 0 **&** FLOPAR(?,304) = Open	Cargo tank (Number 1 & Starboard) in vacuum. Relief valve open

The cycle would involve for each variable referenced in the Monitoring Rule the finding of a Construct Rule that has an **If** component that matches the variable reference (e.g. Cargo tank pressure) and also has the same object reference as all the other variables in the Monitoring Rule (e.g. Number 1, Port). The object reference is then used in the Message as well as ensuring the correct binding between the different tests on the variables.

The collection of tanks also represents systems that interact with each other. An example of such an interaction is:

Rule#	Monitoring Rules	Message/Meaning/Action
3	**If** Rule#1 & Rule#2 apply to **adjacent** tanks	Large pressure differential between cargo tanks **Object (Rule#1)** and **Object (Rule#2).** Possible conditions leading to bulkhead collapse.

This requires some further structural details that describe the adjacency of tanks. Other kinds of relationships can also be expressed (e.g. Connected_To).

Rule#	Structure Rules	Variable/Object/Relation
A1	**If Object** (Number 1, Port)	**Connected_To (Object** (Number 1, Starboard))
A2	**If Object** (Number 1, Port)	**Connected_To (Object** (Number 2, Port))
A3	**If Object** (Number 2, Port)	**Connected_To (Object** (Number 2, Starboard))
A4	**If Object** (Number 2, Port)	**Connected_To (Object** (Number 1, Port))
A5	**If Object** (Number 2, Port)	**Connected_To (Object** (Number 3, Port))

The cargo tanks are also supported by other systems such as the inert gas system that will have rules such as:

Rule#	Monitoring Rules	Message/Meaning/Action
4	If Inert Gas Power fail & {Scrubber pump is running or Seal pump is running or Fan is running}	Pumps cannot be started. Power is not available.

Overseeing requires an exhaustive scan of all the Monitoring Rules because it is looking for patterns that need a response from the students or leads to such a response and the expansion of these rules using the structure rules has to be achieved every 10 seconds. We expect that for a typical ship there would be about 2000 or more monitoring rules of this kind coupled with the 10,000 or more structural rules. At the very best this means some 6000-inference steps (not counting failures) in the time limit of 10 seconds. This requires each inference step to be completed in less than 0.0017 second or about 250 to 500 machine cycles with current processor power (0.6 to 1.2 GHz Machines). The estimated time would take about 1.5 times longer than this best required time. This is possible, but it would have to be handcrafted and all the tests would have to be simple. There would be no time for the simulator (or anything else) to run on the same machine.

3 A Division of Labour

Since the structure of a ship does not normally change during overseeing then much of the inference required for rule construction can be done off-line. Consequently, the structural linking with the Monitoring Rules is pre-compiled by using a mechanism for rule generation from the ship's structure. This takes advantage of the repetition of the cargo organisation. A ship's structure can be expressed as a hierarchy (the context tree). This is not always the case but exceptions can easily fit into such a scheme. The rules that reference a class of ship in terms of the desired expertise are expressed as General Rules. The particular ship drawn from that class for which we need Specific Rules that describe the structure is called the Target System. The associated context tree is the Target System description and is used by a rule generator that will construct the rules for a specific ship. These resulting rules are the System Specific Rules (Figure 1).

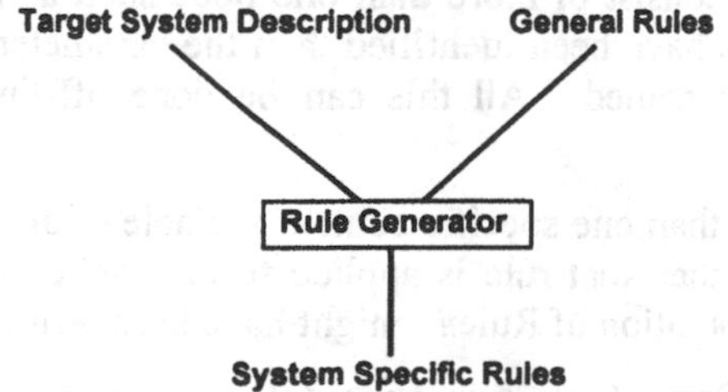

Figure 1. The Merging of Information for Rule Generation

Figure 2 shows a small part of a simplified context tree that represents the structure of a ship. The context tree takes the place of the structural rules that would have been needed for the standard expert system. The root of the tree is SHIP and can always be assumed. The nodes along a particular pathway can be used as object (concept) descriptors as used in the FLIN conceptual database [2] (adjectives and nouns). So in our example rules rewritten below, CARGO TANK indicates the general type of object to which the rules refer. Alternatives might be CARGO PIPE or BALLAST TANK and so on.

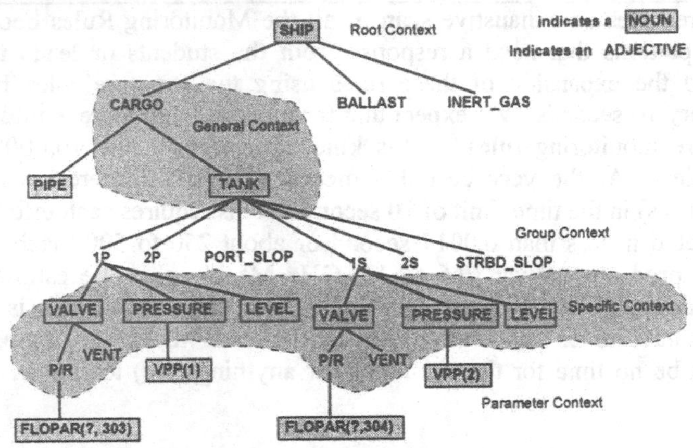

Figure 2. The Context Tree

Rule #	Object Type (General Context)	Monitoring Rules (Specific Context)	Message/Meaning/Action (Group Context)
1	Cargo tank	**If** pressure < 0 **&** P/R valve open	Cargo tank **Object (Rule#1)** in vacuum. Relief valve open
2	Cargo tank	**If** pressure >= 1400 **&** P/R valve open	Very high pressure in cargo tank **Object (Rule#2)**

The general object has parts associated with it. These parts can also be referenced in the same way. These specific objects like P/R VALVE or VENT VALVE or simply just PRESSURE depict general variables, which define the state of the object. Combine both the General and Specific Contexts then two things are identifiable. The first is the set of objects to which the rule applies and the second is the set of variables on each object that need to be tested. In this example the objects will be the set {1P, 2P, PORT_SLOP, 1S, 2S, STRBD_SLOP}. Note that the Group objects can consist of more than one node such as MAIN OXYGEN. Once these group items have been identified then the parameters (the variables in the simulation) can be named. All this can be done off-line to generate the constructed rules [2].

If it is found that more than one specific context variable of an object is identified during rule generation then that rule is applied to the '*or*' of all its possibilities. For example, the pre-condition of Rule#1 might have been written (see figure 2):

For Cargo Tank **If** pressure < 0 *and* valve open

Then this would be interpreted, since there are two options, as:

For Cargo Tank **If** pressure < 0 *and* (P/R valve open *or* vent valve open)

If there is more than one ambiguous specific context variable then every possible combination (the cross product) is generated. This will be referred to as *the ambiguity construct.*

The hierarchy is stored as text in a file where each level is marked by a set of dashes as illustrated in table 1. Repeated structures are easy to reproduce through cut and paste.

```
SHIP
- CARGO
-- TANK
--- 1P
---- VALVE
----- P/R
------ FLOPAR(?.303)
----- VENT
------ FLOPAR(?,288)
---- PRESSURE
----- VPP(1)
--- 2P
```

Table 1. A Fragment of the structure hierarchy as stored on file

Relationships can also be represented in a context tree as shown in figure 3. Here the relationships are between objects that can be identified as single nodes. All the nodes in the context can be considered as relationships and as such the decomposition of the ship does not have to follow physical structures; they can include usage or functional relationships. For example, this may be the relationship of the liquid cargo group of pipes.

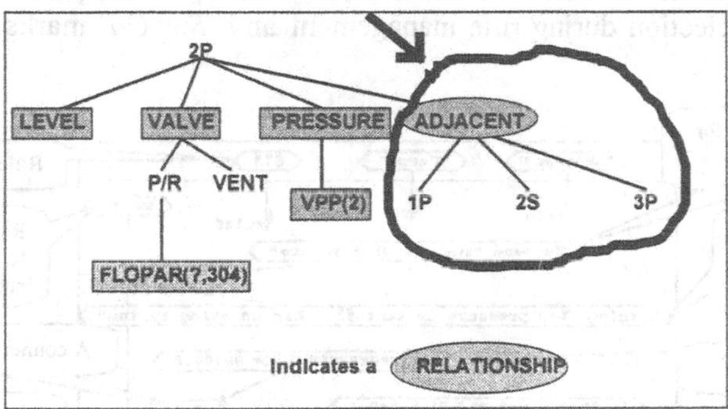

Figure 3. Relationships

4 Rules as Pictures

Since the development tool (ClarityPro) creates functional programs directly through diagrams, it was thus natural to create rules in the same form. Formal representation is essential for computation; nevertheless, formal notation may prematurely displace informal diagrammatic working during the process of developing a program or model [3]. It is conceivable both to be formal and informal at the same time because it is now possible to generate program code directly from diagrams. These diagrams are the Clarity[1] schema and can be interpreted directly into the functional language [4, 5]. A typical rule schematic is shown in Figure 4. For reasons of rule management the single rule number has been replaced by three parameters that define the Main and Sub categories followed by a relative rule number within those categories. These three dimensions now define the identity of any rule. The user may pre-define the allowed categories. Internal to the system these three dimensions are converted into a single rule number.

Functions (and hence their schematic) normally have zero or more input parameters and always a single output. The inputs are at the top of the schematic and the output is at the bottom. However, such a schematic can also be considered to be similar to a completed form. The lozenges represent the form fields and these can be added to and/or changed so that a new rule can be created from an old rule.

Starting at the bottom of the schematic, the lozenge containing **<list ?0>** describes the type of output for the function *cnorm_&*. In this case it will be a list of mixed types (strictly *an unknown* type). This function *cnorm_&* is there to pre-process the rule into a form ready for the rule generation sequence. The user defines the general context of the rule in the next lozenge. In this case "CARGO" "TANK". The next cluster of lozenges expresses the pre-condition of the rule. This also includes all the specific contexts that help identify the variables to be tested and the additional logic connectors. These connectors include *and* (as &&), *not* and *or* (as ||). The different pre-condition lozenges contain tests that are linked together via connecting arrows through these logic functions. The final cluster of lozenges that converge on the function *makelist* defines any number of the messages/ meanings/actions of the rule. In this case, a Warning' is output, 'Keywords' is available for selection during rule management and *'Sw_On'* marks the firing of this rule.

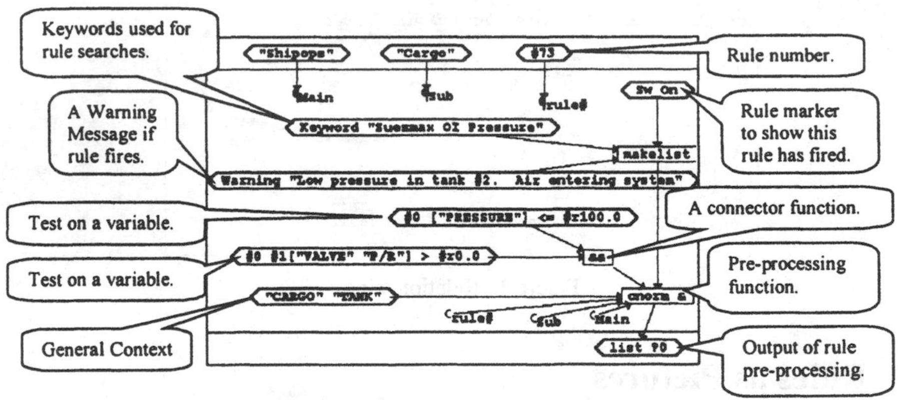

Figure 4. A Rule defined as a function as used in LICOS

There are several other kinds of consequences of the rule firing. This includes 'Action', 'Act', 'Information' and 'Error'. 'Act' and 'Action' provide a means of obeying functions that do something. Functions can also be obeyed in the pre-

[1] A version of Clarity (ClarityLite) minimised for teaching functional programming can be obtained free off the web: http://www.clarity-support.com/

condition provided they return a Boolean result. However, their side effects may be anything (e.g. starting a machine or printing). All processing begins at the bottom of the picture. The parameters are then processed clockwise from a function's output. The order of processing the pre-condition can be important.

5 Rule Pre-Conditions

The usual structure of a rule pre-condition is a set of tests linked together with logic connectors. These connectors are functions. Figure 5 is an example of a set of logic connectors. This schematic includes the pre-condition logic represented by:

({Port Suction Valve > #r0}
or {Stbd Suction Valve > #r0})
and {Drive Valve > #r0}
and (**not** {Discharge Valve > #r0})

Any formally correct Boolean structure may be constructed using these logic connector functions. The process of modifying the diagram is made simple through the ClarityPro environment.

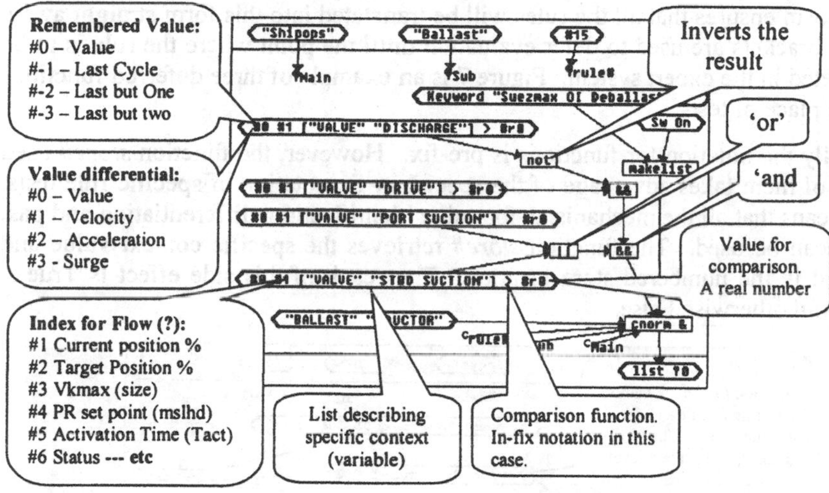

Figure 5. The structure of the pre-condition

The specification of the specific context variable can be extended to include three other elements:

- *Remembered Value:* The system remembers the last three values from previous cycles. The negative integer placed at the beginning of the test indicates which of the last three values is required for the test.
- *Value Differential:* The system uses these last three values to calculate the rates of change associated with a variable. Instead of a negative integer, a positive integer is used to indicate the level of differentiation. Most physical

systems can be described completely in terms of value (e.g. position), velocity (e.g. momentum), acceleration (e.g. force) and surge (e.g. impact).

- *Index to Flow:* The second integer refers only to certain variables in the simulator where there is an unspecified parameter. Such a parameter is marked by a '?' in the context tree. The system just replaces the '?' with the number. FLOPAR(?,303) is an example of a flow measurement that references a range of possible meanings depending in the value of '?'. Some examples are shown in figure 5.

Rule tests can be simply the fact that a specified rule has fired during the cycle. Figure 6 shows that all that's required is to give the number. The assumption is that the number is relative to the same main and sub category as the current rule. If the referenced rule is in a different category or sub-category then instead of the single number the following format is used:

<Ext "Shipops" "Ballast" #2>

The signs < > indicate the lozenge. Round brackets are used with functions that are to be interpreted at the point of rule generation. This is needed, for example, because the expert system assumes an internal system of rule numbering and this mechanism ensures that all the rules will be translated into this form straight away. Square brackets are used to defer evaluation until the point where the rule is to be interpreted in the expert system. Figure 7 is an example of three deferred functions used in place of tests.

Normally the notation for functions is pre-fix. However, the function *store#* used in two of them takes advantage of the special in-fix notation of specific rule tests. This means that all the mechanisms for value identification, differentiation and past cycles can be used. The function *store#* retrieves the specific context value and places it in the numbered store location. The result of this side effect is True if successful otherwise False.

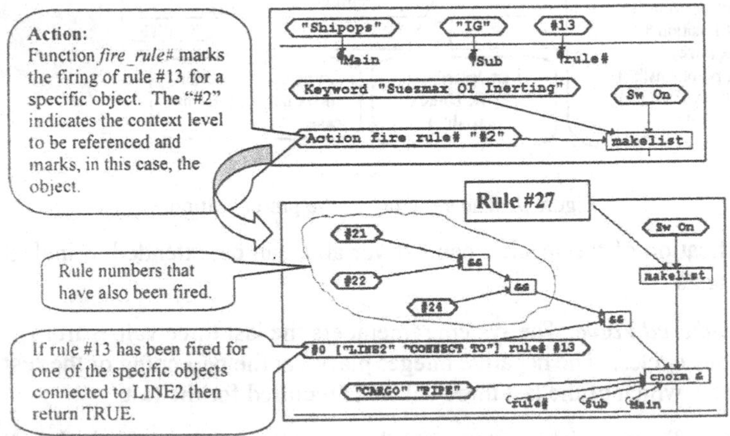

Figure 6. The passing of information between rules

The numeric reference to a memory location with *store#* is global so in principle could be used outside the rule. There is no mechanism here for marking the source of the information other than the number. The only limit to the number of locations is the limit set by the system for an integer.

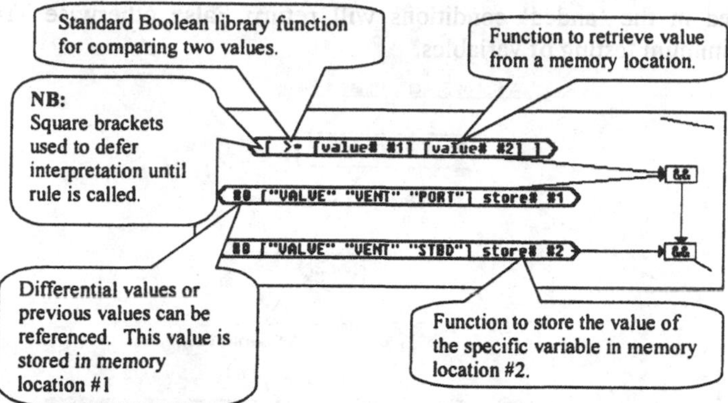

Figure 7. Using functions and memory in a Pre-condition

The final function in figure 7 uses the function *value#* to retrieve the stored values. This uses the normal pre-fix notation. Square brackets are used throughout in place of the normal round bracket so that all evaluations are deferred. Any library or user defined function can be used this way. There are currently about 300 library functions.

Rules can be used to trigger off any pattern directed event that can be programmed in ClarityPro. The limitation is that the actions must conform to the strict rule format. It is also possible to call the complete rule interpreter with a separate set of rules as a rule action. Thus, different monitoring procedures or expertise can be triggered by rules to any depth. However, generality is restricted because global variables such as switches and other inter-rule communication will remain current at all depths.

6 Cycles of Interpretation

The pre-complied system specific rules are in two parts. The first part is the pre-condition and is in conjunctive normal form. The second part is a list of actions that are activated when the condition is True.

The pre-condition tests are ordered such that they are the conjunction of disjunctions (conjunctive normal form). Every Boolean function, which consists of Boolean tests that are linked together by normal logical connectives and brackets, can be converted into this normal form. An example of this is the condition that might be expressed as:

$$(a \wedge d) \vee (b \wedge c)$$

where ‘a’, ‘b’, etc are Boolean tests on variables. This will become in conjunctive normal form:

$$(a \vee b) \wedge (a \vee c) \wedge (d \vee b) \wedge (d \vee c)$$

The function 'Check Rule Boolean Condition' in figure 8 runs through each of the 'ored' conditions and if a True is detected within the 'ored' list testing will stop and return True otherwise False. At the next level up, the first False that is encountered in the 'anded' conditions will return False otherwise True. This ensures minimum testing of variables.

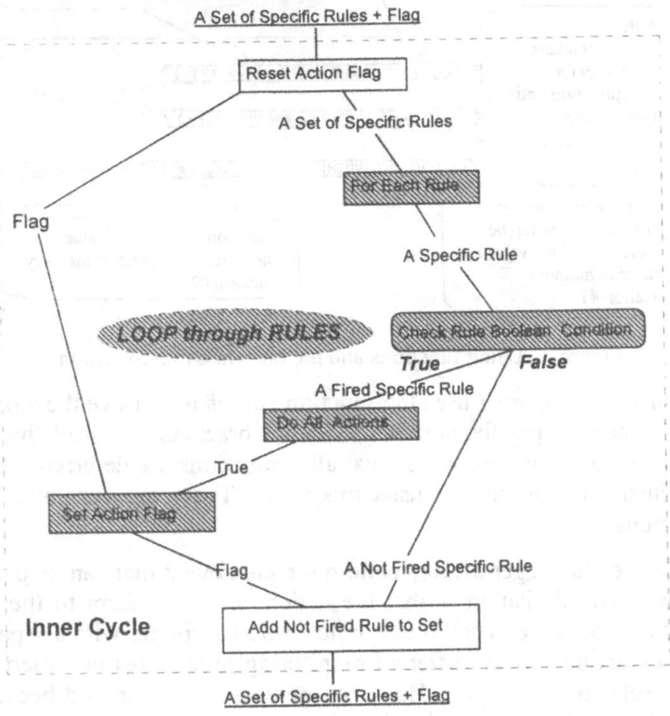

Figure 8. The Inner Cycle through a rule Set

Thus, for each rule in the set, if the pre-condition is True then the actions are obeyed and the rule is then effectively deleted from the set during this outer cycle (figure 9). All unfired rules where the pre-condition was False are collected together for reassessing. This is because the firing of a rule may alter the conditions of other rules so that they are then able to fire on the next round. For example, switches may be set by a fired rule that is tested by other rules. These dependent rule firings will occur in either the same inner cycle or the next one. The Action Flag is set to show that at least one rule has fired on that inner cycle.

The Outer Cycle ensures that the Inner Cycle is repeated until either there are no more rules left (they have all been fired) or no rules have been fired (nothing happened). At one of these two points the Outer Cycle finishes. This Outer Cycle is then repeated every N seconds where N is predefined by the set-up procedures.

This process ensures that the rules are *explored forward chaining and breadth first.* Since the structure has already been combined with the detailed rules the depth of the tree is likely to be shallow. The result is an exhaustive scan of the applicable rules every N seconds. In our case N has to be less than 10.

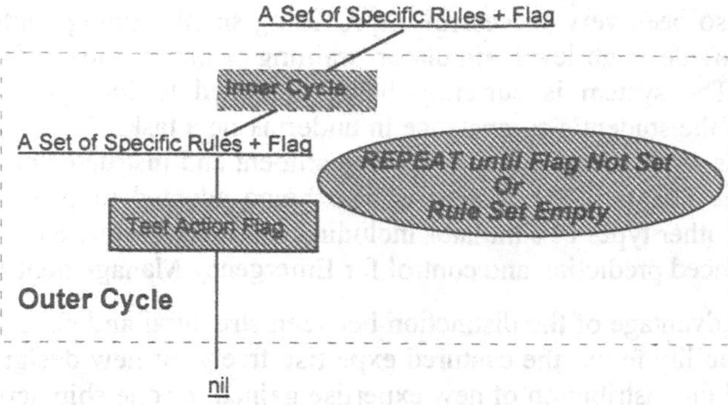

Figure 9. The Outer Cycle through the rule set.

Many processes, if kept simple to express, depend upon order. The mechanism of rule interpretation cannot guarantee that the rules will always be visited in a particular sequence. The only certainty that we have is that the processing within a rule will be consistent. What are also certain is that every rule will be visited at least once in an outer cycle and that every rule that fires will be eliminated on subsequent inner cycles. All switches etc. will be reset only after each complete outer cycle. It is possible in many cases to use this information to force sequencing between rules.

It is also known that any logical function can be expressed in conjunctive normal form. For example, we require firing a rule when all the stripping and suction valves attached to a particular line were **closed**. It is known that the ambiguity construct would '*or*' all the valves together for any particular line but we need an '*and*'. However, using De Morgan's Law we can get a simple logical equivalent by testing the valves for **open** and using an '*or*'. So the statement:

All the valves are **closed** for line 1

becomes:

There are **no** valves **open** for line 1.

The system currently has about **2000** rules that are scanned in about **2** seconds. These rules are generated from a context tree of a ship and about **500** general rules.

7 Conclusion

The WISE Expert System, as part of the 'WISE Cargo' product has been purchased by 15+ companies (primarily ship owners and managers) and is operational in over **35** sites worldwide, including 25 installations on board real vessels, generating an income in excess of $250,000.

There are two primary benefits identified by clients. First, is that by having the system on board it allows them to ensure all the appropriate officers obtain training on the simulator instead of just the few sent to shore based courses. Second, it allows them to either reduce the overall training costs (reduced travel) or to structure the training more effectively by using the higher cost shore based courses to concentrate on teaching the higher level skills and student assessment. The system has also been very successful in providing small training centres with the ability to provide high-level simulator training without the traditional large overheads. The system is currently being extended to incorporate automatic assessment of the student's competence in undertaking a task. The assessment can be provided as feedback in real time to both student and instructor or as hardcopy for use by the clients. The system is also being adapted to provide the same capability for other types of simulator including those for Engine Room operations and also enhanced prediction and control for Emergency Management Systems.

The greatest advantage of the distinction between structural and expert knowledge has been the ability to use the captured expertise freely for new designs of ship as they arise and the distribution of new expertise gained for one ship across all other ship designs. The pre-compilation of this knowledge has also made the expert system responsive enough to be used in real time for operational cargo ships.

Ships officers very often only stay on a vessel for 4-6 months and do not return to the same vessel. Consequently, the 'knowledge' they build up about operating that particular vessel is lost when they leave and has to be learnt by their replacement, thus affecting both safety and efficiency. At the same time, there is widespread recognition that the overall standard of the skills of seafarers is reducing. With this in mind, work is currently in progress to connect WISE Expert with the control system of real ships instead of a simulation. In this context, the WISE Expert 'knowledge database' will provide a repository whereby the knowledge for the ship can be collected along with the general operational knowledge used with the simulator. WISE Expert will then be used to intelligently monitor all the activities onboard relating to the control of the cargo operation and provide warnings or advice to the operators if particular situations are identified or predicted, enhancing the overall safety capable of being provided by the ships operating system [1]. The first such system is expected to be completed during 2006.

References

1 Gillett, R. & Addis T. R., 'Intelligent Software: How it can be used to improve safety and training methods'. GASTECH2000, The 19th International LNG, LPG & Natural Gas Conference & Exhibition, George R. Brown Convention Center, 14-17 November, Houston, Texas, USA. pp 10, (2000),

2. Addis T.R., 'Designing Knowledge_Based Systems'. published Kogan Page. ISBN 0 85038 859 7, ISBN 1 85091 251 3, 1985; Prentice Hall, ISBN 0-13-201823-3; 1986; 2nd Edition Ab-Libris Ltd,. ISBN: 190356118 3 2003

3. Shaw L. G & Woodward J. B 'Modeling Expert Knowledge', Knowledge Acquisition ,vol. 2, pp. 179-206, (1990)

4 Addis T. R. and Townsend Addis J. J 'Avoiding Knotty Structures in Design: Schematic Functional Programming', Journal of Visual Languages and Computing, Vol. 12. pp689-715. (2001)

5. Addis T. R. and Townsend Addis J. J. 'An Introduction to Clarity: A Schematic Functional Language for Managing the Design of Complex Systems'. Vol. 56, No4, April, International Journal of Human Computer Studies, ISSN 1071 5819, pp331-422, (2002)

A Camera-Direction Dependent Visual-Motor Coordinate Transformation for a Visually Guided Neural Robot

Cornelius Weber, David Muse, Mark Elshaw and Stefan Wermter

Hybrid Intelligent Systems, School of Computing and Technology
University of Sunderland, UK. Web: www.his.sunderland.ac.uk

Abstract

Objects of interest are represented in the brain simultaneously in different frames of reference. Knowing the positions of one's head and eyes, for example, one can compute the body-centred position of an object from its perceived coordinates on the retinae. We propose a simple and fully trained attractor network which computes head-centred coordinates given eye position and a perceived retinal object position. We demonstrate this system on artificial data and then apply it within a fully neurally implemented control system which visually guides a simulated robot to a table for grasping an object. The integrated system has as input a primitive visual system with a what-where pathway which localises the target object in the visual field. The coordinate transform network considers the visually perceived object position and the camera pan-tilt angle and computes the target position in a body-centred frame of reference. This position is used by a reinforcement-trained network to dock a simulated PeopleBot robot at a table for reaching the object. Hence, neurally computing coordinate transformations by an attractor network has biological relevance and technical use for this important class of computations.

1 Introduction

There is a view of current developments leading to a major advance in a future personal robot industry, as illustrated by citations such as: "In thirty years I think it [the personal robot industry] will be bigger than the personal computer industry" [16]. Yet a key capability currently limiting robotic expansion is image processing, one function of which is to identify the position of an object and making it available to mechanical actuators, for example for grasping.

The control of the human body is a complex task due to the complexity of the body geometry and the difficulty to extract information from the world by sensors like vision and to transform it into a motor-relevant representation. So to simply grasp an object, we need to *(i)* visually localise an object, *(ii)* infer its position in body-centred coordinates which are relevant for control of the arm and hand, and *(iii)* activate the relevant muscles to perform a grasp.

Here we present a neural model which consists of three systems, *(i)* a visual, *(ii)* a coordinate transform and *(iii)* a motor system, which performs such a task on a simulated robot. The complexity of the human body is schematically addressed by the robot camera which can pan-tilt its gaze direction during the docking. This accounts for the fact that the eyes and/or the head can move with respect to the body, which makes it necessary to transform a visually identified location into a body-centred location as is relevant for the motor control.

In [18] we have implemented a vision controlled robotic docking action that was trained by reinforcement learning. The assumption that the robot camera was fixed to the body allowed a direct match from pixel coordinates to body-centred coordinates. Because of the fixed camera, objects had to be in a confined space so that they were visible. The grasping manoeuvre is shown at the following URL: www.his.sunderland.ac.uk/robotimages/Cap0001.mpg .

In [11] the camera is allowed to move, but it is assumed that it is fixating the target when computing its direction. Hence a reaching map can be defined using only the camera posture. When a robot or the object is moving, however, a camera can hardly fixate the object, in particular when using commercially available, slow pan-tilt camera mounts.

Let us briefly discuss the underlying geometry of the coordinate transformation problem. For simplicity we will in the following not distinguish eye- and head position, accounting for a pivoting camera which is mounted on a robot body. Fig. 1 visualises the geometry of our setup with a PeopleBot robot.[1] If the robot is to grasp the fruit object on the table, then the following coordinates are important for controlling the motors: the distance d of the robot to the target object and the angle θ at which the object is to the left or the right of the robot body. In order to avoid bumping into the table with the robot's "shoulders" when near the table, the angle φ of the robot rotation w.r.t. the table edge will later also be used for motor coordination.

While d and θ are required for motor control, the robot sensory system represents the object only visually, delivering the perceived horizontal and vertical positions h and v of the object in the visual field. Knowing also the camera pan- and tilt angles p and t, it is possible to compute d and θ. We assume a constant elevation of the camera over the target object which allows the distance of the object to be estimated from how low it is perceived, thus from v and t. This compensates for not using a stereo camera. In summary, (d, θ) are a function of (h, v, p, t), and the purpose of the coordinate transform network is to learn and compute this function.

It would be possible, even with complicated human geometries, to compute this function using deterministic vectorial transformations. Humans, however, *learn* sensory-motor coordination, which allows for adaptations during evolution and ontogenesis. In the mammalian cortex transitions between visual and motor representations are made in the posterior parietal cortex (PPC) which lies at a strategic position between the visual cortex and the motor cortex. PPC neurons are modulated by the direction of hand movement, as well as by visual, eye position and limb position signals [2]. These multi-modal responses allow the PPC to carry out computations which transform the location of targets from one frame of reference to another [3, 4].

---

[1] Konstantinos Karantzis implemented the PeopleBot in the gazebo robot simulator.

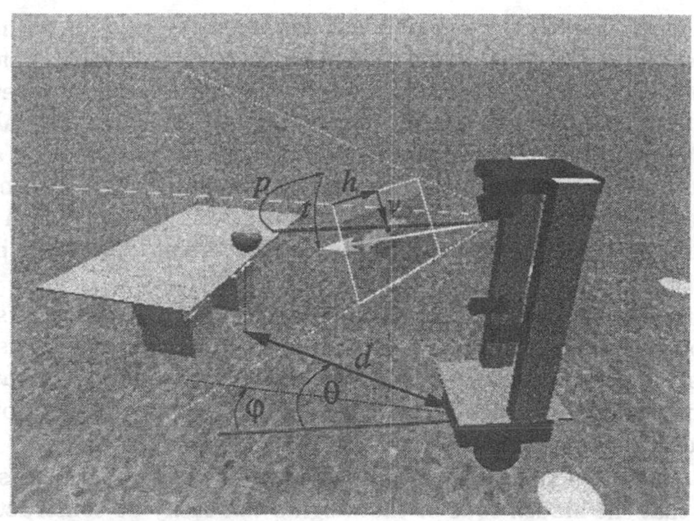

Figure 1: The simulated PeopleBot robot with its short black grippers in its environment. Coordinates are as follows: θ is the angle of the target w.r.t. the forward direction of the robot and d is the distance between the robot and the target object. φ is the robot orientation angle w.r.t. an axis that is perpendicular to the table and will be used later, directly in motor control. θ and d comprise the body-centred representation of the target object which is relevant for motor control but not given directly by sensors. p is the pan angle and t is the tilt angle of the camera. h and v are the horizontal and vertical image pixel coordinates of the perceived target object (the white frame shows the image seen by the robot camera). The body-centred coordinates (θ, d) are to be computed as a function of easily accessible values (h, v) and (p, t).

Models of neural coordinate transformations originally dealt with the "static" case, in which, for example, Cartesian coordinates (c_1, c_2) of an object (e.g. as seen on the retina) are neurally transformed into joint angles (θ_1, θ_2) of an arm required to reach the target [8]. Such a model is static by not accounting for the influence of another variable, such as the rotation of the head. To account for such a modulating influence we need dynamic, adjustable mappings.

A standard way to achieve a dynamic mapping is to feed the two inputs such as Cartesian coordinates c and head rotation r into a hidden layer. These inputs are coded as population vectors $\boldsymbol{x}^c$ and $\boldsymbol{x}^r$ for neurons arranged along a one-dimensional line where the location of an approximately Gaussian-shaped activation hill encodes the value. Both inputs are used in a symmetric way. The working principle of the use of the hidden layer is described as [17]: "One first creates a 2-dimensional [hidden] layer with an activity equal to the [outer] product of the population activity in $\boldsymbol{x}^c$ and $\boldsymbol{x}^r$. Next, a projection from this layer to an output layer implements the output function $\boldsymbol{z} = f(\boldsymbol{x}^c, \boldsymbol{x}^r)$."

Such a network with two one-dimensional input layers, a one-dimensional output layer and a two-dimensional hidden layer has been termed a basis function network [5]. Because of its structure, the output layer is symmetric with the input layers and the network can be used in any direction. Lateral weights within each layer allow for a template fitting procedure during which attractor network activations generate approximately Gaussian-shaped hills of activations. In a "cue integration" mode the network receives input with additive noise at all three visible layers and produces the correct, consistent hills with maximum likelihood [5].

The gain field architecture [14] adds a second hidden layer which subtracts certain inputs to remove unwanted terms from the solution on the first hidden layer. This allows it to encode not only the position of a hill of activation, but also its amplitude. Since this breaks the symmetry between the input layers and the output layer, this network is used only in one direction.

The use of the hidden layer as the outer product of input layers has the advantage that the hidden code or the weights can easily be constructed using algebraic transformations. A learning algorithm for all the weights is not given with these models. A specific disadvantage is the large dimensionality of the hidden layer: if both input layers are two-dimensional, as in our problem, then the hidden layer would have to be represented as a four-dimensional hyper-cube.

Here we propose a network which learns the coordinate transformation. Every unit is connected with all other units by connection weights which are trained according to the Boltzmann machine learning rule [1] (see [9] for an introduction). This rule is biologically plausible using only local, Hebbian and anti-Hebbian learning. After training, the network generates the distribution of the training data using stochastic units. The learning rule furthermore allows to include any number of additional hidden units in order to make the network more powerful in generating a complex data distribution. The hidden code would self-organise during learning without requiring the network designer to construct it. For our data, however, no hidden layer was required. During learning, all three areas receive their respective coordinate as training data in a symmetric fashion, while after learning, missing information in any area can be recovered based on the principle of pattern completion.

Using two-dimensional input areas and artificial test data described in Section 2, we will describe training of the network in Section 3 and show how it performs coordinate transformations in Section 4, as required for the robotic scenario. In Section 5 we show how the coordinate transformation network can be applied as part of a neural control system that docks a robot at a table to grasp a visually identified object. In Section 6 we will discuss the results and underlying assumptions and Section 7 gives a summary.

2 Test Scenario

Using the symbols from Fig. 1, let us introduce the following notation for two-dimensional coordinates: $\boldsymbol{\alpha}^{vis} = (h, v)$ is the position of the object of interest in the camera image. $\boldsymbol{\alpha}^{head} = (p, t)$ is the camera rotation angle. $\boldsymbol{\alpha}^{body} = (\theta, d)$ is the body-centred position of the object of interest. As a first test example we choose an abstract coordinate transformation defined by:

$$\boldsymbol{\alpha}^{body} = \boldsymbol{\alpha}^{vis} + \boldsymbol{\alpha}^{head}, \tag{1}$$

where the individual terms of the vectors are:

$$\theta = h + p \tag{2}$$

$$d = v + t. \tag{3}$$

Eq. 2 describes well the true relation between body-centred, visually perceived and camera position in the horizontal plane. Eq. 3, however, would not describe the true, non-linear, relation between the coordinates in the vertical dimension. Therefore, these equations are just a simplified account of more general coordinate transformations.

The distance d of the object in the real scenario can somehow be computed from v and t given a realistic constraint that the object is on floor-level and assuming an elevated camera position. Hence the coordinates $\boldsymbol{\alpha}^{vis}$ and $\boldsymbol{\alpha}^{head}$ contain sufficient information to compute $\boldsymbol{\alpha}^{body}$. Other body-centred coordinates like distances in x- and y-direction may alternatively be computed.

We represent our coordinate vectors $\boldsymbol{\alpha}^{vis}$, $\boldsymbol{\alpha}^{head}$ and $\boldsymbol{\alpha}^{body}$ on neural sheets as neural activation vectors $\boldsymbol{x}^{vis}$, $\boldsymbol{x}^{head}$ and $\boldsymbol{x}^{body}$, respectively. Such a coding of low-dimensional vectors by high-dimensional neuron activations is called population coding. Neural activations within the $\boldsymbol{x}$ vectors are defined by envelopes of Gaussians centred on the corresponding positions of the $\boldsymbol{\alpha}$ vectors. Fig. 2 depicts the algebraic transformation and the mapping to neural representations. Neural population coding allows arbitrary coordinate representations by replacing the coordinate systems in the lower part of Fig. 2.

3 Architecture and Training

The coordinate transform network architecture is depicted in Fig. 2, top. It consists of three fully connected areas which represent $\boldsymbol{x}^{vis}$, $\boldsymbol{x}^{head}$ and $\boldsymbol{x}^{body}$. The Boltzmann machine learning rule uses randomised unit update rather than structured information flow and lends itself to highly interconnected networks with the possibility to introduce any number of additional hidden units to boost performance. With its binary stochastic units it is powerful in learning a given data distribution. For the specific purpose of function approximation other biologically plausible schemes (e.g. [12]) would also be possible.

The Boltzmann machine has two running modes: in the *clamped phase* the data distribution is forced upon the visible units of the network. The network activation states $\boldsymbol{x}$ are then subject to the distribution $P^{+}_{\boldsymbol{x}}$ where the upper index "+" denotes the *clamped phase*. Since in our case there are no hidden units, the network state consists only of the three visible input areas, i.e.: $\boldsymbol{x} := \{\boldsymbol{x}^{vis}, \boldsymbol{x}^{head}, \boldsymbol{x}^{body}\}$. The other running mode is the *free running phase* in which the distribution $P^{-}_{\boldsymbol{x}}$ over the network states arises from the stochasticity

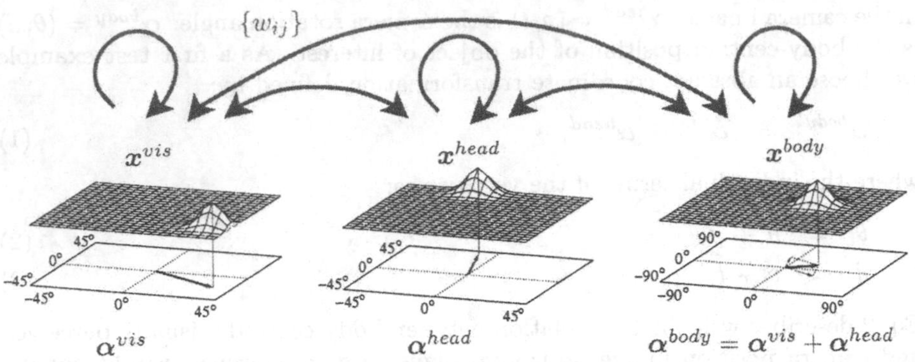

Figure 2: A coordinate transformation on two-dimensional manifolds. **Below**: three two-dimensional vectors, $\boldsymbol{\alpha}^{vis}$, $\boldsymbol{\alpha}^{head}$ and $\boldsymbol{\alpha}^{body}$ and their relation to each other which is also graphically explained by the dotted lines in the right graph. Note the extended range of the body-centred coordinate system, which makes the other vectors projected into that system appear half as long. **Middle**: the neural population code $\boldsymbol{x}^{vis}$, $\boldsymbol{x}^{head}$ and $\boldsymbol{x}^{body}$ representing each vector on two-dimensional sheets of neurons. A hill of neural activation carries the information about the corresponding position of each vector. **Top**, the network architecture: the set of weights $\{w_{ij}\}$ connects every unit with every other in all three layers.

of the units and is determined by the network parameters, such as weights and thresholds. Here, the upper index "−" denotes the *free running phase.*

The goal of learning is that the distribution $P^-_{\boldsymbol{x}}$ generated by the network approximates the data driven distribution $P^+_{\boldsymbol{x}}$ which is given. $P^-_{\boldsymbol{x}} \approx e^{-E(\boldsymbol{x})}$ is a Boltzmann distribution which depends on the network energy $E(\boldsymbol{x}) = \sum_{i,j} w_{ij} x_i x_j$ where w_{ij} denotes the connection weight from neuron j to neuron i. Therefore $P^-_{\boldsymbol{x}}$ can be molded by training the network parameters. Derivation of the "distance"[2] between $P^-_{\boldsymbol{x}}$ and $P^+_{\boldsymbol{x}}$ w.r.t. the network parameters leads to the learning rule

$$\Delta w_{ij} = \epsilon \Big(\sum_{\{\boldsymbol{x}\}} P^+_{\boldsymbol{x}} x_i x_j - \sum_{\{\boldsymbol{x}\}} P^-_{\boldsymbol{x}} x_i x_j \Big) \tag{4}$$

with learning step size ϵ which we set between 0.0025 and 0.001. Computing the left term corresponds to the *clamped phase* of learning, the right term to the *free running phase.* Without hidden units, the left term in Eq. (4) can be re-written as $\sum_{\mu}^{data} x_i^\mu x_j^\mu$ where μ is the index of a data point. Without hidden units thus the *clamped phase* does not involve relaxation of activations.

The right term of Eq. (4) can be approximated by sampling from the Boltzmann distribution. This is done by recurrent relaxation of the network in the

[2]Correctly, the distance has to be termed the Kullback-Leibler divergence. See [9] for a derivation of the learning rule.

free running phase. The stochastic transfer function

$$P(x_i(t+1)=1) = \frac{1}{1+e^{-\sum_j w_{ij}x_j(t)}} \tag{5}$$

computes the binary output $x_i \in \{0,1\}$ of neuron i at time step $t+1$. Repeated relaxation approximates a Boltzmann distribution of the activation states.

During training, the two phases are computed alternating. One randomly generated data point is presented to account for the *clamped phase.* Then a relatively short relaxation of the network, consisting of updating all units for 15 iterations using Eq. (5) is performed to account for the *free running phase.* Units are initialised in this phase by activating every unit with a probability of 0.1, regardless of its position. During testing, we also used the deterministic continuous transfer function

$$x_i(t+1) = \frac{1}{1+e^{-\sum_j w_{ij}x_j(t)}} . \tag{6}$$

Self-connections were omitted in the expectation that they would grow very large, but later assessment showed that this would not have been the case. Instead, a threshold θ_i was added to each unit. It was treated during training as a weight that was connected to an external unit with a constant activation of -1. There are no further weight constraints.

4 Coordinate Transformation Results

We have explored two methods of sampling the training data, described below. Both satisfy Eq. 1. From the two-dimensional $\boldsymbol{\alpha}$ vectors, high-dimensional neural population vectors $\boldsymbol{x}$ are produced, as visualised in Fig. 2. The Gaussian envelopes over the neural activations have a maximum value of 1. The Boltzmann machine learning rule accepts continuous values between 0 and 1 which are treated as probabilities of a neuron being in the active state.

The first method was to uniformly sample $\boldsymbol{\alpha}^{vis}$ and $\boldsymbol{\alpha}^{head}$, and then to produce the position $\boldsymbol{\alpha}^{body}$ dependent on these. This leads to a non-uniform distribution of $\boldsymbol{\alpha}^{body}$ which is biased toward the centre (background shading in Fig. 5 a)). The reason for this is that there are more combinations possible from the visual- and head input to produce a position in the middle of the body centred coordinate system.

The second method was to uniformly sample $\boldsymbol{\alpha}^{body}$ first, and then randomly generate one of $\boldsymbol{\alpha}^{vis}$ or $\boldsymbol{\alpha}^{head}$, and construct the other so that geometrical relations are met, if possible. This was not always the case as some combinations of, e.g. $\boldsymbol{\alpha}^{head}$ and $\boldsymbol{\alpha}^{body}$ would require $\boldsymbol{\alpha}^{vis}$ to be outside of its range. For example if $\boldsymbol{\alpha}^{body}$ denotes an object position 50° (to the right) and $\boldsymbol{\alpha}^{head}$ denotes a head angle of -30° (to the left), then the object would have to be in the visual field at a position of 80° in order to satisfy Eq. (1) and $50^o = 80^o + (-30^o)$, which is outside of the range of the visual field. In these cases a different random input activation was generated until a mapping could be made to produce the

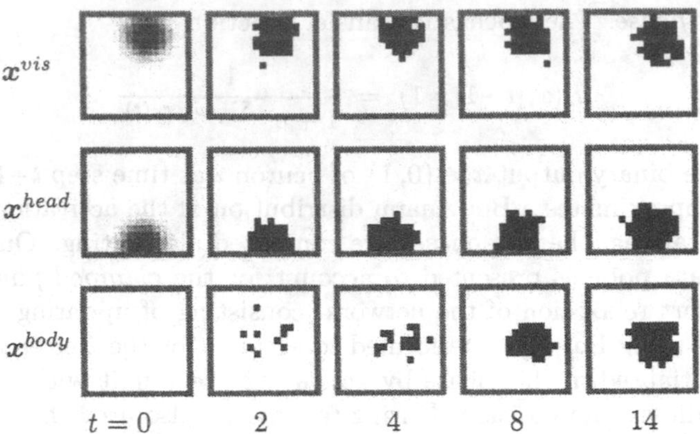

Figure 3: Neural activations produced by the trained network for one example case. At time step $t = 0$ (left column) the network is initialised with continuous Gaussian shaped inputs on two of the three areas, x^{vis} and x^{head}, and zeros within x^{body}. Values are between zero (white) and 1 (dark). In the following iterations, at time steps indicated at the bottom of this figure, the network maintains binary stochastic activations. These account for the positive inputs but also fill in the missing input by generating an appropriate vector x^{body}.

required output. Note that both methods produce the same training data, but in a different probability distribution.

The network was trained to produce the correct vector x^{body} with 50000 data points which took around 5 hours to complete running on a Linux based desktop. The size of each layer was 15×15 units. Even though the network can work in any direction or perform "cue integration" [5] if input is applied to all areas, we will consider only the task where it is initialised with x^{vis} and x^{head} as input vectors. Then it will produce a vector x^{body} that is consistent with these inputs ("function approximation" [5]). x^{vis} and x^{head} will also fluctuate slightly over time, if allowed to change. This is shown in Fig. 3 where we see that the activations representing x^{vis} move slightly downward between time steps 2 and 14. These fluctuations can be avoided by clamping the input units so that the data representation remains fixed on them.

In Fig. 4 we see how constant input x^{vis} and x^{head} effects the output area representing the body centred coordinates. For example x^{head} in Fig. 4 a) represents a head position to the very far right and it contributes a strong positive net input to the right of the area representing the body centred position, as seen in Fig. 4 b). To the left of this area there is an even larger, inhibitory net input. The reason for this is that when the head is turned to the very right, the visual field does not cover the left side of the body, so the object that is acted upon cannot be at the very left of the body. Note that every data point involves a hill of neural activation on every area which implies that the object

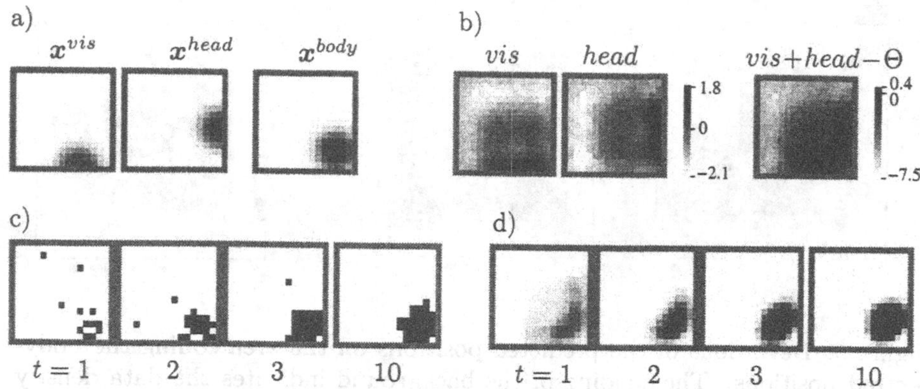

Figure 4: Neural activations for an example case. **a)** shows input vectors x^{vis} and x^{head} and the corresponding correct target vector x^{body}. **b)** Individual net input into the body representation area from the x^{vis} (left) and x^{head} (middle) vectors as well as the sum of both inputs minus thresholds Θ (right). Scale bars to the right indicate the values. **c)** shows the binary vector x^{body} that emerges from the constant input in b) and from further relaxation at time steps given below. It reproduces the target vector as a binary, stochastic code. **d)** shows x^{body} emerging when using the continuous transfer function Eq. (6).

is always assumed to be seen. Thus, based on just one observation, such as x^{head}, a rough estimate of x^{body} can be given even if x^{vis} is undetermined.

Similarly, a visually perceived position incurs a constraint in the body centred target position. If both constraints are combined, as in Fig. 4 b), right, then a relatively small region in the body representation area receives maximal net input. The remaining external influence onto the area is mainly inhibitory. Finally, Fig. 4 c) and d) demonstrate that via recurrent relaxation using the lateral weights, after only two steps a focused pattern of activation emerges around the correct position x^{body}, that is shown in Fig. 4 a). More examples of data and network output pairs are concatenated in an animation which can be seen at: http://www.his.sunderland.ac.uk/supplements/AI05/

The errors produced by the network on the body centred area are illustrated in Fig. 5 a) and b), here after 100000 learning steps with Gaussian centres avoiding the outer-most units, in order to reduce boundary effects. Positions encoded by the network and those of the data were obtained by sliding a Gaussian over the area and selecting the position with maximum overlap to the neural activations. Data are averaged over altogether 20000 data points while using Eq. (5) as stochastic neuronal activation function. On the left, we can see a tendency of the network to generate peripheral positions of x^{body} and thus α^{body} toward the centre. The reason for this can be seen in the background shading of Fig. 5 a), which shows that a greater density of α^{body} has been produced to the centre of its area when homogeneously sampling α^{vis} and α^{head}. The learnt network represents this trend in its weights and biases.

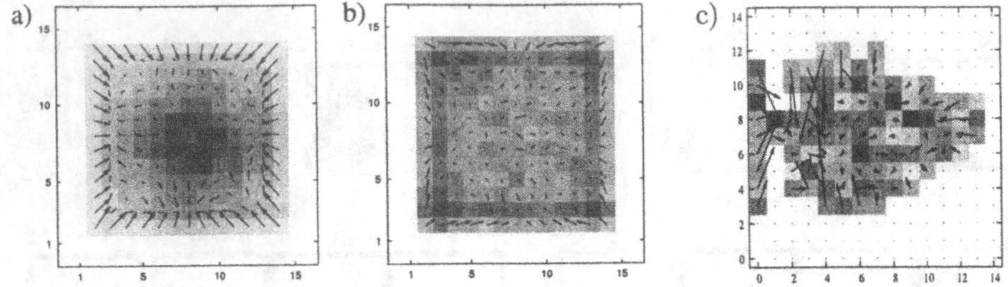

Figure 5: Deviations of the predicted positions on the area coding the body-centred positions. The shading of the background indicates the data density of the generated positions. In **a)**, the distribution is biased toward the centre, as the visual- and head-positions were sampled homogeneously. In **b)**, body-centred positions were sampled uniformly, before generating visual and head-positions. Arrows show the systematic network errors, pointing from the correct target position toward the predicted position. **c)** is a similar plot for the robotic data, where the ordinate denotes θ ranging from -90° to 90° and the abscissa denotes $\sqrt{d}$ with d ranging from 0 to 2 metres. See Section 5 for details.

In order to verify this influence of the inhomogeneity we used the second method of sampling the training data, which ensured that activation hills were uniformly distributed on the body representation area as shown in Fig. 5 b). Comparing it with Fig. 5 a), we see that the strong tendency to predict positions away from the low density data regions around the border has been greatly reduced. We have furthermore averaged the errors over single trials, thus also capturing the noise induced by the stochasticity of the neurons resulting from Eq. (5). The average deviation between the correct body-centred object position and its estimation by the network was 0.79 and 0.67 units for the first and second method of sampling, respectively. With 15 units covering 180° (see Fig. 2) this corresponds to 9.48^o and 8.04^o deviation of the network estimation of α^{body}. This data shows that the network can produce usable and robust solutions of the dynamic coordinate transformation problem.

5 Application within a Robot Control System

The integrated robot control system is shown in Fig. 6. The visual system feeds into the coordinate transform system which then feeds into the motor system. The "eye-move" motor area is only concerned with focusing the camera on the target object. Its connections have been learnt in an error-driven fashion, strengthening (weakening) the weights if the camera movement was too little (too large) to focus an object. Independent of the range of the camera movement, when the robot is moving, the camera moves too slow for centring the object permanently, but fast enough to keep it somewhere in the field of view.

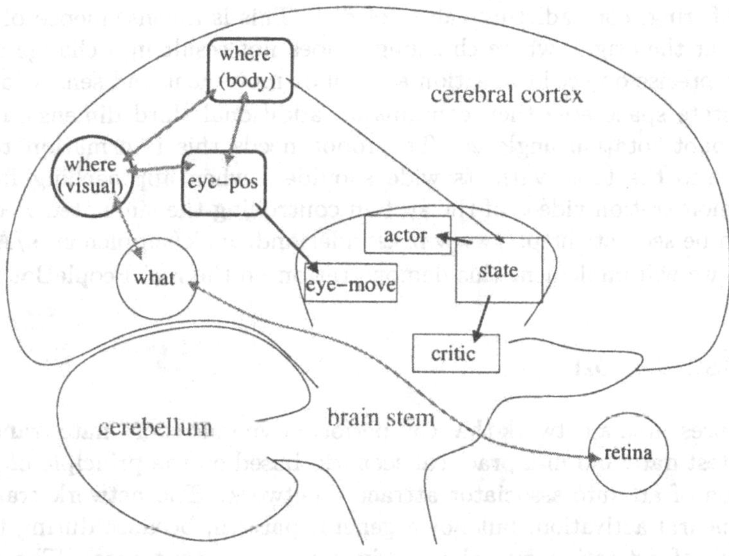

Figure 6: The three areas involved in the coordinate transformation embedded in the full control model and overlaid on a sketch of the brain. The boxes denote the implemented areas of neurons; round in the visual system, oval-boxes in next steps of the coordinate transform system and rectangular in the motor system. Thick arrows represent trained connections, partially in both directions as the arrow heads suggest, the thin arrow denotes mere copying. Not displayed are recurrent within-area connections in each of the coordinate transform areas (bold outlines). Light green arrow colour denotes associative learning while dark red denotes error-driven or actor-critic reinforcement learning of connections which is associated with the basal ganglia.

Apart from the coordinate transform network, the model including the visual and motor systems has been presented before [18]. There it docks the robot to the target object which must be relatively close, since the camera is fixed facing downward. While there the visual "where" representation was directly fed into the "state" area (cf. Fig. 6), now the body-centred "where" representation feeds into the "state" area instead. This body-centred "where" area codes along one axis for the body-centred target object angle θ (cf. Fig. 1), and along the other axis for the square root $\sqrt{d}$ of the distance between the robot and the object (the square root function expands close ranges where higher precision is needed). Fig. 5 c) shows the errors produced by the coordinate transform network. Not all of the area received any data when the robot was moved to randomised positions, as the background shading shows. Large errors along the axis of the angle θ at small distances d can be explained by the training data: similar visual inputs h, v and pan-tilt values p, t were sometimes paired with largely differing, contradicting values of d, θ. This is a consequence of a "singularity" at the origin, where changing θ does not result in a change of other values, imprecise object localisation and robot movement and sensor latencies.

The state space area then contains an additional third dimension coding for the robot rotation angle φ. The robot needs this information to avoid crashing into the table with its wide shoulders when approaching from the side. Demonstration videos of the system controlling the simulated PeopleBot robot can be seen at: http://www.his.sunderland.ac.uk/supplements/AI05/

Next, we will implement this demonstration on the real PeopleBot robot.

6 Discussion

We have presented a network that can perform dynamic coordinate transformations on test data and in a practical scenario based on the principle of pattern completion of an auto-associator attractor network. The network transforms a hill of neural activation, but not a general pattern, because during training such a hill of activation was always given to the output area. Thereby the weights have been trained to produce the competition that allows just one hill to emerge on each area. This would be a limitation in e.g. the lower visual system where this transformation would remove all except the positional information. However, we conceive the network to reside in a higher level of the dorsal "where" stream in the PPC, which is known to abstract from information that is processed in the lateral "what" stream.

As the network will produce a refined output, even if the input is more scattered, we observe an effect similar to attention, which is also attributed to the PPC [7]. This allows the system to handle noisy input data as the emerging activation hill removes the noise, leading to robustness of the network. It should be noted that while such a network architecture allows just one hill of activation for *rate* coded neurons, it would allow more than one hill if these were separated in another dimension such as the *phase* of spiking neurons (e.g. [13]).

There is a restriction on the range over which our network can make a transformation. As we have seen in Fig. 4, location estimates of $\boldsymbol{x}^{vis}$ and $\boldsymbol{x}^{head}$ are added to obtain an estimate of $\boldsymbol{x}^{body}$. It is important that each of the two inputs must convey information about and provide a bias for the location of the target. If for example the head position was irrelevant to the target position, then the visual estimate which *per se* permits many body-centred positions could not be narrowed down any further. This does not imply that the target object is altered by the head position, but it means that only such a target may be chosen which is within the visual field. This is a realistic assumption accounting for all cases in which an agent's hand is visually guided to an object.

Extensions of existing networks have been made to achieve object-centred representations with a basis function network [6] or to transform another's frame of references into a self-centred frame of reference with a gain field architecture [15] which is necessary to perform imitation. We believe that our simplified architecture without any hidden layer also lends itself to such tasks.

We have so far assumed that each area's input arrives in a topographically arranged way and as a Gaussian-shaped activation hill. A specific question is how to learn these input mappings. The three areas convey different information which implies different, possibly independent mechanisms. *(i)* The topographic mapping of the visual object position is particularly evident in the lower visual system. *(ii)* The eye position is represented in several cortical areas, e.g. V6A, 7a, V3a, LIP, MT, MST, PO and the ventral premotor cortex (PMv) [10]. Many of these areas also respond to e.g. visual stimuli and hand position. Therefore, the development of an eye position map might be guided by other, e.g. visual maps, and might take into account factors such as the activations of the eye muscles. Since the eyes and the head can be moved independently (for most robots and their camera this is not the case), another mapping for the head position, possibly dependent on the muscles and vestibular signals, would be required. Finally, *(iii)* the development of the map of a body centred coordinate system might be controlled by factors such as the joint angles of the arm with which to reach the object or factors such as the duration to reach its position by self-movement. Thus, such a map is motor related and might reside in posterior parietal cortex where neurons in the monkey are also modulated by the direction of hand movement, as well as by visual, eye position and limb position signals [2].

7 Summary

We have developed an artificial neural network capable of performing a dynamic coordinate transformation to generate body centred coordinates based on the visual information and head orientation (pan/tilt of a robot's camera). It differs from static coordinate transformations in that the transformed variable (here, a visual object coordinate) is modulated by another coordinate (the head position) in order to obtain the target variable (the object coordinate relative to the agent's body). The network learns in a biologically plausible way and activations converge rapidly to a focused pattern on the output layer. This removes the need to manually solve and implement any intermediate computational steps of the transformation using a large number of additional units as is the case with other systems. The model advances our understanding of this important class of processes in the brain and helps extending the range of robotic applications.

Acknowledgements This is part of the MirrorBot project supported by a EU, FET-IST programme, grant IST-2001-35282, coordinated by Prof. Wermter.

References

[1] D. Ackley, G. Hinton, and T. Sejnowski. A learning algorithm for Boltzmann machines. *Cognitive Science*, 9:147–69, 1985.

[2] C.A. Buneo, M.R. Jarvis, A.P. Batista, and R.A. Andersen. Direct visuomotor transformations for reaching. *Nature*, 416:632–6, 2002.

[3] Y.E. Cohen and R.A. Andersen. A common reference frame for movement plans in the posterior parietal cortex. *Nature Review Neuroscience*, 3:553–62, 2002.

[4] J.D. Crawford, W.P. Medendorp, and J.J. Marotta. Spatial transformations for eye-hand coordination. *J. Neurophysiol.*, 92:10–9, 2004.

[5] S. Deneve, P.E. Latham, and A. Pouget. Efficient computation and cue integration with noisy population codes. *Nature Neurosci.*, 4(8):826–31, 2001.

[6] S. Deneve and A. Pouget. Basis functions for object-centered representations. *Neuron*, 37:347–59, 2003.

[7] S.R. Friedman-Hill, L.C. Robertson, L.G. Ungerleider, and R. Desimone. Posterior parietal cortex and the filtering of distractors. *PNAS*, 100(7):4263–8, 2003.

[8] Z. Ghahramani, D.M. Wolpert, and M.I. Jordan. Generalization to local remappings of the visuomotor coordinate transformation. *J. Neurosci.*, 16(21):7085–96, 1996.

[9] S. Haykin. *Neural Networks. A Comprehensive Foundation.* MacMillan College Publishing Company, 1994.

[10] K. Nakamura, H.H. Chung, M.S.A. Graziano, and C.G. Gross. Dynamic representation of eye position in the parieto-occipital sulcus. *J. Neurophysiol.*, 81:2374–85, 1999.

[11] L. Natale, G. Metta, and G. Sandini. A developmental approach to grasping. In *Developmental Robotics AAAI Spring Symposium*, 2005.

[12] R.C. O'Reilly. Biologically plausible error-driven learning using local activation differences: The generalized recirculation algorithm. *Neur. Comp.*, 8:895–938, 1996.

[13] A. Raffone and C. van Leeuwen. Dynamic synchronization and chaos in an associative neural network with multiple active memories. *Chaos*, 13:1090–104, 2003.

[14] E. Sauser and A. Billard. Three dimensional frames of references transformations using recurrent populations of neurons. *Neurocomputing*, 64:5–24, 2005.

[15] E. Sauser and A. Billard. View sensitive cells as a neural basis for the representation of others in a self-centered frame of reference. In *Proceedings of the Third International Symposium on Imitation in Animals and Artifacts, Hatfield, UK.*, 2005.

[16] T. Doi. Sony vice president. www.sony.net/sonyinfo/qrio/interview , 2004.

[17] A. van Rossum and A. Renart. Computation with populations codes in layered networks of integrate-and-fire neurons. *Neurocomputing*, 58-60:265–70, 2004.

[18] C. Weber, S. Wermter, and A. Zochios. Robot docking with neural vision and reinforcement. *Knowledge-Based Systems*, 17(2-4):165–72, 2004.

An Application of Artificial Intelligence to the Implementation of Virtual Automobile Manufacturing Enterprise

A K Srivastava
School of Technology and Computer Science
Tata Institute of Fundamental Research
Homi Bhabha Road, Mumbai 400 005, INDIA
anoop@tcs.tifr.res.in
www.tcs.tifr.res.in/ãnoop

Abstract

In this paper, we present an application of Artificial Intelligence to the implementation of Virtual Automobile Manufacturing Enterprise. We provide a multi autonomous agent based framework. Our agent based architecture leads to flexible design of a spectrum of virtual enterprises by distributing computation and by providing a unified interface to data and programs. Autonomous agents are intelligent enough and provide autonomy, simplicity of communication, computation, and a well developed semantics. The steps of design and implementation are discussed in depth, in particular an ontology, the agent model, and interaction pattern between agents are given. We have developed mechanisms for coordination between agents using a language, which we call Virtual Enterprise Modeling Language (VEML). VEML is a dialect of Java and includes Knowledge Query and Manipulation Language (KQML) primitives. We have implemented a multi autonomous agent based system, which we call VE System. VE System provides application programmers with potential to globally develop different kinds of VEs based on their requirements and applications. We provide case study of automobile manufacturing enterprise and demonstrate efficacy of our system by discussing its salient features.

1 Introduction

Manufacturing enterprises are now global businesses covering multiple sites around the world and consist of a number of shop floors, service providers and suppliers of materials and components. With advances taking place in information, transportation, networking and communication technology, companies/factories are being organized as a network of units, each unit corresponding to a well defined objective in a classical set up such as production plant, storage plant, transportation hub, customer relation etc. without the necessity of either locating all the units at the same physical location of the plant or owning all the units by the management of the primary plant establishment. This leads to the description of an *Extended Enterprise* where all resources such as stock, space and production capacity of all the enterprises are added together. Such a real-life model has come to be referred to as *Virtual Enterprises* [1]. A Virtual Enterprise (VE) is an enterprise which has no resource of its own but consists of shared and coordinated activities which utilizes the resources of participating enterprises.

Establishments based on such a model have proven cost-effective and have reduced the overheads on establishments to a significant level. Successful operational VEs can be seen in manufacturing/service industries dealing with *Semiconductors, Microelectronics, Electronic Commerce* and a variety of *Demand-Supply Chains.* Needless to emphasize that in VEs, it is essential to have an effective analysis of the demand-supply chains and the effect of demand/supply fluctuations on various raw materials and products. Information technology with increased power of processors, decrease in the cost of memory, evolution and acceptance of the Internet and its rapid growth, the World Wide Web, multimedia and virtual reality technologies have a direct impact on manufacturing. IT has played a very important role in supply chains, modeling of supply chains and reengineering supply chains.

The Virtual Enterprise [1] presents many challenges and opportunities for *Artificial Intelligence* (AI) technology. Adding together the resources of all the participating enterprises of VE stresses technology for information retrieval, networking, communication, coordination, decision making and so on. Satisfying diverse user needs calls for advanced interfaces, user modeling and other emerging techniques. Between users and VE is a gulf filled with a large and evolving network of services that must be selectively arranged to accomplish a particular task.

We argue that a fundamental role for AI in Virtual Enterprise is to perform the underlying monitoring, management, and allocation of services and resources that bring together users and information. While user interfaces and retrieval technologies are important, it is obvious that such technologies will undergo ongoing and dramatic change, which in turn can lead to the restructuring of "how things are done" in VE. In a very real sense, therefore, the underlying architecture of VE must continually search through a growing, shifting, and complex space of content and capabilities for combinations that best serve needs arising at a given moment.

For this reason we view the critical role of AI in Virtual Enterprise as providing an infrastructure that accommodates extreme heterogeneity of content and function, and support continual extension and evolution. This means that:

- Specialized information processing functions must combine flexibly.
- Combinations of functional units and resources to be deployed for any particular task must be the dynamic choices of the system based upon continually changing factors in Virtual Enterprise.
- The capabilities and requirements of any functional unit must be explicitly described, in order for the system or these units themselves to evaluate their applicability and suitability of combinations.

This paper aims to satisfy these criteria with an architecture based on distributed software agents. The agents in this system represent specialized information-processing functions, with additional abilities to reason about their effectiveness and requirements, communicate with other agents, negotiate about terms and resources, and perform other generic agent functions. We call them autonomous agents because we assign these modules autonomy of action (they choose what services to perform for whom with what resources under what terms), under the general constraints imposed by their situations and their relations with other agents [12]. Typical Virtual Enterprise tasks require teaming among numerous specialized agents.

Our description so far has been generic, because the scope of what constitutes an "information processing task" relevant to the Virtual Enterprise is broad. To make our conception more concrete, the types of agents that we have built for Virtual Automobile Manufacturing Enterprise include:

- **User interface agents:** To manage the presentation of information and input from the user.
- **Information service provider agents:** To perform specific services such as search on databases.
- **Facilitator agents:** To support the location of relevant agents and mediation among them.

To realize this vision, it is shown how a software agent oriented specification leads to achieving the above objectives and a flexible design of VEs. Such a specification leads to the design of distributed software agents. First, the notion of VE is given through formalization of an enterprise and a collection of enterprises [21]. Next, under the structure of VE, it is shown how specification leads to a spectrum of VEs [19]. To demonstrate the viability of the proposed coordination schemes, a programming language is designed and developed, which is called Virtual Enterprise Modeling Language (VEML) and it's run-time architecture to construct the descriptions mutually understood by VE agents. Knowledge Query and Manipulation Language (KQML) [2,3,4,5,6,7] which is based on speech act categories for describing protocols and agent communication strategies is used. In particular, we have been able to identify a number of speech acts (and appropriate semantics) that cover a broad range of information services. In addition, we have used speech acts to cover negotiat ion: the process by which a set of agents come to terms on provision of information services and allocation of resources to the various service activities. The Autonomous Agent Based Virtual Enterprise System which is called VE System has been implemented in Java [20]. The VE System provides application programmers with potential to globally develop different kinds of VEs based on their requirements and applications. The ultimate goal of VE System is to effectively turn the various participating enterprises into a unified, dependable, secure and distributed computing infrastructure of VE.

This paper is organized as follows. Section 2 deals with design. Section 3 describes the implementation. Section 4 discusses salient features. Section 5 presents conclusion and future work.

2 Design

The design of virtual enterprise is done considering a case study of automobile manufacturing enterprise. The ontology, agent model, interaction pattern between agents, and VEML design is provided.

2.1 Ontology

VIRTUAL ENTERPRISE: is a set of inter-related UNITS that are totally or partially committed to some common *PURPOSE.*
UNIT: is an entity for *MANAGING* the *ACTIVITIES* to *ACHIEVE* one or more *PURPOSES.* An UNIT may be a manufacturing/processing plant, a subcontractor, a transport provider, a supplier or a warehouse.
CAPACITY: is a quantity (in a given measure unit) that is available for allocation to *ACTIVITIES* over time. The CAPACITY of a RESOURCE contains the number of *ACTIVITIES* that it can simultaneously support.
RESOURCE: is an *ENTITY* with some amount of CAPACITY that is allocable to *ACTIVITIES* over time.
ORDER: is a set of REQUESTS; it is the way a CUSTOMER expresses his requirements in terms of PRODUCTS and delivery conditions. An ORDER can be in one of the following states: under negotiation, confirmed, planned, being executed, completed.
REQUEST: is a statement defining a CUSTOMER's needs, in terms of PRODUCT, quantity, DUE DATE.
PRODUCT: is the final result of a manufacturing *ACTIVITIES* chain. A manufacturing enterprise PURPOSE is to make PRODUCTS.
ENQUIRY: is a process of a CUSTOMER asking for information about PRODUCTS, prices and DUE DATES. This process eventually leads to placing an ORDER.
QUOTATION: is a statement of price, description of PRODUCTS, DUE DATES, and other terms of sale, offered by a supplier to a prospective CUSTOMER.
DUE DATE: is the date when PRODUCTS are due to be available for delivery.
PLANNING: is an *ACTIVITY* whose intended *PURPOSE* is to produce a *PLAN.*
PRODUCTION PLAN: is an *ACTIVITY SPECIFICATION* with an intended *PURPOSE.* A PRODUCTION PLAN produces an assignment of *ACTIVITIES* to UNITS and *TIME INTERVALS.*
ROUGH PRODUCTION PLAN: is a PRODUCTION PLAN based on aggregate information and setting *TIME INTERVALS* for production in the

UNITS considered to be feasible candidates.
FINE PRODUCTION PLAN: is a PRODUCTION PLAN based on more detailed information, and setting *CALENDER DATES* for production in specific UNITS.
ACTIVITY: something done over a particular *TIME INTERVAL.*
SPECIFICATION: is a set of *CONSTRAINTS.*
CONSTRAINTS: is a *RELATIONSHIP* expressing an assertion that can be evaluated with respect to a given *PLAN* as something that may hold and can be elaborated in some language.

2.2 Agent Model

The agent model of virtual automobile manufacturing enterprise proposed by us is shown in fig. 1.

1. **End User Application Customer (EUAC)**: a) Enquire about the product e.g. availability of the product, b) Due date i.e. delivery period of the product, c) Price (negotiation may be done by the customer), d) Requirements of the customer also should be incorporated i.e. modifications may be asked by the customer.
2. **Order Acquisition Agent (OAA)**: a) Acquiring orders from customer. This agent is responsible for following actions: (i) Credit Checking: The suitability of dealing with the customer is checked using standard database or using the historical records within the company, (ii) Order suitability: Whether the customer order can be serviced at all given the capacity available, alliance that the company has embarked on etc. b) Negotiation with the customers about price, due date etc., c) Handling customer requests for modifying or canceling respective orders, d) Querying with RMA regarding product.

This agent captures the order information directly from customers and communicates these orders to the RMA. When a customer order is changed, it is communicated to RMA. When plans violate constraints imposed by the customer (such as due date violation), the order acquisition agent participates in negotiating with the customer.
3. **Resource Management Agent (RMA)**: a) Maintaining inventory control of raw-materials, sub-assemblies that come from suppliers or sub-contractors etc. (decision on outsourcing or alliances in supplying these items are taken), b) In-process inventory control.

Resource Management Agent performs the functions of the inventory management and purchasing. It dynamically manages the availability of resources so that the schedule can be executed. It estimates resource demand and determines resource order quantities. It is responsible for selecting suppliers that minimizes costs and maximizes delivery. It generates EDI purchase requests and monitors their fulfillment. The inputs to the resource agent are the schedule from the scheduler, the availability or unavailability of resources from suppliers, the arrival of resources from the factory floor and the consumption of resources from the dispatcher. The outputs of the resource agent include the arrival of

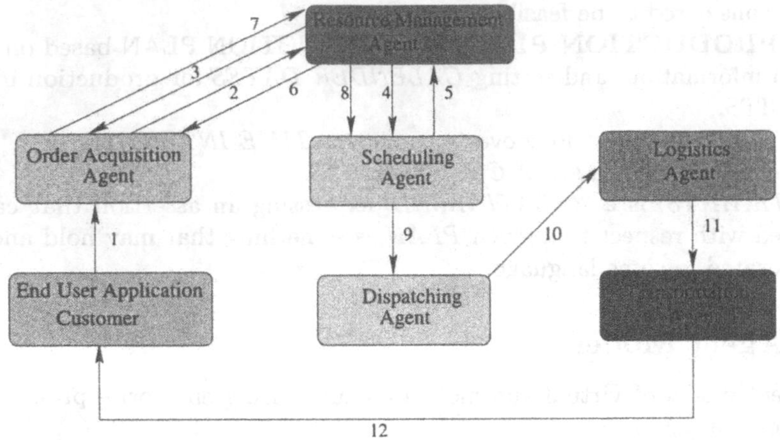

Figure 1: Communication Pattern Between Agents

the resources, the availability of the resources and the orders sent to the suppliers. The resource agent generates purchase orders and monitors the delivery of resources. When resources do not arrive as expected, it assists the scheduler in exploring the alternatives to the schedule by generating alternative resource plans.

4. **Scheduling Agent (SA)**: a) Scheduling and rescheduling activities in the factory exploring hypothetical what-if scenario's for potential new orders and generating schedules that are sent to the dispatching agent for execution.

The inputs to the scheduling agent are the production requests from the logistics agent, resource problems from the resource agent, and the deviations from the current schedule from the dispatching agent. Its output is a detailed schedule. The scheduling agent assigns resources and start times to activities that are feasible while at the same time optimizing certain criteria such as minimizing WIP or tardiness. It can generate a schedule from scratch or repair an existing schedule that has violated some constraints. In anticipation of domain uncertainties such as machine breakdowns, material unavailability, etc., the agent may reduce the precision of a schedule by increasing the degrees of freedom in the schedule for the dispatcher to work with. For example, it may temporarily pad a schedule by increasing an activity's duration, or resource pad an operation by either providing a choice of more than one resource or increasing the capacity required so that more is available. The scheduling agent also acts as a coordinator when infeasible situations arise. It has the capability to explore tradeoffs among the various constraints and goals that exist in the plant.

5. **Dispatching Agent (DA)**: a) Inventory control of the finished goods that come from factory, b) Scheduling or routing the warehouse material handling equipments.

This agent performs the order release and real time floor control functions as directed by the scheduling agent. It operates autonomously as long as the factory performs within the constraints specified by the scheduling agent. When deviation from schedule occur, the dispatching agent communicates them to the scheduling agent for repair. The inputs to the dispatching agent are the schedule from the scheduling agent, the status of the factory floor and the availability of the resources. The outputs are the deviations from the current schedule and the starting of the activities. Given degrees of freedom in the schedule, the dispatcher makes decisions as to what to do next. In deciding what to do next, the dispatcher must balance the cost of performing the activities, the amount of time in performing the activities, and the uncertainty of the factory floor. For example: (i) Given that the scheduler specified a time interval for the start time of a task, the dispatcher has the option of either starting the task as soon as possible, or starting the task as late as possible, (ii) Given that the scheduler did not specify a particular machine for performing the task the dispatcher may use the most cost effective machine (minimize costs) or use the fastest machine (minimize processing time).

6. **Transportation Agent (TA)**: a) Deciding on the mode of shipping depending upon the order's capability (also decides on the alliance in shipping if possible), b) Arranging transportation to retailer/customer, as the case may be, c) Scheduling the fleet of the vehicles, d) Tracking the vehicles.

This agent is responsible for the assignment and scheduling of transportation resources in order to satisfy inter-plant movement requests specified by the Logistics Agent. It will be able to consider a variety of transportation assets and transportation routes in the construction of its schedules.

7. **Logistics Agent (LA)**: a) To co-ordinate multiple plants, multiple suppliers and multiple distribution center domain of the enterprise to achieve the best possible results in terms of the goals of the supply chain, which include on time delivery, cost minimization, etc., b) It manages the movement of products or materials across the supply chain from the supplier of raw materials to the customer of finished goods.

2.3 Communication Pattern Between Agents

The Virtual Enterprise is a set of independent and asynchronous entities that interact with each other through message passing. To illustrate the distributed nature of an enterprise, consider the supply chain function of a virtual enterprise. The supply chain functions span the operations of an enterprise from order entry, through production planning and distribution. The supply chain consists of several agents such as an order acquisition agent, resource management agent, scheduling agent, transportation agent, logistics agent and dispatching agent. When an order is 'generated' by customer (1), the OA agent asks the RMA if the order can be met? (2). The RMA decides whether or not the order is satisfied from inventory, production or both. If production is needed, the RMA asks SA if it is possible to schedule the activities needed to satisfy the outstanding order, (4). If SA decides that it can schedule these activities, it notifies the RMA that we can fit the activity in our current schedule,

Source	Destination	message #	message content	Performative
EUAC	OAA	1	query/ incoming order from customer	ask-one
OAA	RMA	2	can we meet the order ?	ask-one
RMA	OAA	3	yes, we can	reply
RMA	SA	4	can we schedule and meet order requirement?	ask-one
SA	RMA	5	yes we can / no, we can not	reply
RMA	OAA	6	yes we can / no, we can not	reply
OAA	RMA	7	order accepted	broadcast
RMA	SA	8	confirm request	tell
RMA	SA	9	production is complete and send for dispatching	achieve
SA	DA	10	tell logistics agent for dispatching	tell
LA	TA	11	tell transportation agent for vehicles	tell
TA	EUAC	12	transportation agent sends the product to customer	tell

Figure 2: Interaction summary between EUAC, OAA, RMA, SA, DA, LA and TA

(5). The RMA tells the OAA that we can meet the order, (6). If the stock is available, the RMA tells the OAA to accept the order otherwise, (3). The OAA then confirms the customer order and tells the RMA, (7). The RMA tells the SA that order is accepted, (8). The SA informs the DA after completing the production, (9). The DA informs the LA for dispatching, (10). The logistics agent tells the transportation agent regarding transportation, (11). The transportation agent then arranges for transportation to the customer, (12).

The interaction is shown in fig. 1 and fig. 2.

2.4 Virtual Enterprise Modeling Language (VEML)

VEML is a dialect of the Java programming language directly enabling software agent oriented programming and development of VE. VEML includes KQML primitives. KQML is a language and an associated protocol to support the high level communication between autonomous agents. KQML is an abstraction, a collection of primitives plus the assumption of a simple model for inter-agent communication. There is no such thing as an implementation of KQML in the sense that KQML is not a compiled language. VEML is a compiled language. The VEML grammar includes Java grammar with additional keywords and statements.

VEML is a tool to build software applications that dynamically interact and communicate with their immediate environment (user, local resources and computer system) and/or the world, in an autonomous (or semi-autonomous), task oriented fashion. VEML simplifies programming on the Internet by providing synchronous and asynchronous communication among agents with the help of message passing. Universal naming is possible in VEML. VEML supports communication among multiple inter generating computations/nodes. It is a language for programs to use to communicate attitudes about information, such as querying, stating, achieving, believing, requiring, subscribing and offering. The complete grammar, syntax and semantics of VEML is given in chapter 3 of the thesis of A K Srivastava. [1]

2.4.1 Methods For Coordination Between Agents

Since all agent communication is via synchronous and asynchronous message passing, there is a need to have the methods for coordination purpose.

msg.send()

The send method is used by the sender agent to send message to the receiver agent. The address of the receiver agent is specified in the message. This method sends a message to the receiver agent and does not expect a reply.

msg.setReplyWith()

The setReplyWith method is used by the sender agent to send a message to the receiver agent and indicates to the receiver that the sending agent expects a reply. The receiver agent need not to give the reply. (Note: to receive the expected reply, the receiving agent must register a handler. This mode of operation is termed as "*asynchronous*" send).

msg.sendAndAwaitReply(String performative, String contents, String receiver)

The sendAndAwaitReply method is used by the sender agent to send the message to the receiver agent and wait for reply. This method performs a "*synchronous*" send as opposed to an "*asynchronous*" send.

sendMsgAndAwaitReply()

The sendMsgAndAwaitReply method creates, sends and receives a message in one call.

getSender()

The getSender method is used to get the sender agent's name.

getPerformative()

The getPerformative method is used to get the performative used for sending message.

getContents()

The getContents method is used to get the contents of the message sent.

getReceiver()

The getReceiver method is used to get the receiver agent's name.

registerHandler(String performative, Handler handler)

The registerHandler method is used to register the handler (e.g. ask-one, reply etc.).

getMessage()

The getMessage method is used to get the message.

[1] http://www.tcs.tifr.res.in/ãnoop

agent.shutdown()
The shutdown method is called by the agent to shutdown itself and the agent will be deregistered from the ANS.
doClient()
doClient method is used by the client agent to send the content of the message to the server agent and wait for the reply.
doServer()
doServer method is used by the server agent to start the server process and receive the content of the message from the client agent.

3 Implementation

To test the validity of what has been described, a VE System is implemented, which demonstrates virtual automobile manufacturing enterprise [18]. The application programs are written in VEML which get preprocessed into Java programs by VEML compiler. Java program uses agent library and get eventually compiled into Java byte code, for execution atop any Java Virtual Machine (JVM).

3.1 Architecture

Figure 3. shows the architecture of VE System, which comprises the following components: (a) Front-end: a GUI handles all of the user interactions. The front end is implemented in VEML. Front end is a screen shot of VE showing the form, which user has to fill for different purposes. The user has to place the order in the format provided in the form. (b) Back-end: a virtual enterprise engine where the agents actually "live" and interact with one another. The back end is implemented in VEML and KQML. The back-end implements a request response service: a client sends a request to the back-end, the back-end services that request. The front-end and back-end communicates with one other via TCP/IP sockets.

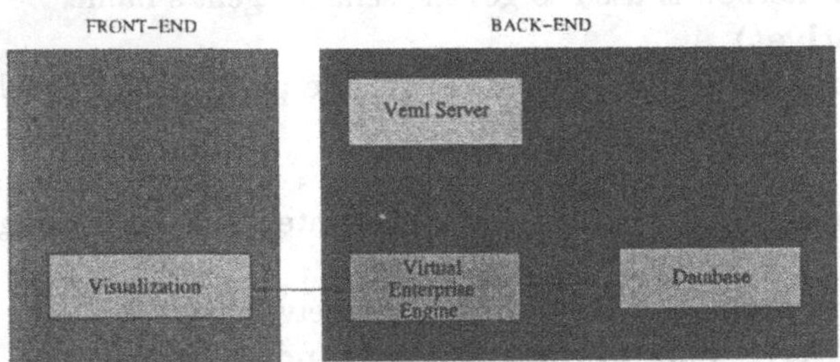

Figure 3. Architecture of Virtual Enterprise System

4 Salient Features

The salient features of VE System are as follows:

4.1 Scheduling Agent

The scheduling agent uses the software engineering technique of PERT/CPM to manage the tasks in its assembly line. The RMA gives the SA a list of ready made products.

4.2 Resource Management Agent

The resource management agent maintains a negotiation algorithm that it uses to compute the price of any product for which a request comes up. The RMA maintains a database which consists of ready made products and its respective quantities. The database also consists of the list of spare parts / raw materials required and their quantities.

4.3 Naming, Security, and Direct Connection

Agents can have any number of logical names that don't contain the hostname. There is no way for an agent to "overhear" a conversation between two other agents. This provides security. Agents can establish direct connections with each other for bulk data transfer.

4.4 Agent Creation and Run

Each agent runs within an individual Java thread. Each agent gets registered with the VE facilitator. The facilitator maintains registry of all agents. Since agents are Java threads, which are light weight processes, a large number of threads can be created. There is no limitation on the number of agents.

4.5 Third Party Creation of Agents

We have used protocols and semantics for defining more extensible agent communications. "This protocol is open to allow third-party agents (with their own unique strategies) to participate in the agent coordination". We envision developers creating sophisticated commerce agents that require a non-trivial amount of resources to complete it's market analysis. Such agents could potentially be run more efficiently on a user's local machine and communicate/negotiate with other agents via open protocol. Agents can be developed in any language e.g. C, Lisp, Prolog, Java and VEML. This system supports protocol like TCP/IP, SMTP, and FTP.

4.6 Routers

The router in this system provides an easy-to-use link between application and network viz. (1) Routers are a content independent message routers, (2) All routers are identical, just an executing copy of the same program, (3) A router handles all messages going to and from it's associated agent i.e. each agent has it's own separate router process. Thus it is not necessary to make extensive changes in the program's internal organisation to allow it to asynchronously receive messages from a variety of independent sources, (4) The router provides this service for the agent and provides the agent with a single contact point for the communication with the rest of the network, (5) It provides both client and server functions for the application and can manage multiple simultaneous connections with other agents, (6) Routers relies solely on its performatives and arguments, (7) A router directs a message to a particular Internet address as specified by the message, (8) When an application exits, the router sends another message to the facilitator, removing the application from the Facilitator's database, and (9) Routers can be implemented with varying degree of sophistication although they can guarantee to deliver all messages.

4.7 Facilitator

The facilitator agent of this system performs following useful services: (1) Maintain a registry of service names, (2) Forward message to named services, (3) Routes messages based on the content, (4) Provides matchmaking between information providers and clients, (5) Provides mediation and translation services, (6) This is a simple software agent which maintains the database of active agents, (7) This provides the registry of agent names and addresses, (8) It is used by all the agents as they arise to register their names and addresses and to subsequently locate other agents to which messages are to be sent, and (9) It accepts register and unregister performatives to maintain it's database and responds to ask-one and ask-all etc.

4.8 Scalability

When an agent is created, it acquires a Java thread. So, depending on the number of agents created, it acquires that many number of threads. These threads are software programs. Each thread defines a separate path for execution. Multi tasking threads require less overhead than multi tasking processes. Processes are heavyweight tasks that require their own separate address spaces. Interprocess communication is expensive and limited. Context switching from one process to another is also costly. Threads on the other hand are lightweight. They share the same address space and cooperatively they share the same heavyweight process. Interthread communication is inexpensive and context switching from one thread to the next is low cost.

Multi threading enables to write a very efficient programs that make maximum use of the CPU because idle time can be kept to a minimum. Java manages threads and makes multi threading especially more convenient, because many of the details are handled by the programmer. Hence the issue in this case is not the processes occupied by agents in the operating system rather it is the memory. Each agent or thread consumes memory from the operating system. So a large number of agents will have large memory requirement.

4.9 Performance and Efficiency

The system performance guarantees to agents so that the agents can meet real time constraints. The parameters of argument are time to complete the process, cost factor, bandwidth requirement and transfer of code. This system is a single unified framework with message passing in which wide range of distributed applications can be implemented efficiently and easily. This system uses a network service by remotely invoking its operations. The results are transmitted back over the network to the sending agent which processes them depending on the result. The service and client platforms have to provide an infrastructure to support agents. Messages can be transmitted from one agent of a machine to the other agent on the same machine or the other machine in a heterogeneous network. The station based agents system helps to reduce communication costs, bandwidth requirements, and improves performance by becoming more efficient. This consumes less memory. In a complex large system like automobile manufacturing enterprise the impact is much more with respect to time.

5 Conclusion and Future Work

This paper presents an application of AI to the implementation of virtual enterprise which is a multi autonomous agent based system. We have considered automobile manufacturing enterprise as an example scenario and have provided an ontology, agent model, and interaction pattern between agents. We have developed an agent oriented virtual enterprise modeling language and have provided the methods used for working of the agents. Finally, the architecture and salient features of VE system are provided. Here our focus is in supporting the best communication, co-ordination and problem solving mechanism available with minimum programming effort on the developer's side. Hence this architecture can be directly applied in practice. As all the facts surrounding software agents recommends, Virtual Enterprises are just one area for a new generation of automated information services. AI has a large role to play in improving the generality, robustness and overall competence of these services. We believe that the field of AI has an equally important role to play in architectural infrastructure (in concert with other technologies, of course). In a Virtual Enterprise, our typical problem is an abundance of available information and information services. Efficiently bringing together the right agents with the right resources for the right tasks is the measure of the VE's effectiveness.

Our future work is interfacing of VEML with web and CORBA and give a VEML-CORBA based architecture for autonomous agents communication in cooperative service and network management. The agents themselves are completely autonomous. Machine Learning techniques need to be applied in more effective manner to make the agents tremendously smart.

References

[1] C. Makatsoris and C. B. Beasnt. Semiconductor Virtual Enterprises: Requirements and Solution Proposals. In Anton JEZERNIK and Bojan DOLSAK, editors, Proceedings of DMMI'97, Porloroz, Slovenia, 3-9 September, 1997.

[2] Tim Finin, Don McKay, and Rich Fritzson. An Overview of KQML: A Knowledge Query and Manipulation Language. Technical report, Department of Computer Science, University of Maryland, Baltimore County, March 1992.

[3] Lockheed Martin C^2 Integration Systems, 590, Lancaster Ave., Frazer, PA 19355-1808. *Software User's Manual for KQML*, August 1997.

[4] Software Design Document for KQML. Technical report, Unisys Corporation, 70 East Swedesford Road, Paoli, PA 19301, March 1995.

[5] James Mayfield, Yannis Labrou, and Tim Finin. Desiderata for Agent Communication Language. In *proceedings of the 1995 AAAI Spring Symposium on Information Gathering in Distributed Environments*, March 1995.

[6] Tim Finin, Rich Fritzson, Don McKay, and Robin McEntire. KQML-An Information and Knowledge Exchange Protocol. In *Knowledge Building and Knowledge Sharing*. Ohmsa and IOS Press, 1994.

[7] Jeffrey M. Bradshaw. An Introduction to Software Agents. In J M Bradshaw, editor, *Software Agents*. MIT Press, 1996.

[8] M. Shaw, R. Blanning, T. Strader, and A. Whinston, editors. *Handbook on Electronic Commerce*, chapter1. Springer Verlag, 2000.

[9] A K Srivastava, Simulation of a Multi Intelligent Agent Based System, Proceedings of 8th International Conference on Computer Modelling and Simulation UKSim 2005, April 2005,St. John's College, Oxford, UK.

[10] A K Srivastava and R K Shyamasundar, Towards a System for Designing Virtual Enterprises, Proceedings of 14^{th}International Conference on CARFOF '98", December 1998,Coimbatore.

[11] A K Srivastava, Intelligent Agent Based Virtual Enterprise System, Poster proceedings of AI 2004, Queens' College, Cambridge University, U.K. 13-15 Dec.2004.

[12] A K Srivastava and R K Shyamasundar, Application of Software Agents Based Framework Methodology to the Control of Virtual Enterprises, Proceedings of 1^{st}IMS, Selladurai, February, 1998, Coimbatore.

SESSION 5:

MEDICAL APPLICATIONS

Web-based Medical Teaching using a Multi-Agent System

Victor Alves, José Neves, Luís Nelas*, Filipe Marreiros**
Universidade do Minho
{valves,jneves}@di.uminho.pt
*Radiconsult S.A.
luis.nelas@radiconsult.com
**Centro de Computação Gráfica
filipe.marreiros@ccg.pt

Abstract

Web-based teaching via Intelligent Tutoring Systems (ITSs) is considered as one of the most successful enterprises in artificial intelligence. Indeed, there is a long list of ITSs that have been tested on humans and have proven to facilitate learning, among which we may find the well-tested and known tutors of algebra, geometry, and computer languages. These ITSs use a variety of computational paradigms, as production systems, Bayesian networks, schema-templates, theorem proving, and explanatory reasoning. The next generation of ITSs are expected to go one step further by adopting not only more intelligent interfaces but will focus on integration. This article will describe some particularities of a tutoring system that we are developing to simulate conversational dialogue in the area of Medicine, that enables the integration of highly heterogeneous sources of information into a coherent knowledge base, either from the tutor's point of view or the development of the discipline in itself, i.e. the system's content is created automatically by the physicians as their daily work goes on. This will encourage students to articulate lengthier answers that exhibit deep reasoning, rather than to deliver straight tips of shallow knowledge. The goal is to take advantage of the normal functioning of the health care units to build on the fly a knowledge base of cases and data for teaching and research purposes.

1. Introduction

Technologies as broadband networks, where hypermedia, virtual reality and artificial intelligence constitute the founding base of the so called e-learning world, are a quaint reality. Information and knowledge systems developed under the form of front-ends supported by Web technology have proliferated. In fact, small farms of e-learning sites in the Internet exist that integrate and distribute information worldwide, namely to physicians, patients or students, just to name a few. They have developed themselves in a way so ubiquitous that they are becoming victims of their own popularity.

Technological problems related to the maintenance of a high number of specific sites directing the stream of information, knowledge and services and serving several users have been well described in the literature [1]. To overcome these drawbacks, work is being done on the consolidation and integration methodologies of multiple small Web sites in an only entity: the so called e-learning holding portal (portal is a new internet word that started to catch up very strongly in the last few years. It refers usually to a main guide that includes a search engine, plus additional content, such as current news or entertainment info, designed to keep someone at the portal for as long as possible). Operational efficiency and cost reduction can be achieved using holding portals throughout information centralization, directing business or educational processes, and linking users for eventual collaboration, going from the e-business, e-procurement, e-health up to e-learning.

The vitality of a holding portal lies in its integration potential, in support of communities of virtual entities and in the gathering, organization and diffusion of information. Any good strategy for the creation of such a system should capitalize in this point. The departments, schools, or entities usually have different architectures, different people in charge, and duplicated information. Thus it would be desirable to join these different states into one (i.e. in terms of a holding).

1.1 Medical Teaching

Today more than ever, learning medicine is a huge challenge. It requires developing a vast range of manual, intellectual, visual and tactile skills as well as taking into account large amounts of factual information. As the result of medical research everyone is faced to a constant impact upon clinical practice. Continued medical education is essential. Traditionally, medical teaching is based on texts, lectures and bedside teaching, with self-guided individual learning from books being the most common. It is believed that traditional medical teaching and individual learning in particular, can be complemented with electronic systems delivered on the Internet/Intranet. Indeed, one of the advantages of electronic systems in teaching is that it opens the road to increase the learner's involvement. The learner can set the pace, choose the content and select the mode of presentation according to the requirement of his/her individual preferences and situations. Awareness of the knowledge constructing process is increased, as well as the satisfaction gained from learning. As an overall result, medical teaching can be more effective and efficient.

1.2 e-Learning

The electronic learning, which will be referred to as e-Learning, can be defined basically as the electronic systems in teaching/learning that are produced through Web technology. Among its components are found distributed contents in multiple formats, learning experience administration, network community of apprentices, content developers and experts. Thus, the term e-Learning refers to the use of Internet technologies to provide an extensive spectrum of solutions that improve knowledge and performance in teaching/learning [2,3].

One of the main impacts of e-Learning in education resides in the fact that it provides opportunities to create resources that turn the learning process flexible. This implies a different relation between teachers and students and even between institutions, in the sense that the students participate on their own formation and the vertical hierarchy tends to become increasingly more horizontal.

1.3 Multi-agent systems

Multi-agent Systems (MAS) may de seen as a new methodology in distributed problem-solving via theorem proving, i.e. agent-based computing has been hailed as a significant break-through in distributed problem solving and/or a new revolution in software development and analysis [21-23]. Indeed, agents are the focus of intense interest on many sub-fields of Computer Science, being used in a wide variety of applications, ranging from small systems to large, open, complex and critical ones [4,5]. Agents are not only a very promising technology, but are emerging as a new way of thinking, a conceptual paradigm for analyzing problems and for designing systems, for dealing with complexity, distribution and interactivity. It may even be seen as a new form of computing and intelligence.

To develop such systems, a standard specification method is required, and it is believed that one of the keywords for its wide acceptance is simplicity [6]. Indeed, the use of intelligent agents to understand students and their knowledge, and to infer the most appropriate strategy of teaching from the interaction with the students offers the potential to set an appropriate software development and analysis practice and design methodology that do not distinguish between agent and human until implementation. Being pushed in this way the design process, the construction of such systems, in which humans and agents can be interchanged, is simplified, i.e. the modification and development in a constructive way, of multiagent based e-learning systems with a human-in-the-loop potential aptitude is becoming central in the process of agent-oriented software development and analysis [1,7].

This model has provided a clear means of monitoring the agent's behaviour with significant impact in their process of knowledge acquisition and validation [8] and will be now applied in the development of intelligent agents that will support the e-learning system.

1.4 Intelligent Tutoring Agents

One of the present approaches in the field linked to electronic systems in medical teaching and Artificial Intelligence (AI), is the design of tutoring agents that supervise the user's actions in a data processing environment to provide aid.

Specifically, tutoring agents are interface agents that cooperate with the users (e.g. students, health professionals) to reach an objective [9,10].

The idea is that computers may be employed to understand students and their state of knowledge, and to infer the most appropriate strategy of tutoring. Nevertheless, several factors delayed the development of the intelligent tutoring agents, namely the scarce knowledge that they have on cognition and human behaviour. These systems will improve following the progress on these areas (e.g. the problem of adapting the environment to the needs of the students [11]).

The complexity problem of intelligent tutoring agents design is due in part to the monolithic architecture in which it is based. An approach to the design of these systems, and others inside the AI field, tries to solve this problem applying a strategy of the type "divide and conquer", which give rise to the so called multi-agent systems or agencies [12]. These types of systems are formed by a series of agents that work like computational entities with complete autonomy and that communicate among themselves to carry out a concrete task.

To incorporate in this architecture a certain degree of user adaptability, enabling personalized learning, intelligent agents should be developed in such a way that each agent adapts itself in function of the system's necessities [13-16]. By **intelligent** we mean that the agent pursues its objectives and executes its tasks so that it optimizes some measure related to its good performance [8,17,18].

2. The Multi-agent System

In this section we describe our efforts and experience designing a MAS for e-learning in the medical arena. At the core of the designed system lays the data warehouse and a large amount of data (e.g. medical images, video, or text). This information is complemented with the knowledge base that defines its structure and classifies and defines the relationships between its parts. The upper level was developed in terms of a multi-agent system that accesses the information and presents it according to the meta-information and the specific task they are designed to do, which could be anything from pure textual referencing to a guided tour through a defined subject matter, to a three-dimensional annotated image reconstruction of an organ system (e.g. the students and health professional's interfaces). It was also developed a set of intermediate agents which will allow us updating and adding to the content database, authoring tools and medical data, and in doing so, will have to assure consistency within the meta-information (e.g., the medical data provider and the necessary teaching resources) (Figure 1). In terms of the internal representation of the information, suitable accepted formats, standards and protocols were used. At this early stage of the project, several options are kept open, but only when medical standards are not available. It was mandatory to have great flexibility in the automated database manipulation process, avoiding the risk of fixation on certain software and/or hardware vendors, enabling the system scaling as the project grows.

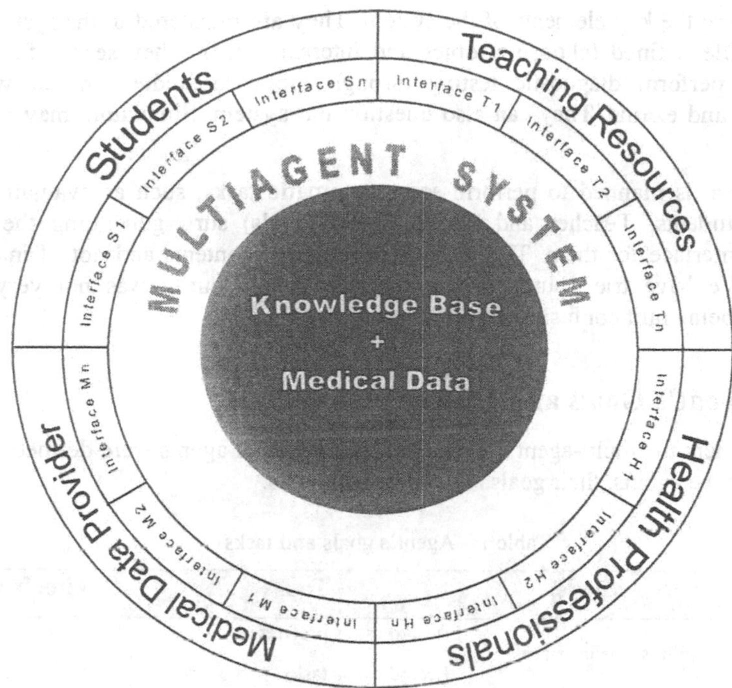

Figure 1 – Software structure layout

2.1 The Multi-Agent System architecture

We now report on the agents we developed, starting with a brief description of the basic type of agents and specifying the way they interact. To pursue this objective they were grouped into four complementary sets corresponding to the Medical Data Provider interfaces, the Health Professionals interfaces, the Teaching Resources interfaces and the Students interfaces (Figure 1).

The Medical Data Provider interfaces provide new medical data from medical equipment, mainly from medical imaging and from Electronic Medical Records (EMR).

The Health Professionals interfaces are used mainly by physicians that supply new medical information (e.g. image classification, case studies) to the system and use the existent information to help in their patient diagnostic task (e.g. look for a collection of cases similar to the patient he is studying).

The Teaching Resources interfaces supply new educational contents. Here they create and update case studies, exercises and contents for the e-learning process. They consult and link their teaching contents to the knowledge base and medical information stored by the system (with patient identity hidden). It should be pointed out that most of the teachers that use these interfaces are physicians in the Hospital that use the Health Professionals Interfaces for their clinical practices.

Students are the key elements of the system. They are registered in the system and their profile defined (choosing topics and interest areas). They search for study material, perform diagnostic testing through the case studies and answer to exercises and exams. They can also question the system. Simulators may also be provided.

The System is planned to perform some automatic tasks, such as evaluating the user's (Students, Teacher and Health Professionals) surf, generating the most suitable interface for them. This is done in terms of contents and not of interface design. We have tried out dynamic interface design but it was not very well accepted being quit confusing for the user.

2.2 Agent's Goals and Tasks

To implement the multi-agent system, six basic types of agents were defined. Table 1 presents the agents, their goals and their main tasks.

Table 1 – Agent's goals and tasks

Agents	Goals	Tasks	Interfaces
Profile Agents	Optimise the interface	Record user's preference Record user's tasks	Students Health Professionals
Evaluator Agents	Evaluate the user interface	Evaluate user's preferences and tasks Suggest interface improvements	
Information Producer Agents	Prepare information for the system (e.g., contents, medical images, case-studies, interfaces)	Add or change contents and systems functionality	
Research Agents	Find information with quality according to the user	Research information on Knowledge Base	Students Teaching Resources Health Professionals
Questions Agents	Reply to user questions	Try to get answers for students' questions. Question teaching resources about new topics Learn to deduct new answers	Students Teaching Resources
Anonymize Agents	Hide patient identification in data	Produce anonymized replica of medical information	Medical Data Provider Health Professionals

2.3 Agents Interaction

We have split the system in five parts. The first four are the main areas and the last one represents the system core.

2.3.1 Medical Data Provider Interfaces

The following scheme describes how Medical Data Provider Interfaces supply information to the system. When Medical Data Provider sends data to the Knowledge Base an Anonymize Agent replicates anonymous data that may be used by the Information Producer Agent to create new contents for educational proposes. The process of information production may involve joining other data that exists in the Knowledge Base. The two agents use a communication method to announce their state through the Black Board (a shared memory) (Figure 2).

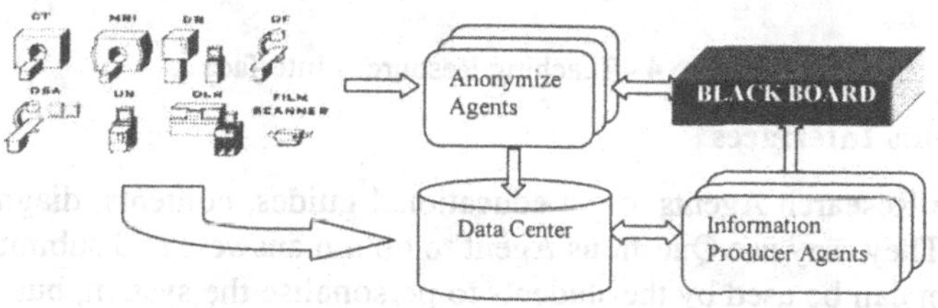

Figure 2 – Medical Data Provider

2.3.2 Health Professionals Interfaces

Health Professionals are other suppliers of information to the system. The system's response is similar to the Medical Data Provider Interfaces. They also need to retrieve information from the system in order to perform better diagnostics. Research Agents are responsible to make available the most suitable information for the health professional (Figure 3).

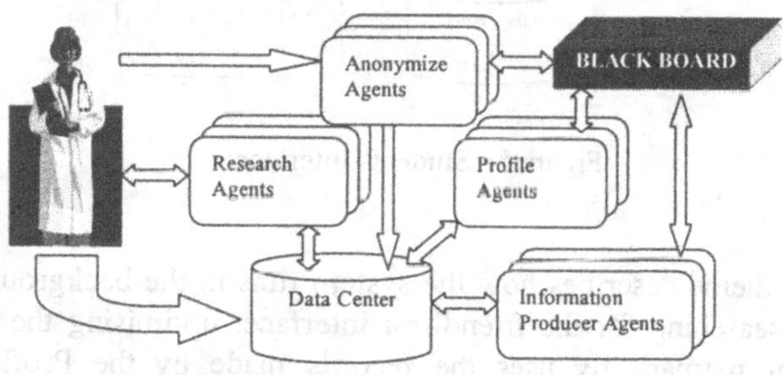

Figure 3 - Health Professional Interface

2.3.3 Teaching Resources Interfaces

Teaching Resources represent essentially teachers that can supply the system with new contents and answer questions made by the students. Teachers use a Research Agent to find relevant information and use them to produce new materials. The Profile Agent is responsible for starting the improvement of the available interface, learning preferences and analysing preferences of each user. The Questions Agent tries to get the best answer for unsolved questions (Figure 4).

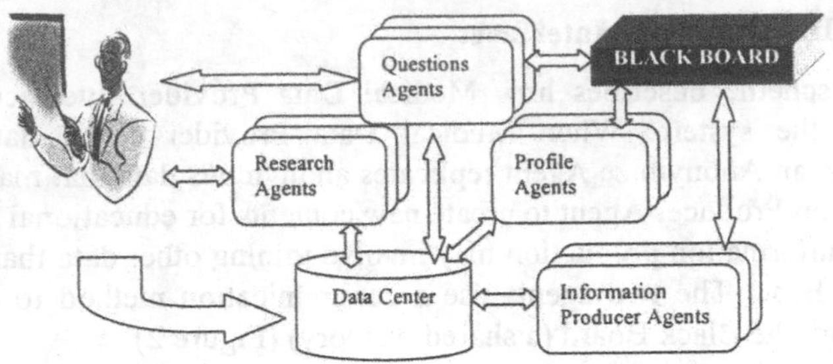

Figure 4 - Teaching Resources Interface

2.3.4 Students Interfaces

Students use Research Agents to get educational guides, contents, diagnostic tests, exams, etc. They may use Questions Agent to obtain answers and submit questions. Profile Agent can be used by the students to personalise the system, but it works all the time trying to deduct what will be the best system configuration for each individual (Figure 5).

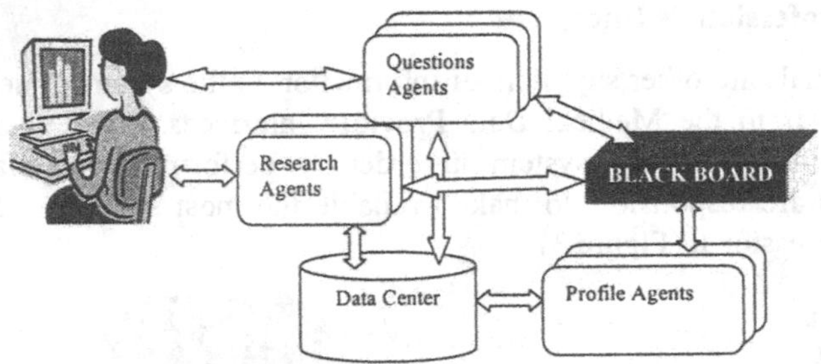

Figure 5 - Students Interface

2.3.5 System

The following scheme describes how the system runs in the background, trying to improve itself, searching for the friendliest interface, optimising the system. The Evaluator Agent permanently uses the records made by the Profile Agent. It suggests to the Information Producer Agent changes to the interface.

Establishing a partnership with the user is crucial for the success of the system, like in the traditional education where the students have quick answers for their challenges (Figure 6).

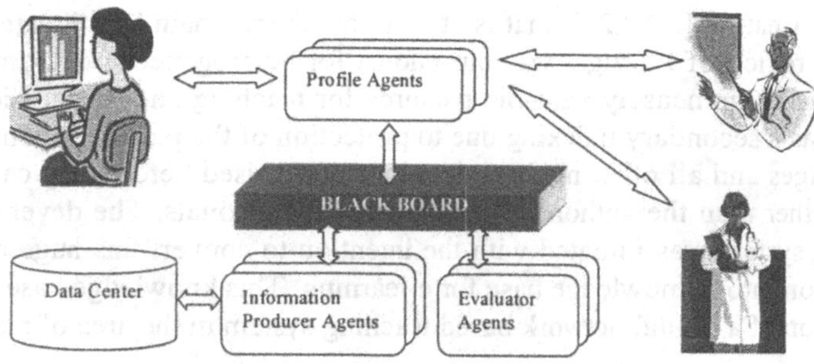

Figure 6 – Multi-agent profile adjustment

3. The Multi-agent System implementation

In order to achieve these benefits, electronic systems in medical teaching must meet well defined requirements. On the infrastructural side, client/server network architecture is required, where a Storage Area Network (SAN) holds the data warehouse, medical data (e.g. medical imaging) and most of the specific software agents that deliver medical content. This approach enables continuous content updates and assessment. The network should allow fast transfers with low latencies to avoid waiting times. Finally, the client computers where the learners work on should be easy to set up and economical. Fortunately, the new academic and Hospital networks currently being built meet these requirements. Thanks to the availability of commodity standards that the internet is founded upon, it will be able to implement the system on widely available, scalable network hardware. On the client side, internet technology will ensure platform independence. This is paramount once it keeps down costs of ownership and allows adapting to the rapidly developing marketplace for computer hardware and system software. In table 2, an overview of the technologies and tools used are presented.

Table 2 – Development technologies/tools used

Technology/tools	Objective
Oracle version 9, Tools: WebDB	Relational Database
Linux	Operating System and Blackboard implementation
PHP for Oracle	Web programming
Apache	Web server
Adobe Acrobat (PDF)	Document format
Java Servelets	Web programming
C (GTK)	Agents' programming
CGI and PERL	Agents' programming
DICOM Services	Storage, Send and Viewer Plug-in

The priority in terms of implementation was to cover the medical imaging field going from data acquisition and storage to physicians, teachers and student's interfaces. The AIDA system, an Agency for Integration, Archive and Diffusion of

Medical Information [5,19,20], that is at work at several main health care facilities in the north region of Portugal was our choice for heterogeneous data integration. These data is an immensely valuable resource for teaching and diagnostic aid. All these data has a secondary indexing due to protection of the patient's identification. Studies, images and all other medical data are anonymised before they can be used by others rather than the authorised health care professionals. The development of our tutoring system was initiated with the intention to convert this huge repository of information into a knowledge base for e-learning. This knowledge base will form the foundation of a digital network based teaching system in the area of medicine.

3.1 Computational Architecture

The system presents itself with critical features like system's failure or system's breakdowns, so that a scalable three layer computational architecture was conceived (Figure 7):

- **Layer I** - Web applications server's layer where the users interface and the system's software will run;
- **Layer II** - Data Base and application server's layer where the medical data acquisition and handling software will run; and
- **Layer III** - Storage server's layer where the data will be archived (e.g., medical images, clinical data, reports, knowledge base).

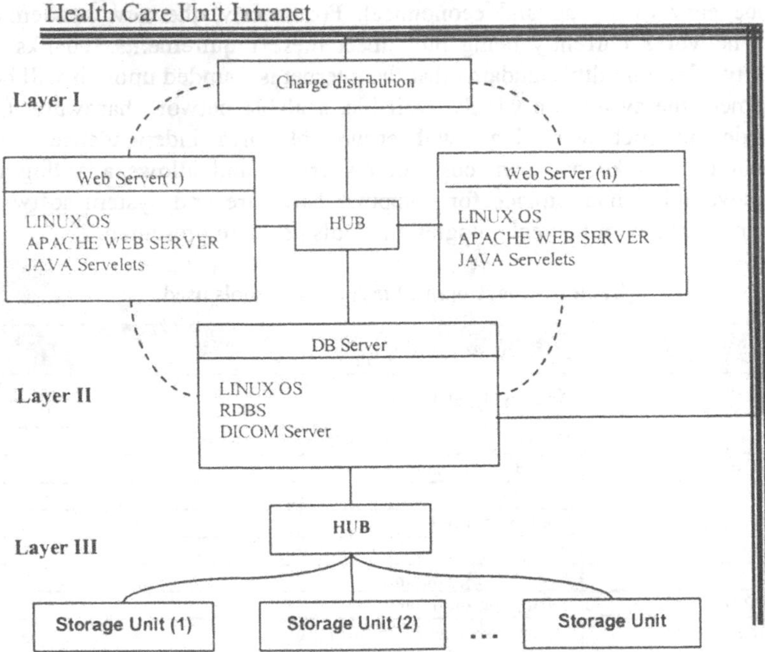

Figure 7 – The three layer computational architecture

3.2 System Building and the Project Team

In this project we had the collaboration of four System Engineers in the programming tasks, a graphic designer for interface designing, four XRay Technicians specialized in the various areas of the medical imaging equipment (Computer Tomography, Digital XRay, Magnetic Resonance and Mamography), three physicians (a Neuroradiologist and two radiologists) and some support from the equipment manufacturers field engineers (*CIT – Centro de Imagiologia da Trindade* (medical imaging company) is a Hitachi Reference Site, in particular to the CT systems).

The system was tested and is being partially used at *Hospital da Ordem da Trindade* (Hospital) and is currently under assessment and in the implementation phase at *ISCS-N Instituto Superior de Ciências de Saúde do Norte* (University).

Despite the system was previously thought for a particular use in the University's medical e-learning field, the sub-systems that implement partial functionalities ended up being desired by the institutions involved. Some are currently in use in some health care Units as well as diagnostic centres.

As the size of the project and its responsibility grew, it meant that we had to do some backup to our supporting of the systems and have currently the development team monitoring and supporting it, receiving feed back and developing new interfaces for new arising situations (Figure 8).

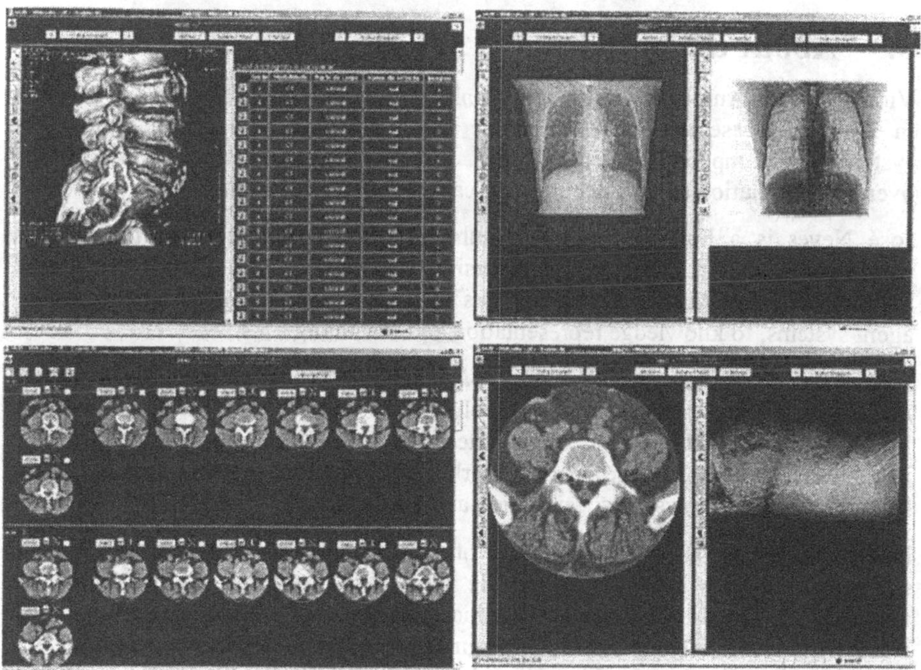

Figure 8 – Interface screen shots

4. Conclusion

The concept that computer systems should be capable of adapting themselves to suit the needs either of individuals or of different classes of users is an apparently attractive, if slightly unusual, one. Early applications of the adaptive system concept have been rather disappointing and problems have proved far harder to deal with than was first expected. Will the dream of having intelligent tutoring agents in the medical arena go the same way?

In this paper we provide an answer to such a question, by presenting a unifying perspective of an adaptive system which facilitates the integration of different sub-systems. Indeed, it uses the more recent advances in problem solving methodologies that use multi-agent systems when applied to the development and evolution of e-learning systems, in this case in the medical arena.

The key success factor of this project was the involvement in the developing team of physicians from the Radiology Department, (Neuroradiologists and Radiologists), Technicians (XRay Technicians) as the image makers, Engineers and Graphic Designer motivated to work and listen to their needs as well as for making the interface with the requesting Physicians, investigators, students and teachers from the University and their teams, who took the trouble of analysing, experimenting and giving the feedback needed to help us implement the necessary changes and interfaces to make things more attractive and functional.

5. About the authors

Victor Alves is Auxiliary Professor at Minho University where he received his PhD in 2002. His research interests include medical image processing, multi-agent systems and computer aided diagnostics. In this project he is responsible for the overall coordination and for agent specification and development.

José Neves is a Full Professor at Minho University. He received his PhD in Computer Science at Heriot Watt University, Scotland, in 1982. He is the leader of the Artificial Intelligence Group and his interests range from research in multi-agent systems, to knowledge representation and reasoning.

Luís Nelas is senior consultant of *Radiconsult.com- Consultoria Informática e Radiologia.* His research interests include Computer Aided Diagnostics and Medical Imaging. He is particularly interested in developing systems to aid in quality and efficiency of the imaging workflow production process. In this project he is responsible for system specification and assessment

Filipe Marreiros is a Masters student of Computer Graphics and Virtual Environments at Minho University. He is also a researcher at the *Centro de Computação Gráfica* (Computer Graphics Center) in Guimarães, Portugal. His research interests include Medical Imaging, User-Centered Interface Design and Scientific Visualization. In this project he is responsible for the graphic interface design and implementation.

6. Acknowledgements

We are indebted to *Radiconsult.com- Consultoria Informática e Radiologia, CIT-Centro de Imagem da Trindade, Instituto Superior de Ciências de Saúde do Norte*, and to *Hospital da Ordem da Trindade*, for their help in terms of experts, technicians and machine time. We wish to endorse a special thanks to Dr. Rui Cabral Mota for his great comments and suggestions which assumed major relevance in the system assessment from the physician and teacher point of views.

References

1. Machado, J., PhD Thesis, "Intelligent Agents as Objects of Virtual Reality Distributed Systems" (In Portuguese), Departamento de Informática, Escola de Engenharia, Universidade do Minho, Braga, Portugal, 2002.
2. Rosenberg, M. J., "E-Learning: Strategies for Delivering Knowledge in the Digital Age". New York: McGraw-Hill Professional Publishing, 2000.
3. Hartley, D. E., "On-Demand Learning: Training in the New Millennium". Boston, MA: HRD Press, 2000.
4. Gruber, T.R. "The role of common ontology in achieving sharable, reusable knowledge bases", in Proceedings of the Second International Conference (KR'91), J. Allen, R. Filkes, and E. Sandewall (eds.), pages 601-602 Cambridge, Massachusetts, USA, 1991.
5. Abelha, A., PhD Thesis, "Multi-agent systems as Working Cooperative Entities in Health Care Units" (In Portuguese), Departamento de Informática, Universidade do Minho, Braga, Portugal, 2004.
6. Heinze, C., Papasimeon, M., and Goss, S., "Specifying Agent Behaviour with Use Cases, in Design and Applications of Intelligent Agents" – Proceedings of the Third Pacific Rim International Workshop on Multiagentes PRIMA 2000, eds. C. Zhang and V. Soo, 128-142 (Lecture Notes in Artificial Intelligence, 1881) 2000.
7. Neves, J., Alves V., Nelas L., Maia M., and Cruz R. "A Multi-Feature Image Classification System that Reduces the Cost-of-Quality Expenditure", in Proceedings of the Second ICSC Symposium on Engineering of Intelligent Systems, Paisley, Scotland, UK, pages 594-554, 2000.
8. Alves, V., PhD Thesis, "Distributed Problem Solving – A breakthrough into the areas of artificial Intelligence and Health" (In Portuguese), Departamento de Informática, Escola de Engenharia, Universidade do Minho, Braga, Portugal, 2002.
9. Sleeman, D., & Brown, S. (Eds.). "Intelligent Tutoring Systems". Computers and People Series. London: Academic Press, 1982.
10. Burns, H. L., Parlett, J. W. & Redfield, and C. L. (Eds.). "Intelligent Tutoring Systems: Evolutions in Design". Hillsdale, NJ: Lawrence Erlbaum Associates, 1991.
11. Gauthier, G. , Frasson, C. & VanLehn, K. (Eds.). "Intelligent Tutoring Systems", Lecture Notes in Computer Science, Vol. 1839, Berlin: Springer Verlag, 2000.
12. Bradshaw, J. M. (Ed.) "Software agents", Cambridge, MA: MIT Press, 1997.

13. Bigus, J.P. & Bigus, J. "Constructing Intelligent Agents using Java". NY: John Willey & Sons, 2001.
14. Hendler, J.A. (Ed.) "Intelligent Agents: Where AI meets Information Technology", Special Issue, IEEE Expert, 1996.
15. Maes, P., "Modeling Adaptive Autonomous Agents", Artificial Intelligence Magazine, 1995.
16. Maes, P., "Agents that Reduce Work and Information Overload", Communications of the ACM, 1994.
17. Weiss, G. (Ed.), "Multiagent Systems: A Modern Approach to Distributed Artificial Intelligence". Cambridge, MA: MIT Press, 1999.
18. Edwards, P., Bayer, D., Green, C. L., Payne, T., "Experience with Learning Agents which Manage Internet-Based Information". AAAI Spring Symposium on Machine Learning for Information Access, AAAI Press, Menlo Park, CA, 1996, pp.31-40, 2001
19. Alves, V., Neves, J., Maia, M., Nelas. L., "Computer Tomography based Diagnosis using Extended Logic Programming and Artificial Neural Networks". Proceedings of the International NAISO Congress on Information Science Innovations ISI2001, Dubai, U.A.E., 2001.
20. Alves V., Neves J., Maia M., Nelas L., "A Computational Environment for Medical Diagnosis Support Systems". ISMDA2001, Madrid, Spain, 2001.
21. Neves, J., Machado, J., Analide, C., Novais, P., and Abelha, A."Extended Logic Programming applied to the specification of Multi-agent Systems and their Computing Environment", in Proceedings of the ICIPS'97 (Special Session on Intelligent Network Agent Systems), Beijing, China, 1997.
22. Faratin, P., Sierra C. and N. Jennings "Negotiation Decision Functions for Autonomous Agents" in Int. Journal of Robotics and Autonomous Systems, 24(3-4):159-182, 1997.
23. Wooldridge, M., "Introduction to MultiAgent Systems", 1st edition, John Wiley & Sons, Chichester,

Building an Ontology and Knowledge Base of the Human Meridian-Collateral System[1]

C.G. Cao and Y.F. Sui
Key Laboratory of Intelligent Information Processing, Institute of Computing Technology, Chinese Academy of Sciences, Beijing 100080, China
{cgcao,yfsui}@ict.ac.cn

Abstract

Meridian-collateral knowledge is a profound and complex part of the whole traditional Chinese medicine (TCM). It is the basis for many TCM-related computer applications. This work aimed to develop a sharable knowledge base of the human meridian-collateral system for those applications. We began the work by building a frame ontology of the meridian-collateral system (called OMCAP); and then developed a large-scale sharable instance base (called IMCAP), which was, with the aid of the tool OKEE. The OMCAP consists of 89 categories and 38 slots, and the IMCAP contains 1549 instance frames.

1. Introduction

The theory of meridians and collaterals is one of the profound theories of traditional Chinese medicine (TCM). It was systematically developed by ancient Chinese medical theorists and practitioners in their prolonged practice over thousands of years. The theory is closely related to acupuncture therapy, and is the foundation of acupuncture, moxibustion, massage, qigong, and clinical practice of other related fields of TCM [1][2][3][4][5][6].

In this paper, we introduce a frame-based domain ontology of the meridian-collateral system, called OMCAP, which is in the spirit of the Generic Frame Protocol [7], with a few significant extensions. With the OMCAP ontology, we have built a large-scale sharable instance base, called IMCAP (Instances of Meridians, Collaterals, Acupoints and acu-mox Prescriptions), which contains instance frames of categories in the OMCAP. The knowledge base is intended to be used in TCM-related applications such as automated diagnosis and therapy, medical instruction and training, and natural language processing.

In the beginning of OMCAP and IMCAP development, we obtained a list of influential knowledge sources recommended by our experts [1][2][3][4][5][6]. We conducted a comprehensive survey to identify the categories, instances, relations,

[1] This work is supported by the Natural Science Foundation (#60496326 and #60273019), and the National 973 Programme (#2003CB317008).

constraints and so forth in the human meridian-collateral system. The results of the survey outline the four major components of the OMCAP, mainly in the spirit of Gruber's view of ontologies [8]: A set of basic and common categories (e.g Integer, String and Terms); a set of categories which are not unique in the theory of meridians and collaterals, but are necessary to define the OMCAP; a set of categories (including Acupoints, Meridians, Colleterals, and Acu-Mox Prescriptions) and their relations (including has-all-disjoint-subcategories, has-disjoint-subcategories, and has-all-subcategories); and a set of formal axioms for constraining the interpretation of those categories and their relations.

In addition to being a language for describing the instance frames of categories, the OMCAP plays two other significant roles. Firstly, slots in a category are 'place-holders' for the instance frames of that category, and they are to be filled in during the knowledge acquisition process. Secondly, axioms in the OMCAP can be used both in knowledge inference and knowledge verification during the knowledge acquisition procedure: When acquired knowledge violates such axioms, the knowledge engineer is alarmed to identify and resolve the problems.

The rest of the paper is organized as follows. Section 2 presents the frame-based language for the OMCAP and IMCAP and discusses a few issues in developing the OMCAP and IMCAP. Section 3 introduces a tool for building and managing ontologies and knowledge bases. Section 4 presents the two-year effort of building ontology OMCAP and instance base IMCAP. Section 5 discusses a few issues regarding the OMCAP and IMCAP, and concludes the paper.

2. A Frame-Based Language for the Ontology OMCAP and IMCAP

Before presenting the frame-language for the OMCAP and IMCAP, we need to discuss two general yet important issues in ontology building, namely categories and taxonomic relations.

To develop the OMCAP, we need to start from a few common categories, such as Integer, Float, Boolean, Char, String, Terms, and CTime (i.e. ChineseTime, formatted in YYYYMMDDHHMMSS), Of course, in addition to the common categories above, we need to consider TCM-specific common categories, including the categories Zang-Fu Organs and its subcategories Zang Organs and Fu Organs, and Five Elements, and Illnesses. These common categories are already available and widely used in other ontologies as well [9][10][11][12].

In the meridian-collateral system itself, there are four broad categories, i.e. Acupoints, Meridians, Collaterals, and Acu-Mox Prescriptions, and each of these categories has subcategories.

To build a domain ontology, we define a taxonomical relation between categories and their instance. In our practice with ontological engineering, we have encountered and summarized several common and specific taxonomic relations among categories and instances, including has-all-disjoint-subcategories, has-disjoint-subcategories, has-all-subcategories, has-subcategories, subcategory-of, has-all-instances, has-instances, and instance-of. They offer much freedom in representing taxonomies in the setting of traditional Chinese medicine.

Before we proceed, we introduce a few useful notions:

1. CAT denotes the set of all categories in the OMCAP. It includes the common categories and TCM-specific categories.
2. listof is a category constructor, which makes a list category from some other category in CAT. For example, listof Acupoints is a new category, and its instances are lists whose elements are acupoints. For the listof constructor, we introduced four functions, i.e. elements, first-element, last-element, and length, which give the set of all elements, the first element, last element and length of a list, respectively.
3. LC denotes the set of all lists of categories in CAT, i.e. $LC=\{(C_1, \ldots, C_n) | C_i \in CAT, n \geq 2\}$. In other words, $LC=BC^2 \cup BC^3 \cup \ldots$
4. For $C \in CAT$ or $C \in LC$, dom(C) denotes the set of instances of C.
5. INS is the set of instances in the OMCAP, i.e. $INS = \cup_{C \in CAT \cup LC} dom(C)$.

With the notions, we turn to the taxonomic relations. Given a category C, has-all-disjoint-subcategories and has-disjoint-subcategories both reflect the subcategories of C, but the differences is that the value of the former gives all the subcategories of C which are disjoint, whereas although the value of the latter gives all the subcategories of C, they are non-disjoint. Formally, we have the following axioms:

Ax-1: $\forall C \in CAT\ \forall L \in LC$ [has-all-disjoint-subcategories(C; L)

$\leftrightarrow \forall C1 \neq C2 \in elements(L)$ [$dom(C1) \cap dom(C2) = \phi \wedge \cup_{C3 \in elements(L)} dom(C3) = dom(C)$]]

Ax-2: $\forall C \in CAT\ \forall L \in LC$ [has-disjoint-subcategories(C; L)

$\leftrightarrow \forall C1 \neq C2 \in elements(L)$ [$dom(C1) \cap dom(C2) = \phi \wedge \cup_{C3 \in elements(L)} dom(C3) \subset dom(C)$]]

There are also situations where the subcategories of a category may not be disjoint. To describe this non-disjointness, we designed the two relations has-all-subcategories and has-subcategories, and they satisfy the following constraints:

Ax-3: $\forall\ C \in CAT\ \forall L \in LC$ [has-all-subcategories(C; L)

$\leftrightarrow \exists\ C1, C2 \in elements(L)$ [$dom(C1) \cap dom(C2) \neq \phi \wedge \cup_{C3 \in elements(L)} dom(C3) = dom(C)$]]

Ax-4: $\forall\ C \in CAT, \forall L \in LC$ [has-subcategories(C; L)

$\leftrightarrow \exists\ C1, \exists C2 \in elements(L)$ [$dom(C1) \cap dom(C2) \neq \phi \wedge \cup_{C3 \in elements(L)} dom(C3) \subset dom(C)$]]

The relation subcategory-of is irreflexive, and describes the category-subcategory relation. It satisfies the following axiom:

Ax-5: $\forall$ C1, $C2 \in CAT$ [subcategory-of(C1; C2) $\leftrightarrow dom(C1) \subset dom(C2)$]

Similarly, we have three category-instance relations. They satisfy the following axioms:

Ax-6: $\forall C \in CAT\ \forall L \in LC$ [has-all-instances(C; L) $\leftrightarrow$ elements(L) = dom(C)]

Ax-7: $\forall C \in CAT\ \forall L \in LC$ [has-instances(C; L) $\leftrightarrow$ elements(L) $\subset$ dom(C)]

Ax-8: $\forall C \in CAT\ \forall I \in INS$ [instance-of(I; C) $\leftrightarrow$ I $\in$ dom(C)]

Now, it is the point to introduce the frame-based representation for the OMCAP and IMCAP. Fig. 1 presents the overall syntax of the representation. The frame representation is in the spirit of the Generic Frame Protocol [7], but with a few significant extensions to be explained in the following subsections.

As depicted in Fig. 1, a category definition starts with the keyword defcategory, followed by a category name. The body of a category frame is a collection of statements of three kinds: include statements, slot definitions, and category knowledge (see line 2 of Fig. 1). In the following subsections, we will explain the representation and a few important notions in more details.

Firstly, to facilitate domain category reusability, we introduced a notion called category inclusion – A category can be included in another category (called host category). In the OMCAP, there are two kinds of category inclusion, i.e. explicit inclusion and default inclusion (or implicit inclusion). Explicit inclusion requests a statement like "include: Category-001" to be declared in the host category. But, this is not required in the case of default inclusion.

In our OMCAP, explicit inclusion is transitive under the relation subcategory-of(C1, C). That is, we have:

Ax-9: $\forall C, C1, C2 \in CAT$ [subcategory-of(C1,C) $\wedge$ include(C, C2) $\rightarrow$ include(C1, C2)]

In addition to category reusability, category inclusion plays another important role in our ontology OMCAP, i.e. category knowledge inheritance, and we will discuss this in section 2.3.6.

Secondly, we discuss the facets of slots. A slot may have a number of facets for constraining its interpretation. One facet, i.e. value category, is mandatory. It is stated using the syntax ":category <value-category>", where <value-category> may be a basic category, common category, a defined category, a category constructed from existing categories using the constructor listof, or the special category Aggregator. In the last case, we call the slot an aggregating slot. An aggregating slot of a category C represents a number of slots either in C, or inherited from the supercategories of C, or in some included categories of C. The slot value of the aggregating slot is determined by the component slots; in other words, when one asks "what is the value of an aggregating slot", the answer is produced by obtaining the values of the component slots. (For an example, see the category Acupoints in section 4.2, where regional-anatomy is an aggregating slot for the slots regional-vasculature and regional-innervation).

```
1.    defcategory <category-name>
      '{'
          <category-statements>
      '}'

      <category-name>::=<string>

2.    <category-statements>::={<category-statement>}
      <category-statement>::=<include-statements>
                             |<category-knowledge>
                             |<slot-definitions>
3.    <include-statements>::=include: <included-category>{, <included-category >}
4.        <slot-definitions>::= slot: <slot-name> <facet-statements>
5.    <facet-statements>::=:category <value-category>
                          [:domain <value-set>]
                          [:default <default-slot-value>]
                          [:unit <unit>]
                          [:instance-slot-value <isv-values>]
6.    <category-knowledge>::=<slot-name>:<slot-value>
7.    defprivatecategory <category-name>
      '{'
          <category-statements>
      '}'

      <private-category-name>::=<string>

8.    definstance <instance-name>: <category-name>
      '{'
          <instance-statements>
      '}'
      <instance-statements>::={<slot-name>:<slot-value>}
```

Fig.1. A frame-based language for the OMCAP and IMCAP

The facet ":instance-slot-value <isv-values>" is a special one. Before introducing the facet ":instance-slot-value <isv-values>", we first explain an important phenomenon in the meridian-collateral domain and others as well. As we have observed, a great number of categories are defined directly by referring to their instances; in other words, those categories can not be fully comprehended without referring to the intents of their instances. For instance, in all the knowledge sources of meridians and collaterals, categories and instances are generally presented together. To a large extent, this phenomenon is due to the fact that the categories of meridians and collaterals are formed based on an induction or summarization of properties of their instances. Meanwhile, because the ontology OMCAP and the instance base IMCAP are primarily hand-crafted, we decided to lift some of the intents of instances to their categories to make the latter more explicit as well as more human-comprehensible. We call this *instance lifting*, and represent the lifted intents through a new facet ":instance-slot-value <isv-values>".

Thirdly, we discuss slot inheritance. When a category is included in a host category, whether explicitly or by default, the host category can directly use the slots defined in the included category, which relieves us of redefining those slots in the host[2]. Therefore, category inclusion is an implementation of slot inheritance. A second kind of slot inheritance is realized through the relations subcategory-of(C1, C) and instance-of(I, C), where C1 (the subcategory) can use all the slots defined in C, and the instance I can use all the slots in C. Moreover, C1 can also use the slots defined in the categories included in C, as shown in the axiom Ax-9.

Fourthly, we discuss category knowledge and its inheritance. In a category, we can specify two kinds of category knowledge: public knowledge and private knowledge. Given a category, its public knowledge is the knowledge which is shared by, or inheritable to, all of its subcategories and instances, whereas its private knowledge is about the category itself and is *not* inheritable. As indicated in line 6 of Fig. 1, the category knowledge of a category C, whether public or private, appears as slot-value pairs, where slots are defined in the supercategories or included categories of the category C.

Unfortunately, there are no universal rules for determining what knowledge of a category is private – this is essentially a domain-dependent issue. In the OMCAP, the taxonomic knowledge of a category C is private except for the relation subcategory-of; that is, each of the following slot-value pairs, if appeared in the category, is private knowledge of the category: has-all-disjoint-subcategories: <subcategories>, has-disjoint-subcategories: <subcategories>, has-all-subcategories: <subcategories>, has-subcategories: <subcategories>, has-all-instances: <instances>, and has-instances: <instances>

To explicitly represent private knowledge of categories, we introduced the notion of private category: When a private category is included in a host category, its slot-value pairs is taken to be private knowledge of the host category.

To define private categories, we introduced the keyword defprivatecategory, as shown in line 7 of Fig. 1. The category Terms is a typical private category, and can be used to represent (private) terminological knowledge for a category, such as Chinese pinyin, original name, and informal definition of the category. For more details see section 4.1.

An instance frame begins with the keyword definstance, followed by the name of the instance and the name of the category which the instance belongs to (see line 8 of Fig. 1). The body of an instance frame is a collection of slot-value pairs.

3. OKEE: A Tool for the OMCAP and IMCAP

---

[2] Of course, we can redefine a slot included in a host category. This slot will have a *new* definition, and overwrite the definition of the slot in the included category.

We have been developing an Ontology and Knowledge Engineering Environment (OKEE) for building and managing both domain ontologies and knowledge bases. An earlier version of OKEE was reported elsewhere in [12], and it provided a set of facilities for defining categories and slots, checking syntactical errors, analyzing category inclusions, and analyzing both category frames and instance frames for inconsistency.

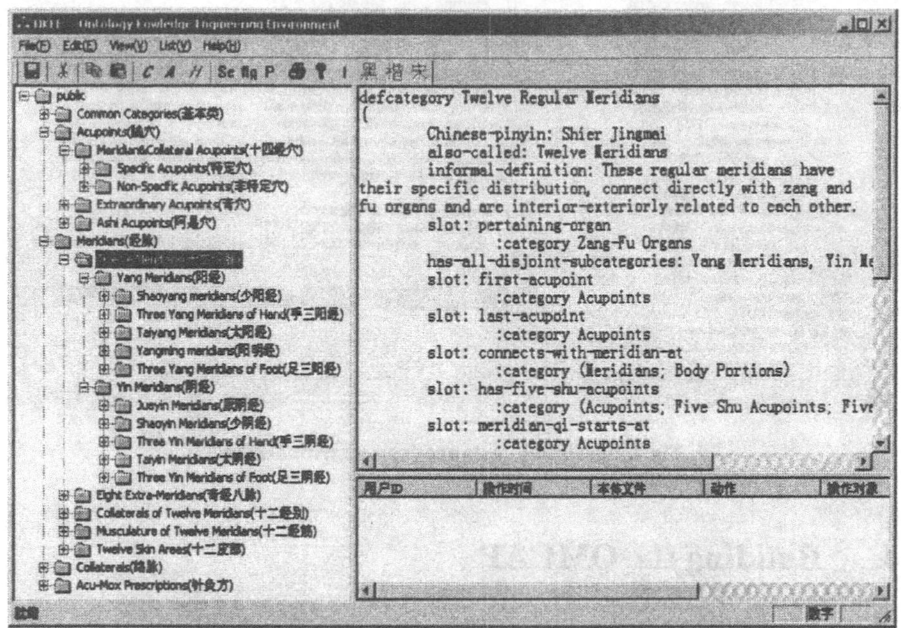

Fig.2. Defining the OMCAP with OKEE

Our work with the OMCAP and IMCAP provided us with several opportunities to extend OKEE. The extensions are not merely TCM-specific, and they are also useful in building other domain ontologies. With the extended OKEE, we defined the categories in the OMCAP and instance frames of those categories in the IMCAP (see Fig. 2 and Fig. 3). Currently, the knowledge base consists of 89 categories, 38 slots, and 1549 instance frames.

The left side window of Fig.2 shows (part of) the top five levels of the taxonomy of categories, and its right window shows the editing area for the category Twelve Regular Meridians. The right window of Fig.3 shows the editing area for one of the instances, i.e. Lung Meridian, of the category Twelve Regular Meridians.

OKEE also provides a compiler to transform the frame representation into an internal representation, called io-models, for fast retrieval and reasoning [11][12]. And a multi-agent system has recently been developed as a component of OKEE, which can reason with clinical problems based on the OMCAP and IMCAP.

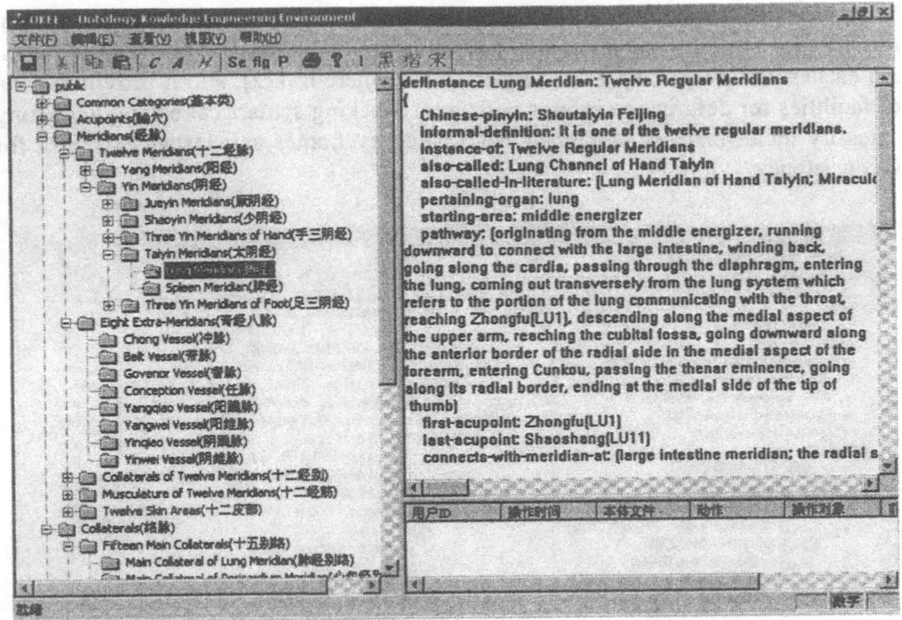

Fig.3. Specifying instance frames with OKEE

4. Building the OMCAP

4.1 Common Categories for OMCAP

As discussed in section 2, in addition to the basic categories such as Integer, Float, Boolean, Char, String, and CTime, we need a few more common categories to define the OMCAP. These include Terms, Five Elements, Illnesses, Zang-Fu Organs, Zang Organs, and Fu Organs.

4.2 Categories and Axioms of Acupoints

Generally, each acupoint can be described from many aspects, as depicted in Fig.4. Below, we explain the slots in some detail.

The category Acupoints has three disjoint subcategories: Meridian&Collateral Acupoints, Extraordinary Acupoints, and Ashi Acupoints. Further, the category Meridian&Collateral Acupoints has two disjoint subcategories, i.e. Specific Acupoints and Non-Specific Acupoints.

The slot code refers to the code information defined in [5]. For example, the code of Zhongfu is LU1. The slot belongs-to is used to represent a meridian and collateral to which an acupoint belongs. Note that, in the human meridian-collateral system, only the twelve regular meridians, governor vessel and conception vessel have acupoints. Altogether, these fourteen meridians have 361 acupoints [1][2].

```
defcategory Acupoints
{
        informal-definition: Acupoints in meridians. Each acupoint has its own location, anatomy,
    and indications.
        has-all-subcategories: Meridian&Collateral Acupoints, Extraordinary Acupoints, Ashi
    Acupoints
        slot: code
                :category String
        slot: belongs-to
                :category Meridians
        slot: locations
                :category listof String
        slot: regional-anatomy
                :category Aggregator
                :domain regional-vasculature, regional-innervation
        slot: regional-vasculature
                :category listof String
        slot: regional-innervation
                :category listof String
        slot: has-specificity
                :category Boolean
                :default false
        slot: conjunction-acupoint-of
                :category listof Meridians
        slot: function
                :category listof String
        slot: indications
                :category listof Illnesses
        slot: needling-method
                :category String
        slot: needling-precaution
                :category String
        slot: moxibustion
                :category String
                :domain applicable, inapplicable
                :default applicable
}
```

Fig.4. The category Acupoints

Each acupoint has a specific location, and thus has a regional anatomy. For these, we designed two slots location and regional-anatomy. Note that the slot regional-anatomy is an aggregating slot, and its slot value is determined by the two slot values of regional-vasculature and regional-innervation.

The slot has-specificity is a special Boolean slot. It is true for an acupoint, if and only if the acupoint is an instance of Specific Acupoints. Formally, we have

Ax-10: $\forall$ a: Acupoints [has-specificity(a) $\leftrightarrow$ instance-of(a; Specific Acupoints)]

For an acupoint, its slot conjunction-acupoint-of may or may be not defined. If defined, it means that the acupoint is a point where a number of meridians (indicated in the slot value conjunction-acupoint-of) intersect.

The slot function indicates the function of an acupoint in acu-mox treatment. It is the basis on which an acu-mox prescription is made or interpreted. The values of the slot indications give a list of illnesses which the acupoint can be used (possibly together with other acupoints) to treat.

The slots needling-method and needling-precaution give the needling method of an acupoint and the precaution during acupuncture. The slot moxibustion states whether moxibustion is applicable to an acupoint. The facet ":domain" specifies the domain of the slot moxibustion can take values, and ":default applicable" indicates that the default value of moxibustion.

```
defcategory Meridian&Collateral Acupoints
{
        Chinese-pinyin: Shisi Jing Xue
        has-all-disjoint-subcategories: Specific Acupoints, Non-Specific Acupoints
}
defcategory Specific Acupoints

{
        Chinese-pinyin: Teding Xue
        subcategory-of: Meridian&Collateral Acupoints
        has-all-subcategories: Five Shu Acupoints, Source Acupoints, Collateral
  Acupoints, Back Shu Acupoints, Front Mu Acupoints, Eight Confluential Acupoints, Eight
  Strategic Acupoints, Xi Acupoints, Xiahe Acupoints, Conjunction Acupoints
}
```

Fig.5. The category Meridian&Collateral Acupoints and one of its subcategories

After the introduction to the Acupoints, we pay our attention to one of its most important (sub)subcategories, i.e. Specific Acupoints. In traditional Chinese medicine, some acupoints of meridians are located in specific positions, and have specific curative effects in treating certain illnesses. This category is further classified into ten subcategories, as shown in Fig.5.

Among the specific acupoints, the Five Shu Acupoints is a particular subcategory. Each of the twelve regular meridians has five shu acupoints, and therefore we have five different subcategories of the category Five Shu Acupoints, i.e. Jing-Well Acupoints, Ying-Spring Acupoints, Shu-Stream Acupoints, Jing-River Acupoints, and He-Sea Acupoints.

4.3 Categories and Axioms of Meridians and Collaterals

As stated in the introduction, the human meridian-collateral system is composed of two major parts, namely the meridian system and collateral system. The meridian system includes twelve regular meridians, eight extra-meridians, collaterals of twelve meridians, musculature of twelve meridians, and twelve skin areas. The collateral system consists of fifteen main collaterals, minute collaterals, and superficial collaterals.

Fig.6 depicts the category Meridians. To describe the circulation of a meridian, we identified seven slots, i.e. starting-area, ending-area, first-acupoint, last-acupoint, pathway, connects-with-meridian-at (defined in Twelve Regular Meridians), and contains-acupoints-in-order. The starting-area and ending-area tell the areas where the meridian starts and end, and the first-acupoint and last-acupoint indicate the first and last acupoints of the meridian, respectively[3]. The pathway of a meridian gives the whole circulation path of a meridian. The value of the slot connects-with-meridian-at tells where a meridian connects with another meridian.

The slot contains-acupoints-in-order indicates the acupoints that a meridian owns and the order of those acupoints. The slot value of contain-acupoints-in-order is listof Acupoints, and the first and last elements of this list are the slot values of first-acupoint and last-acupoint, respectively. Formally, we have the following axiom:

Ax-11: ∀ m: Meridians ∀loa: listof Acupoints [contain-acupoints-in-order(m; loa) → first-element(loa)=first-acupoint(m) ∧ last-element(loa)=last-acupoint(m)]

In the category Meridians, the slot has-specific-acupoints gives all the specific acupoints on a meridian, and we will further explain the slot below.
In the Meridians, the category Twelve Regular Meridians is a major subcategory. According to traditional Chinese medicine [1][2], Twelve Regular Meridians is classified into two subcategories, i.e. Yin Meridians and Yang Meridians, which are further classified into sub-subcategories, respectively, as previously depicted in the left window in Fig.2.

Now we turn to the collaterals. According to traditional Chinese medicine [1][2], while the meridians constitute the main trunk and run longitudinally and interiorly within the body, collaterals are branches of the meridians and run transversely and superficially from the meridians.

The category Collaterals has three disjoint subcategories, namely Fifteen Main Collaterals, Minute Collaterals and Superficial Collaterals. The category Fifteen Main Collaterals has the twelve instances of collaterals which separate from the twelve regular meridians, the collaterals of the conception and governor vessels, and the main collateral of the spleen. They are named respectively after the names or acupoints from where they start, and their main function is to strengthen the association of the yin and yang meridians and the interior-exteriorly related meridians on the body surface.

---

[3] The starting area and first acupoint of a meridian generally does not coincide. For example, the lung meridian starts from the middle energizer, but the first acupoint of the meridian is Zhongfu (LU1). This applies to the ending area and last acupoint of a meridian, too.

```
defcategory Meridians
{
        Chinese-pinyin: Jingmai
        Informal-definition: The meridians constitute the main trunk and run
longitudinally and interiorly within the body
        slot: function
                :category listof String
        slot: starting-area
                :category String
        slot: ending-area
                :category String
        slot: first-acupoint
                :category Acupoints
        slot: last-acupoint
                :category Acupoints
        slot: pathway
                :category listof String
        slot: indications
                :category listof Illnesses
        slot: contains-acupoints-in-order
                :category listof Acupoints
        slot: number-of-acupoints
                :category Integer
        slot: has-specific-acupoints
                :category (Specific Acupoints; Acupoints)
        has-all-subcategories: Twelve Regular Meridians, Eight Extra-Meridians,
Collaterals of Twelve Meridians, Musculature of Twelve Meridians, Twelve Skin Areas
}
```

Fig.6. The category Meridians

4.4 Categories of Illnesses and Acu-Mox Prescriptions

The meridian-collateral theory is closely related to acupuncture therapy. A special kind of knowledge, i.e. acu-mox prescriptions, is of practical value in clinical treatment. In this section, we focus on the categories and instances of acu-mox prescriptions.

The slot acu-mox-prescription links acu-mox prescriptions with concrete illnesses. The category Acu-Mox Prescriptions is defined Fig.7. The first two slots give the indications and contraindications of prescriptions. The slot prescription prescribes the acupoints and needling or moxibustion methods to be applied to those prescribed acupoints.

```
defcategory Acu-Mox Prescriptions
{
        slot: indications
                :category listof Illnesses
        slot: source
                :category TCMLiterature
        slot: contraindications
                :category listof Illnesses
        slot: prescription
                :category listof (Methods; Acupoints)
        slot: supplementary-acupoints
                :category (Illnesses; Methods; Acupoints)
}
definstance gastric ulcer: Illnesses
{
        acu-mox-prescription: acu-mox-for-gastric-ulcer
}
definstance acu-mox-of-gastric-ulcer: Acu-Mox Prescriptions
{
        indications: gastric ulcer
        source: Acupuncture and Moxibustion
        prescription: (puncture; Zhongwan), (puncture; Zusanli)
        supplementary-acupoints: (vomiting; puncture; Neiguan)
}
```

Fig.7. The category Acu-Mox Prescriptions and one of its instances

The prescribed acupoints may not be effective in situations where some other illnesses are present in a patient. Usually, supplementary acupoints are selected. These acupoints are represented using the slot supplementary-acupoints.

As illustration, an instance frame of Illnesses (i.e. gastric ulcer) is given with an acu-mox prescription in Fig.7. In the acu-mox prescription, the supplementary acupoints are also described: if vomiting, then puncture Neiguan(PC6) in addition to Zhongwan(CV12) and Zusanli(ST36).

5. Conclusion

To our best knowledge, ontology building for traditional Chinese medicine has been little researched. In building the ontology OMCAP and the instance base IMCAP, we encountered several problems, and proposed a few generic and efficient solutions, which we believe contribute to current medical ontology research [e.g. 9, 10].

Based on the OMCAP ontology, we have built the knowledge base of the human meridian-collateral system in the past three years or so. The knowledge base is composed of the OMCAP and IMCAP, and it currently contains 89 categories, 38 slots, and 1549 instance frames, which altogether occupy a space of about 331 kilobytes. We believe that the method can be used in ontology building for other branches of traditional Chinese medicine. And we also believe that the new notions and ideas in our work can be used in general medical ontology research.

References

1. Shi, D.B. & Gao, X.M. & He, X.D. & Zhang, C.R. & Li, Q.Y. & Xiao, J.P. The medical volume of the encyclopedia of China. Publishing House of Encyclopedia of China, Beijing, 1991
2. Yin, H.H. & Zhang, B.N. (eds) Basic theories of traditional Chinese medicine (29th edition). Shanghai Publisher of Science and Technology, Shanghai, 2000
3. Liu, G.W. (ed) A complement work of modern acupuncture and moxibustion. Huaxia Publishing House, Beijing, 1998
4. Cheng, X.N. (ed) Chinese acupuncture and moxibustion (revised edition). Beijing Foreign Language Press, Beijing, 2003
5. Academy of traditional Chinese medicine. Thesaurus of Traditional Chinese Medicine, Beijing, 1999
6. Zhang, Q.W. (ed) A practical Chinese-English dictionary of traditional Chinese medicine. Shandong Science and Technology Press, Shandong, 2001
7. Chaudhri, V.K. & Farquhar, A. & Fikes, R. & Karp, P.D. & Rice, J.P. Generic frame protocol 2.0. KSL-97-05, Stanford University, 1997
8. Gruber, T.R. A translation approach to portable ontology specifications. International Journal of Knowledge Acquisition 1993: 199-220
9. Zhou, X.B. Ontology and knowledge extraction from modern medical text. MS Thesis, Institute of Computing Technology, Chinese Academy of Sciences, July 2003
10. Cao, C.G. & Wang, H.T. & Sui, Y.F. Knowledge modeling and acquisition of traditional Chinese herbal drugs and formulae from text. International Journal of Artificial Intelligence in Medicine 2004; 32: 3-13
11. Gu, F. & Cao, C.G. Multi-domain ontology language NKIL. Technical Report, Institute of Computing Technology, Chinese Academy of Sciences, 2003
12. Si, J.X. & Cao, C.G. & Wang, H.T. & Gu, F. & Feng, Q.Z. & Zhang, C.X. An environment for multi-domain ontology development and knowledge acquisition. In: Han, Y.B. & Tai, S. & Wikarski, D. (eds) Engineering and deployment of cooperative information systems. Lecture Notes in Computer Science 2480, Berlin: Springer-Verlag, 2001: 105-116

The Effect of Principal Component Analysis on Machine Learning Accuracy with High Dimensional Spectral Data

Tom Howley, Michael G. Madden,
Marie-Louise O'Connell and Alan G. Ryder
National University of Ireland, Galway, Ireland
thowley@vega.it.nuigalway.ie, michael.madden@nuigalway.ie,
ML.OConnell@nuigalway.ie, alan.ryder@nuigalway.ie

Abstract

This paper presents the results of an investigation into the use of machine learning methods for the identification of narcotics from Raman spectra. The classification of spectral data and other high dimensional data, such as images, gene-expression data and spectral data, poses an interesting challenge to machine learning, as the presence of high numbers of redundant or highly correlated attributes can seriously degrade classification accuracy. This paper investigates the use of Principal Component Analysis (PCA) to reduce high dimensional spectral data and to improve the predictive performance of some well known machine learning methods. Experiments are carried out on a high dimensional spectral dataset. These experiments employ the NIPALS (Non-Linear Iterative Partial Least Squares) PCA method, a method that has been used in the field of chemometrics for spectral classification, and is a more efficient alternative than the widely used eigenvector decomposition approach. The experiments show that the use of this PCA method can improve the performance of machine learning in the classification of high dimensionsal data.

1 Introduction

The automatic identification of illicit materials using Raman spectroscopy is of significant importance for law enforcement agencies. High dimensional spectral data can pose problems for machine learning as predictive models based on such data run the risk of overfitting. Furthermore, many of the attributes may be redundant or highly correlated, which can also lead to a degradation of prediction accuracy.

This problem is equally relevant to many other application domains, such as the classification of gene-expression microarray data [1], image data [2] and text data [3]. In the classification task considered in this paper, Raman spectra are used for the identification of acetaminophen, a pain-relieving drug that is found in many over-the-counter medications, within different mixtures. Typically, methods from a field of study known as chemometrics have been applied to this particular problem [4], and these methods use PCA to handle the high dimensional spectra. PCA is a classical statistical method for transforming attributes of a dataset into a new set of uncorrelated attributes called principal components (PCs). PCA can be used to reduce the dimensionality of a dataset, while still retaining as much of the *variability* of the dataset as possible. The goal of this research is to determine if PCA can be used to improve the performance of machine learning methods in the classification of such high dimensional data.

In the first set of experiments presented in this paper, the performance of five well known machine learning techniques (Support Vector Machines, k-Nearest Neighbours, C4.5 Decision Tree, RIPPER and Naive Bayes) along with classification by Linear Regression are compared by testing them on a Raman spectral dataset. A number of pre-processing techniques such as normalisation and first derivative are applied to the data to determine if they can improve the classification accuracy of these methods. A second set of experiments is carried out in which PCA and machine learning (and the various pre-processing methods) are used in combination. This set of PCA experiments also facilitates a comparison of machine learning with the popular chemometric technique of Principal Component Regression (PCR), which combines PCA and Linear Regression.

The main contributions of this research are as follows:

1. It presents a promising approach for the classification of substances within complex mixtures based on Raman spectra, an application that has not been widely considered in the machine learning community. This approach could also be applied to other high dimensional classification problems.
2. It proposes the use of NIPALS PCA for data reduction, a method that is much more efficient than the widely used eigenvector decomposition method.
3. It demonstrates the usefulness of PCA for reducing dimensionality and improving the performance of a variety of machine learning methods. Previous work has tended to focus on a single machine learning method. It also demonstrates the effect of reducing data to different numbers of principal components.

The paper is organised as follows. Section 2 will give a brief description of Raman spectroscopy and outline the characteristics of the data it produces. Section 3 describes PCA, the NIPALS algorithm for PCA that is used here and the PCR method that incorporates PCA into it. Section 4 provides a brief description of each machine learning technique used in this investigation. Experimental results along with a discussion are presented in Section 5. Section 6 describes related research and Section 7 presents the conclusion of this study.

2 Raman Spectroscopy

Raman spectroscopy is the measurement of the wavelength and intensity of light that has been scattered inelastically by a sample, known as the Raman effect [5]. This Raman scattering provides information on the vibrational motions of molecules in the sample compound, which in turn provides a chemical fingerprint. Every compound has its own unique Raman spectrum that can be used for sample identification. Each point of a spectrum represents the intensity recorded at a particular wavelength. A Raman dataset therefore has one attribute for each point on its constituent spectra.

Raman spectra can be used for the identification of materials such as narcotics [4], hazardous waste [6] and explosives [7].

Raman spectra are a good example of high dimensional data; a Raman spectrum is typically made up of 500-3000 data points, and many datasets may only contain 20-200 samples. However, there are other characteristics of Raman spectra that can be problematic for machine learning:

- *Collinearity:* many of the attributes (spectral data points) are highly correlated to each other which can lead to a degradation of the prediction accuracy.
- *Noise:* particularly prevalent in spectra of complex mixtures. Predictive models that are fitted to noise in a dataset will not perform well on other test datasets.
- *Fluorescence:* the presence of fluorescent materials in a sample can obscure the Raman signal and therefore make classification more difficult [4].
- *Variance of Intensity:* a wide variance in spectral intensity occurs between different sample measurements [8].

3 Principal Component Analysis

In the following description, the dataset is represented by the matrix X, where X is a $N \times p$ matrix. For spectral applications, each row of X, the p-vector x_i contains the intensities at each wavelength of the spectrum sample i. Each column, X_j contains all the observations of one attribute. PCA is used to overcome the previously mentioned problems of high-dimensionality and collinearity by reducing the number of predictor attributes. PCA transforms the set of inputs $X_1, X_2, \ldots, X_N$ into another set of column vectors $T_1, T_2, \ldots, T_N$ where the T's have the property that most of the original data's information content (or most of its variance) is stored in the first few T's (the principal component scores). The idea is that this allows reduction of the data to a smaller number of dimensions, with low information loss, simply by discarding some of the principal components (PCs). Each PC is a linear combination of the original inputs and each PC is orthogonal, which therefore eliminates the problem of collinearity. This linear transformation of the matrix X is specified by a $p \times p$ matrix P so that the transformed variables T are given by:

$$T = XP \quad \text{or alternatively } X \text{ is decomposed as follows: } X = TP^T \tag{1}$$

where P is known as the *loadings matrix.* The columns loadings matrix P can be calculated as the eigenvectors of the matrix $X^T X$ [9], a calculation which can be computationally intensive when dealing with datasets of 500-3000 attributes. A much quicker alternative is the NIPALS method. The NIPALS method does not calculate all the PCs at once as is done in the eigenvector approach. Instead, it calculates the first PC by getting the first PC score, t_1, and the first vector of the loadings matrix, p'_1, from the sample matrix X. Then the outer product, $t_1 p'_1$, is subtracted from X and the residual, E_1, is calculated. This residual becomes X in the calculation of the next PC and the process is repeated until as many PCs as required have been generated. The algorithm for calculating the nth PC is detailed below [10]:

1. Take a vector x_j from X and call it t_n:$t_n = x_j$
2. Calculate p'_n: $p'_n = t'_n X / t'_n t_n$
3. Normalise p'_n to length 1: $p'_{nnew} = p'_{nold} / ||p'_{nold}||$
4. Calculate t_n: $t_n = X p_n / p'_n p_n$
5. Compare t_n used in step 2 with that obtained in step 4. If they are the same, stop (the iteration has converged). If they still differ, go to step 2.

After the first PC has been calculated (i.e. t_1 has converged), X in steps 2 and 4 is replaced by its residual, for example, to generate the second PC, X is replaced by E_1, where $E_1 = X - t_1 p'_1$.

See Ryder [4], O'Connell *et al.* [8] and Conroy *et al.* [6] for examples of the use of PCA in the classification of materials from Raman spectra.

3.1 Principal Component Regression

The widely used chemometric technique of PCR is a two-step multivariate regression method, in which PCA of the data is carried out in the first step. In the second step, a multiple linear regression between the PC scores obtained in the PCA step and the predictor variable is carried out. In this regression step, the predictor variable is a value that is chosen to represent the presence or absence of the target in a sample, e.g. 1 for present and -1 for absent. In this way, a classification model can be built using any regression method.

4 Machine Learning

4.1 Support Vector Machine

The SVM [11] is a powerful machine learning tool that is capable of representing non-linear relationships and producing models that generalise well to unseen data. For binary classification, a linear SVM (the simplest form of SVM) finds an optimal linear separator between the two classes of data. This optimal separator is the one that results in the widest margin of separation between the two classes, as a wide margin implies that the classifier is better able to classify unseen spectra. To regulate overfitting, SVMs have a complexity parameter, C, which determines the trade-off between choosing a large-margin classifier and the amount by which misclassified samples are tolerated. A higher value of C means that more importance is attached to minimising the amount of misclassification than to finding a wide margin model. To handle non-linear data, kernels (e.g. Radial Basis Function (RBF), Polynomial or Sigmoid) are introduced to map the original data to a new feature space in which a linear separator can be found. In addition to the C parameter, each kernel may have a number of parameters associated with it. For the experiments reported here, two kernels were used: the RBF kernel, in which the kernel width, σ, can be changed, and the Linear kernel, which has no extra parameter. In general, the SVM is considered useful for handling high dimensional data.

4.2 k-Nearest Neighbours

k-Nearest Neighbours (k-NN) [12] is a learning algorithm which classifies a test sample by firstly obtaining the class of the k samples that are the closest to the test sample. The majority class of these nearest samples (or nearest single sample when $k = 1$) is returned as the prediction for that test sample. Various measures may be used to determine the distance between a pair of samples. In these experiments, the Euclidean distance measure was used. In practical terms, each Raman spectrum is compared to every other spectrum in the dataset. At each spectral data point, the difference in intensity between the two spectra is measured (distance). The sum of the squared distances for all the data points (full spectrum) gives a numerical measure of how close the spectra are.

4.3 C4.5

The C4.5 decision tree [13] algorithm generates a series of if-then rules that are represented as a tree structure. Each node in the tree corresponds to a test of the intensity at a particular data point of the spectrum. The result of a test at one node determines which node in the tree is checked next until finally, a leaf node is reached. Each leaf specifies the class to be returned if that leaf is reached.

4.4 RIPPER

RIPPER [14] (Repeated Incremental Pruning to Produce Error Reduction) is an inductive rule-based learner that builds a set of prepositional rules that identify classes while minimising the amount of error. The number of training examples misclassified by the rules defines the error. RIPPER was developed with the goal of handling large noisy datasets efficiently whilst also achieving good generalisation performance.

5 Experimental Results

5.1 Dataset

In the following experiments, the task is to identify acetaminophen. The acetaminophen dataset comprises the Raman spectra of 217 different samples. Acetaminophen is present in 87 of the samples, the rest of the samples being made up of various pure inorganic materials. Each sample spectrum covers the range 350-2000 cm^{-1} and is made up of 1646 data points. For more details on this dataset, see O'Connell *et al.* [8].

5.2 Comparison of Machine Learning Methods

Table 1 shows the results of six different machine learning classification methods using a 10-fold cross-validation test on the acetaminophen dataset. The first column shows the average classification error achieved on the raw dataset (RD). The three remaining columns show the results of using each machine learning method in tandem with a pre-processing technique:

Table 1: Percentage Classification Error of Different Machine Learning Methods on Acetaminophen Dataset

Method	Pre-processing Technique RD	ND	FD	FND
Linear SVM	**6.45** *(C=100)*	**2.76** *(C=1)*	**3.23** *(C=10000)*	**0.92*** *(C=0.1)*
RBF SVM	**5.07** *(C=1000, σ=0.1)*	**2.76** *(C=1000, σ=0.001)*	**1.84** *(C=10000, σ=10)*	**0.92*** *(C=10, σ=0.01)*
k-NN	11.06 *(k=1)*	7.83 *(k=1)*	**4.61** *(k=10)*	**4.15** *(k=1)*
C4.5	10.14	7.83	**1.84**	**1.38**
RIPPER	15.67	11.06	**3.69**	**2.3**
Naive Bayes	25.35	13.82	25.81	**5.53**
Linear Reg.	27.65	16.13	25.35	20.28

- ND: dataset with each sample normalised. Each sample is divided across by the maximum intensity that occurs within that sample.
- FD: a Savitzky-Golay first derivative [15], seven-point averaging algorithm is applied to the raw dataset.
- FND: a normalisation step is carried out after applying a first derivative to each sample of the raw dataset.

Table 1 shows the lowest average error average achieved by each classifier and pre-processing combination. For all these methods, apart from k-NN, the WEKA [12] implementation was used. The default settings were used for C4.5, RIPPER and Naive Bayes. For SVMs, RBF and Linear kernels with different parameter settings were tested. The parameter settings that achieved the best results are shown in parentheses. The Linear SVM was tested for the following values of C: $0.1, 1, \ldots, 10000$. The same range of C values were used for RBF SVM, and these were tested in combination with the σ values of: $0.0001, 0.001, \ldots, 10$. For k-NN, the table shows the value for k (number of neighbours) that resulted in the lowest percentage error. The k-NN method was tested for all values of k from 1 to 20. The results of each machine learning and pre-processing technique combination of Table 1 were compared using a paired t-test based on a 5% confidence level and using a corrected variance estimate [16]. The lowest average error over all results in Table 1 of 0.92% (i.e. only two misclassifications, achieved by both Linear and RBF SVM) is highlighted in bold and indicated by an asterisk. Those results which do not differ significantly (according to the t-test) are also highlighted in bold.

On both the raw (RD) and normalised (ND) dataset, both SVM models perform better than any of the other machine learning methods, as there is no significant difference between the best overall result and the SVM results on RD and ND, whereas a significant difference does exist between the best overall result and all other machine learning methods on RD and ND. This confirms the notion that SVMs are particularly suited to dealing with high dimensional data and it also suggests that SVMs are capable of handling a high degree of collinearity in the data. Linear Regression, on the other hand, performs poorly with all pre-processing techniques. This poor performance can be attributed to its requirement that all the columns of the data matrix are *linearly independent* [9], a condition that is violated in highly correlated spectral data. Similarly, Naive Bayes has recorded a high average error on the RD, ND and FD data. This is presumably because of its assumption of independence of each of the attributes. It is clear from this table that the pre-processing techniques of FD and FND improve the performance of the majority of the classifiers. For SVMs, the error is numerically smaller, but not a significant improvement over the RD and ND results. Note that Linear Regression is the only method that did not achieve a result to compete with the best overall result.

Overall, the SVM appears to exhibit the best results, matching or outperforming all other methods on the raw and pre-processed data. With effective pre-processing, however, the performance of other machine learning methods can be improved so that they are close to that of the SVM.

5.3 Comparison of Machine Learning methods with PCA

As outlined in Section 3, PCA is used to alleviate problems such as high dimensionality and collinearity that are associated with spectral data. For the next set of experiments, the goal was to determine whether machine learning methods could benefit from an initial transformation of the dataset into a smaller set of PCs, as is used in PCR. The same series of cross-validation tests were run, except in this case, during each fold the PC scores of the training data were fed as inputs to the machine learning method. The procedure for the 10-fold cross-validation is as follows:

1. Carry out PCA on the training data to generate a loadings matrix.
2. Transform training data into a set of PC scores using the first P components of the loadings matrix.
3. Build a classification model based on the training PC scores data.
4. Transform the held out test fold data to PC scores using the loadings matrix generated from the training data.
5. Test classification model on the transformed test fold.
6. Repeat steps 1-5 for each iteration of the 10-fold cross-validation.

With each machine learning and pre-processing method combination, the above 10-fold cross-validation test was carried out for P=1 to 20 principal components.

Table 2: Percentage Classification Error of Different Machine Learning Methods with PCA on Acetaminophen Dataset

Method	Pre-processing Technique RD	ND	FD	FND
Linear SVM	**5.07** *(P=18, C=0.1)*	**1.84** *(P=13, C=0.1)*	**3.23** *(P=14, C=0.01)*	**0.46** *(P=4, C=0.1)*
RBF SVM	6.91 *(P=19, C=100,* *σ*=0.001)	**2.76** *(P=16, C=10,* *σ*=0.001)	**2.23** *(P=12, C=10,* *σ*=0.001)	**0.46** *(P=5 C=10,* *σ*=0.001)
k-NN	11.06 *(P=17,k=3)*	5.99 *(P=10,k=1)*	**2.3** *(P=14,k=1)*	**0.0*** *(P=4,k=5)*
C4.5	7.83 *(P=20)*	7.37 *(P=19)*	7.37 *(P=5)*	**1.38** *(P=6)*
RIPPER	11.98 *(P=20)*	8.29 *(P=8)*	6.45 *(P=5)*	**2.3** *(P=3)*
Naive Bayes	38.71 *(P=1)*	10.6 *(P=8)*	11.52 *(P=5)*	3.23 *(P=2)*
PCR (PCA+Linear Reg.)	9.22 *(P=16)*	5.53 *(P=20)*	8.29 *(P=11)*	**1.38** *(P=80)*

Therefore, 20 different 10-fold cross-validation tests were run for Naive Bayes, for example. For those classifiers that require additional parameters to be set, more tests had to be run to test the different combinations of parameters, e.g. C, σ, and P for RBF SVM. The same ranges for C, σ and k were tested as those used for the experiments of Table 1.

Table 2 shows the lowest average error achieved by each combination of machine learning and pre-processing method with PCA. The number of PCs used to achieve this lowest average error is shown in parentheses, along with the additional parameter settings for the SVM and k-NN classifiers. As with Table 1, the best result over all the results of Table 2 is highlighted in bold and denoted by an asterisk, with those results that bear no significant difference from the best overall result also highlighted in bold. Again, the pre-processing method of FND improves the performance of the majority of the classifiers, Naive Bayes being the exception in this case. In comparing the best result of Table 1 with the best result of Table 2 for each machine learning method (all in the FND column), it can be seen that the addition of the PCA step results in either the same error (C4.5 and RIPPER) or a numerically smaller error (Linear SVM, RBF SVM, k-NN and Linear Regression). The improvement effected by the inclusion of this PCA step is particularly evident with the Linear Regression technique. Note that this combination of PCA and Linear Regression is equivalent to PCR.

Despite the fact that for the SVM and k-NN classifiers, there is no significant difference between the best results with or without PCA, it is noteworthy that the SVM and k-NN classifiers with PCA were capable of achieving such low errors with far fewer attributes, only four PCs for the Linear SVM and k-NN and 5 PCs for the RBF SVM. This makes the resulting classification model much more efficient when classifying new data. In contrast, PCR required a much greater number of PCs (80) to achieve its lowest error. (This result was discovered in the experiment detailed in the next section.)

To make an overall assessment of the effect of using PCA in combination with machine learning, a statistical comparison (paired t-test with 5% confidence level) of the 28 results of Table 1 and Table 2 was carried out. This indicates that, overall, a significant improvement in the performance of machine learning methods is gained with this initial PCA step. It can therefore be concluded that the incorporation of PCA into machine learning is useful for the classification of high dimensional data.

5.4 Effect of PCA on Classification Accuracy

To further determine the effect of PCA on the performance of machine learning methods, each machine learning method (using the best parameter setting and pre-processing technique) was tested using larger numbers of PCs. Each method was tested for values of P in the range 1-640.

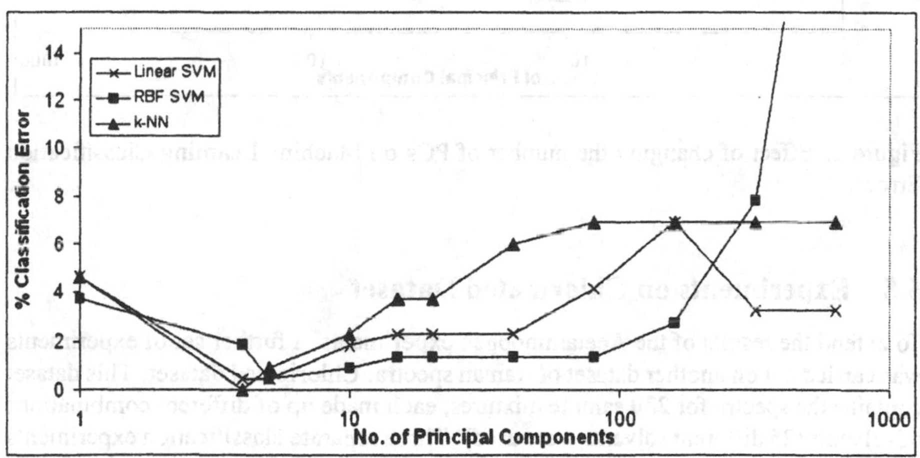

Figure 1: Effect of changing the number of PCs on Machine Learning Classification Error

Figures 1 and 2 shows the change in error for each of the methods versus the number of PCs retained to build the model. It can be seen from these graphs that as PCs are added, error is initially reduced for all methods. Most methods require no more than six PCs to achieve the lowest error. After this lowest error point, the behaviour of the methods differ somewhat. Most of the classifiers suffer drastic increases in error within the range of PCs tested: Naive Bayes, PCR, RBF SVM, RIPPER and k-NN (although not to the same extent as the previous examples). In contrast, the error for C4.5 never deviates too much from its lowest error at six PCs. This may be due to its ability to prune irrelevant attributes from the decision tree model. The Linear SVM initially seems to follow the pattern of the majority of classifiers, but then returns to a more acceptable error with the higher number of PCs. Overall, it is evident that all of the classifiers, apart from PCR, will achieve their best accuracy with a relatively small number of PCs; it is probably unnecesary to generate any more than twenty PCs. However, the number of PCs required will depend on the underlying dataset. Further experiments on more spectral data, or other examples of high dimensional data, are required to determine suitable ranges of PCs for these machine learning methods.

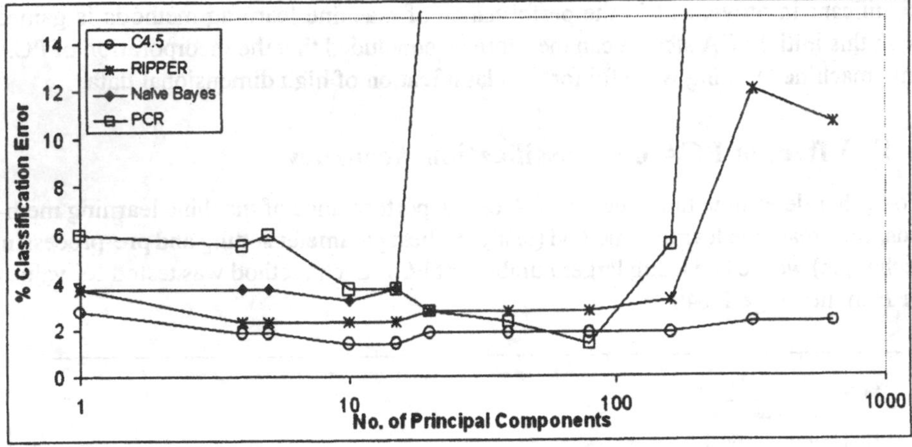

Figure 2: Effect of changing the number of PCs on Machine Learning Classification Error

5.5 Experiments on Chlorinated Dataset

To extend the results of the Acetaminophen experiments, a further set of experiments was carried out on another dataset of Raman spectra: Chlorinated dataset. This dataset contains the spectra for 230 sample mixtures, each made up of different combinations of solvents (25 different solvents were used). Three separate classification experiments were based on this dataset. In each case the task is to identify a specific chlorinated solvent. As can be seen from the results of Table 3, these experiments focussed on only two pre-processing techniques: the normalisation (ND) is used as the baseline method for comparison and the first derivative with normalisation (FND) is used as it produced the best results on the Acetaminophen dataset. This table directly compares the performance of each machine learning and pre-processing combination without PCA against the same combination with PCA. Again, for many of the machine learning methods, the use of PCA appears to improve performance. However, two major

Table 3: Comparison of Machine Learning with and without PCA on Chlorinated Dataset: Percentage Classification Error (N=No PCA, Y=PCA used)

	Dichloromethane				Trichloroethane				Chloroform			
	ND		FND		ND		FND		ND		FND	
Method	N	Y	N	Y	N	Y	N	Y	N	Y	N	Y
LSVM	1.74	0.43	1.74	2.17	5.65	2.61	6.09	2.61	3.91	1.74	5.22	4.78
RBF	0.43	0.43	0.87	1.74	5.22	2.61	6.09	2.61	4.35	3.91	5.22	4.35
k-NN	8.26	9.13	10.43	9.57	16.09	13.35	13.48	11.74	23.91	19.13	20.00	20.00
C4.5	3.04	8.26	0.43	8.26	7.39	16.09	3.91	16.52	3.91	14.78	3.04	16.96
RIP.	6.52	14.78	0.43	12.17	11.30	18.70	6.09	13.04	3.04	18.70	3.04	16.09
NB	43.04	41.30	37.83	26.09	53.48	49.13	40.87	34.35	56.09	51.74	40.00	35.22
Reg.	10.87	10.00	13.04	18.70	18.70	16.96	26.52	16.52	13.91	12.17	25.22	18.70

exceptions stand out: C4.5 and RIPPER, both of which are forms of a rule-leaning algorithm. Both of these methods suffer a notable loss of accuracy when PCA is employed. This is in contrast with the results on Acetaminophen, in which C4.5 and RIPPER gained a small improvement with PCA on the ND dataset, and achieved identical accuracy (to when no PCA was used) on the FND dataset. A comparison of the non-PCA results with those obtained with PCA shows no significant difference. However, if the results of these rule-based algorithms are omitted, a significant difference is observed that confirms the results achieved on the Acetaminophen dataset.

To determine the cause of the drop in performance of C4.5, an analysis was carried out on the decision trees produced by C4.5 when trained on the normalised Chloroform dataset. When the original dataset is used, C4.5 generates a tree of size 11. When the first 27 PCs (this number resulted in the best performance) scores are used as input, C4.5 generates a much more complex tree of size 35. Furthermore, the main branch of this tree is based on PC24 and many samples are classified at a leaf based on PC26. A key point is that PCs are ordered according to their contribution to the total variance; PCs 24 and 26 account for very little (less than 0.2%) of the total variance in the scores data. Any model that assigns a strong weighting to these attributes is in danger of overfitting to the training data and could therefore exhibit poor generalisation ability. A similar comparison of the non-PCA and PCA trees produced from the Acetaminophen dataset shows that a size difference exists, but is not as great: the tree based on original data has size 7 and the tree based on PC scores data has size 13. Of more importance is the fact that, for the Acetaminophen dataset, the tree based on PC scores selected PC3 and PC2 as key attributes; these attributes account for a much greater percentage of the total variance (about 38%).

This analysis shows that the performance of C4.5 may be adversely affected by the use of PC transformed data when compared with its performance on the original data. This occurs when key nodes of the tree are based on PC scores of low variance. Apart from abandoning PCA for decision trees altogether, one alternative is to use the original data and PC scores combined, thus allowing C4.5 to select both from the original set of attributes and from the linear combination attributes. Popelinsky and Brazdil [17] found this approach of adding PC attributes rather than replacing the original attributes to give better results. (They do not report the differences, however.) They found what they described as modest gains in the use of additional PC scores to the dataset when the C5.0 decision tree (a later commerical version of C4.5) was used. We tested this approach on the normalised versions of the spectral datasets with C4.5. In three of the classification tasks, the error achieved was identical to that achieved without PCA; a minor improvement was found for the Trichloroethane dataset. One drawback with this approach is that it increases the dimensionality of the data instead of reducing it, which is one of the main motivations for employing PCA.

6 Related Research

The work presented here extends previous research carried out by the authors into the use of machine learning methods with various pre-processing techniques for the classification of spectral data [8]. That work is extended in this paper by using these machine learning methods in combination with the NIPALS PCA technique, and investigating the effect of different numbers of principal components on classification accuracy. The most closely related research to this work can be found in Sigurdsson *et al.* [18], where they report on the use of neural networks for the detection of skin cancer based on Raman data that has been reduced using PCA. They achieve PCA using singular value decomposition (SVD), a method which calculates *all* the eigenvectors of the data matrix, unlike the NIPALS method that was used here. In addition, they do not present any comparison with neural networks on the raw data without the PCA step.

As far as the authors are aware, few studies have been carried out that investigate the effect of using PCA with a number of machine learning algorithms. Popelinsky [19] does analyse the effect of PCA (again, eigenvector decomposition is used) on three different machine learning algorithms (Naive Bayes, C5.0 and an instance-based learner). In this paper, the principal component scores are added to the original attribute data and he has found this to result in a decrease in error rate for all methods on a significant number of the datasets. However, the experiments were not based on particularly high dimensional datasets. It is also worth noting that there does not appear to be much evidence of the use of NIPALS PCA in conjunction with machine learning for the classification of high dimensional data.

7 Conclusions

This paper has proposed the use of an efficient PCA method, NIPALS, to improve the performance of some well known machine learning methods in the classification of high dimensional spectral data. Experiments in the classification of Raman spectra have shown that, overall, this PCA method improves the performance of machine learning when dealing with such high dimensional data. Furthermore, through the use of PCA, these low errors were achieved despite a major reduction of the data; from the original 1646 attributes of the Acetaminophen dataset to at least six attributes. Additional experiments have shown that it is not necessary to generate more than twenty PCs to find an optimal set for the spectral dataset used, as the performance of the majority of classifiers degrades with increasing numbers of PCs. This fact makes NIPALS PCA particularly suited to the proposed approach, as it does not require the generation of all PCs of a data matrix, unlike the widely used eigenvector decomposition methods. This paper has also shown that the pre-processing technique of first derivative followed by normalisation improves the performance of the majority of these machine learning methods in the identification of Acetaminophen. Further experiments on the Chlorinated dataset confirmed the benefits of using PCA, but also highlighted that poor results can be achieved when PCA is used in combination with rule-based learners, such as C4.5 and RIPPER.

Overall, the use of NIPALS PCA in combination with machine learning appears to be a promising approach for the classification of high dimensional spectral data. This approach has potential in other domains involving high dimensional data, such as gene-expression data and image data. Future work will involve testing this approach on more spectral datasets and also on other high dimensional datasets. Further investigations could also be carried out into the automatic selection of parameters for the techniques considered, such as the number of PCs, kernel parameters for SVM and k for k-NN.

Acknowledgements

This research has been funded by Enterprise Ireland's Basic Research Grant Programme. The authors are also grateful to the High Performance Computing Group at NUI Galway, funded under PRTLI I and III, for providing access to HPC facilities.

References

[1] Peng, S., Xu, Q., Ling, X., Peng, X., Du, W., Chen, L.: Molecular Classification of Cancer Types from Microarray Data using the combination of Genetic Algorithms and Support Vector Machines. FEBS Letters **555** (2003) 358–362

[2] Wang, J., Kwok, J., Shen, H., Quan, L.: Data-dependent kernels for small-scale, high-dimensional data classification. In: Proc. of the International Joint Conference on Neural Networks (to appear). (2005)

[3] Joachims, T.: Text categorisation with support vector machines. In: Proceedings of European Conference on Machine Learning (ECML). (1998)

[4] Ryder, A.: Classification of narcotics in solid mixtures using Principal Component Analysis and Raman spectroscopy and chemometric methods. J. Forensic Sci **47** (2002) 275–284

[5] Bulkin, B.: The Raman effect: an introduction. New York: John Wiley and Sons, Inc (1991)

[6] Conroy, J., Ryder, A., Leger, M., Hennessy, K., Madden, M.: Qualitative and quantitative analysis of chlorinated solvents using Raman spectroscopy and machine learning. In: Proc. SPIE - Int. Soc. Opt. Eng. Volume 5826 (in press). (2005)

[7] Cheng, C., Kirkbride, T., Batchelder, D., Lacey, R., Sheldon, T.: In situ detection and identification of trace explosives by Raman microscopy. J. Forensic Sci **40** (1995) 31–37

[8] O'Connell, M., Howley, T., Ryder, A., Leger, M., Madden, M.: Classification of a target analyte in solid mixtures using principal component analysis, support vector machines and Raman spectroscopy. In: Proc. SPIE - Int. Soc. Opt. Eng. Volume 5826 (in press). (2005)

[9] Hastie, T., Tibshirani, R., Friedman, J.: The Elements of Statistical Learning. Springer (2001)

[10] Geladi, P., Kowalski, B.: Partial Least Squares: A Tutorial. Analytica Chemica Acta **185** (1986) 1–17

[11] Scholkopf, B., Smola, A.: Learning with Kernels: Support Vector Machines, Regularization, Optimization, and Beyond. MIT Press (2002)

[12] Witten, I., Frank, E.: Data Mining: Practical Machine Learning Tools and Techniques with Java Implementations. Morgan Kaufmann Publishers (2000)

[13] Quinlan, R.: Learning Logical Definitions from Relations. Machine Learning **5** (1990)

[14] Cohen, W.: Fast Eeffective Rule Induction. In: Proc. of the 12th Int. Conference on Machine Learning. (2002) 115–123

[15] Savitzky, A., Golay, M.: Smoothing and differentiation of data by simplified least squares procedures. Anal. Chem. **36** (1964) 1627–1639

[16] Nadeau, C., Bengio, Y.: Inference for generalisation error. In: Advances in Neural Information Processing 12. MIT Press (2000)

[17] Popelinsky, L., Brazdil, P.: The Principal Components Method as a Preprocessing Stage for Decision Tree Learning. In: Proc. of PKDD Workshop (Data Mining, Decision Support, Meta-learning and ILP). (2000)

[18] Sigurdsson, S., Philipsen, P., Hansen, L., Larsen, J., Gniadecka, M., Wulf, H.: Detection of Skin Cancer by Classification of Raman Spectra. IEEE Transactions on Biomedical Engineering **51** (2004)

[19] Popelinsky, L.: Combining the Principal Components Method with Different Learning Algorithms. In: Proc. of ECML/PKDD IDDM Workshop (Integrating Aspects of Data Mining, Decision Support and Meta-Learning). (2001)

AUTHOR INDEX